THE ANCIENT LIBRARY OF QUMRAN
AND MODERN BIBLICAL STUDIES

THE
ANCIENT LIBRARY
OF QUMRAN
AND
MODERN BIBLICAL
STUDIES

by

Frank Moore Cross, Jr.
HARVARD DIVINITY SCHOOL

The Haskell Lectures
1956-1957

DOUBLEDAY & COMPANY, INC.

GARDEN CITY, NEW YORK

1958

dead sea scrolls

"relation to
new testamen

Library of Congress Catalog Card Number 58–5933

This book is dedicated to

G. ERNEST WRIGHT

in gratitude

Preface

THE STUDY of the scrolls and fragments of scrolls from the wilderness of the Dead Sea has barely begun. Only a small part of the fund of discoveries is published. Although much of the unpublished material will duplicate or confirm what already is known or suspected, there is much which is of revolutionary import. Positions which must be won now by complicated combinations of bits and tatters of evidence will automatically establish themselves once the vast corpus is laid out for all to see. Certain new documents will sweep away much of the flatulent nonsense now swelling the secondary literature on the scrolls, delivering sober scholars from the burden of continuing controversy, or rather freeing them to enter into new debates.

The time has not yet come, obviously, when it is possible or desirable to attempt total, much less final syntheses in the several major areas of Qumrân research. Nevertheless, Qumrân studies are ready to enter into a new phase. It is not too early to discern some of the coherent patterns emerging from the mass of fact accumulated by a decade of discoveries in the wilderness of Judah. And it is time to lay many of the early discussions to rest. The combination of newly found and partially published documentary material and the results of recent archaeological research has established new positions from which the entire field of inquiry can be viewed in a fresh perspective.

Decisive gains have been made by the paleographer and archaeologist. The study of early Jewish scripts has reached a stage of precision, thanks to the wealth of typological data furnished by recent finds and excavations, which now permits the specialist to date the Qumrân manuscripts within the interval of a half century. Five seasons of excavation at the community center of the scroll sect have been completed. The evidence dredged up by these researches has fixed the chronological framework of the sect's life in the desert within narrow and immovable limits.

Although the new documents from recent discoveries have had only preliminary examination, the importance of the data which have been extracted from them can scarcely be overestimated. In the first find, a narrow sample of the literature composed by the sect was recovered. Now we know the full scope of their religious writings. Historical allusions in the documents of the first discovery were scarce and never quite explicit. In the new manuscripts allusions are rare, to be sure, but Greek kings, Hasmonaean rulers, and a Roman official, all well known to the historian, are named by name. Alongside the few biblical manuscripts from the first cave, all of them of more or less traditional character, we can place now more than a hundred texts, many of non-traditional types. For the reconstruction of the religious and community life of the people of Qumrân, for the tracing of the early development of the Old Testament text, for the determination of the historical relationships of the Qumrân sect, these data are crucial. They enable us to proceed with some boldness to fresh attempts at historical synthesis.

This volume contains the text of the Haskell Lectures for 1956–57, delivered to the Graduate School of Theology, Oberlin College, March 12–21, 1957. The form of the book is shaped by its origin in a series of lectures. Each of the lectures after the first deals with a single, but major area of scroll research. No serious effort is made to give a comprehensive treatment of the field of scroll study as a whole. Each lecture records, however, an attempt to achieve in a given area a synthesis or at least a systematic interpretation of the facts now available. Old and new, published and unpublished data are drawn upon.

The text of the lectures was written with public presentation in view, and at the same time expanded by extensive footnoting, not merely for the usual purposes of documentation, but to enable the writer to elaborate on the restricted material suitable to his text. The longer notes are written at two levels; most contain technical discussions, especially at points where unpublished material or unpublished views are alluded to in the text; at the same time a number of explanatory notes are directed to the reader with less background in the field under discussion than the academic audience to whom the lectures were originally addressed.

There are many acknowledgments to be made. First of all I wish to thank Professor David Noel Freedman. He has been a constant source of encouragement, criticism, and aid. To the Haskell Lectureship Committee, especially to Professor Herbert G. May and Dean Leonard Stidley, I owe a debt of gratitude for hospitality shown me during my pleasant days in Oberlin on the occasion of the delivery of the lectures. To Professor W. F. Albright, my former teacher and perennial mentor, Professor Krister Stendahl, and Mr. John Strugnell who have read my manuscript and offered many helpful suggestions; to R. P. Roland de Vaux, Mr. G. Lankester Harding, and the members of the scroll staff in Jerusalem whose influence is evident throughout the pages of this book; and to my patient wife, who wishes, I am sure, that the scrolls had been fed to the goat responsible for their discovery; to all these I wish to acknowledge my indebtedness and express my thanks.

July 13, 1957   F. M. C., Jr.

Contents

LIST OF ABBREVIATIONS AND SIGLA

Antiq.	Flavius Josephus, *Jewish Antiquities*
ASOR	American Schools of Oriental Research
ATR	*Anglican Theological Review*
BA	*Biblical Archaeologist*
BASOR	*Bulletin of the American Schools of Oriental Research*
CBQ	*Catholic Biblical Quarterly*
Découvertes	J. T. Milik, *Dix ans de découvertes dans le Desert de Juda* (Paris, 1957).
DJD I	D. Barthélemy, O.P., J. T. Milik, *et al.*, *Qumrân Cave I. Discoveries in the Judaean Desert I* (Oxford, 1955)
DSS I	M. Burrows, John C. Trever, and W. H. Brownlee, eds., *The Dead Sea Scrolls of St. Mark's Monastery*, Vol. I (New Haven, 1950)
DSS II	M. Burrows, John C. Trever, and W. H. Brownlee, eds., *The Dead Sea Scrolls of St. Mark's Monastery*, Vol. II:2 (New Haven, 1951)
ET	*Evangelische Theologie*
Gen. Apoc.	N. Avigad and Y. Yadin, *A Genesis Apocryphon. A Scroll from the Wilderness of Judaea* (Jerusalem, 1956)
Geschichte[3]	E. Schürer, *Geschichte des jüdischen Volkes im Zeitalter Jesu Christi*, 3. Aufl. (Leipzig, 1901)
HTR	*Harvard Theological Review*
IEJ	*Israel Exploration Journal*
JAOS	*Journal of the American Oriental Society*
JBL	*Journal of Biblical Literature*
JBR	*Journal of Bible and Religion*
JJS	*Journal of Jewish Studies*
JNES	*Journal of Near Eastern Studies*
JQR	*Jewish Quarterly Review*
JSS	*Journal of Semitic Studies*
LXX	Septuagint
MT	Masoretic Text
NTS	*New Testament Studies*
OMG	E. L. Sukenik and N. Avigad, *'ôṣar ham-mĕgillôt haggĕnûzôt* (Jerusalem, 1954)

PAAJR   *Proceedings of the American Academy of Jewish Research*
PEQ   *Palestine Exploration Quarterly*
Rapport I   R. de Vaux, "Fouille au Khirbet Qumrân," *RB* 60 (1953), pp. 83–106
Rapport II   R. de Vaux, "Fouilles au Khirbet Qumrân. Rapport préliminaire sur la deuxième campagne," *RB* 61 (1954), pp. 206–36
Rapport III   R. de Vaux, "Fouilles de Khirbet Qumrân. Rapport préliminaire sur les 3e, 4e, et 5e campagnes," *RB* 63 (1956), pp. 533–77
RB   *Revue biblique*
RHPR   *Revue d'histoire et de philosophie religieuses*
RHR   *Revue de l'histoire des religions*
ST   *Studia Theologica*
SzHK   K. Elliger, *Studien zum Habakuk-Kommentar vom Toten Meer* (Tübingen, 1953)
TLZ   *Theologische Literaturzeitung*
ThR   *Theologische Rundschau*
TSK   *Theologische Studien und Kritiken*
TWzNT   *Theologisches Wörterbuch zum Neuen Testament*, ed., G. Kittel (Stuttgart)
ThZ   *Theologische Zeitschrift*
VT   *Vetus Testamentum*
War   Flavius Josephus, *The Jewish War*
ZAW   *Zeitschrift für die alttestamentliche Wissenschaft*
ZDPV   *Zeitschrift des Deutschen Palästina-Vereins*
ZNW   *Zeitschrift für die neutestamentliche Wissenschaft*
ZTK   *Zeitschrift für Theologie und Kirche*

The sigla used in designating the manuscripts of Qumrân follow the standard system adopted in the series, *Discoveries in the Judaean Desert*. A full listing is given in *DJD I*, pp. 46–48. Among the more important documents discussed in the text or notes are the following:

1QS [*sérek hay-yaḥad*]   The sectarian Rule of the Community, exemplar from Cave I, Qumrân. Published in *DSS II*.

1QSa, 1QSb   Adjuncts to the Rule of the Community (1QS). Published in *DJD I* as 1Q28a and 1Q28b.

pap4QSe   A papyrus exemplar of the Rule of the Community, from Cave IV, Qumrân. Unpublished.

1QH [*hôdāyôt*]   The sectarian roll of Psalms of Thanksgiving from Cave I. Published in *OMG*.

1QM [*milḥāmāh*]	The sectarian War of the Children of Light Against the Children of Darkness. Published in *OMG*.
1QIsaᵃ	A scroll of Isaiah from Cave I, Qumrân, exemplar a. Published in *DSS I*.
1QpHab. [*péšer* Habakkuk]	The commentary on Habakkuk from Cave I. Published in *DSS I*.
1Q Apoc.	The Genesis Apocryphon from Cave I. Published in *Gen. Apoc.*
4QpNah.	A commentary on Nahum from Cave IV. Partially published by Allegro, *JBL* 75 (1956), pp. 89–95.
4Q Testimonia	The sheet of testimonia from Cave IV. Published by Allegro, *JBL* 75 (1956), pp. 174–87.
4Q T. Levi	The Testament of Levi from Cave IV. Partially published by Milik, *RB* 62 (1955), pp. 398–406.
4QExᵃ	An Exodus manuscript in Paleo-Hebrew script from Cave IV. Partially published by Skehan, *JBL* 74 (1955), pp. 182–87.
4QDeut. 32	A manuscript in which Deuteronomy 32 is preserved. Published by Skehan, *BASOR* 136 (Dec., 1954), pp. 12–15.
4QExᵃ	An Exodus manuscript in Jewish script from Cave IV. Unpublished.
4QSamᵃ	A manuscript of I and II Samuel from Cave IV. Partially published by Cross, *BASOR* 132 (Dec., 1953), pp. 15–26.
4QSamᵇ	A manuscript of I and II Samuel from Cave IV. Partially published by Cross, *JBL* 74 (1955), pp. 147–72.
CD	The Cairo Damascus Document
6QD	A copy of the Damascus Document from Cave VI, Qumrân. Published by Baillet, *RB* 63 (1956), pp. 513–23.
4Q Prayer of Nabonidus	A document belonging to a lost Daniel literature. Published by Milik, *RB* 63 (1956), pp. 407–15.

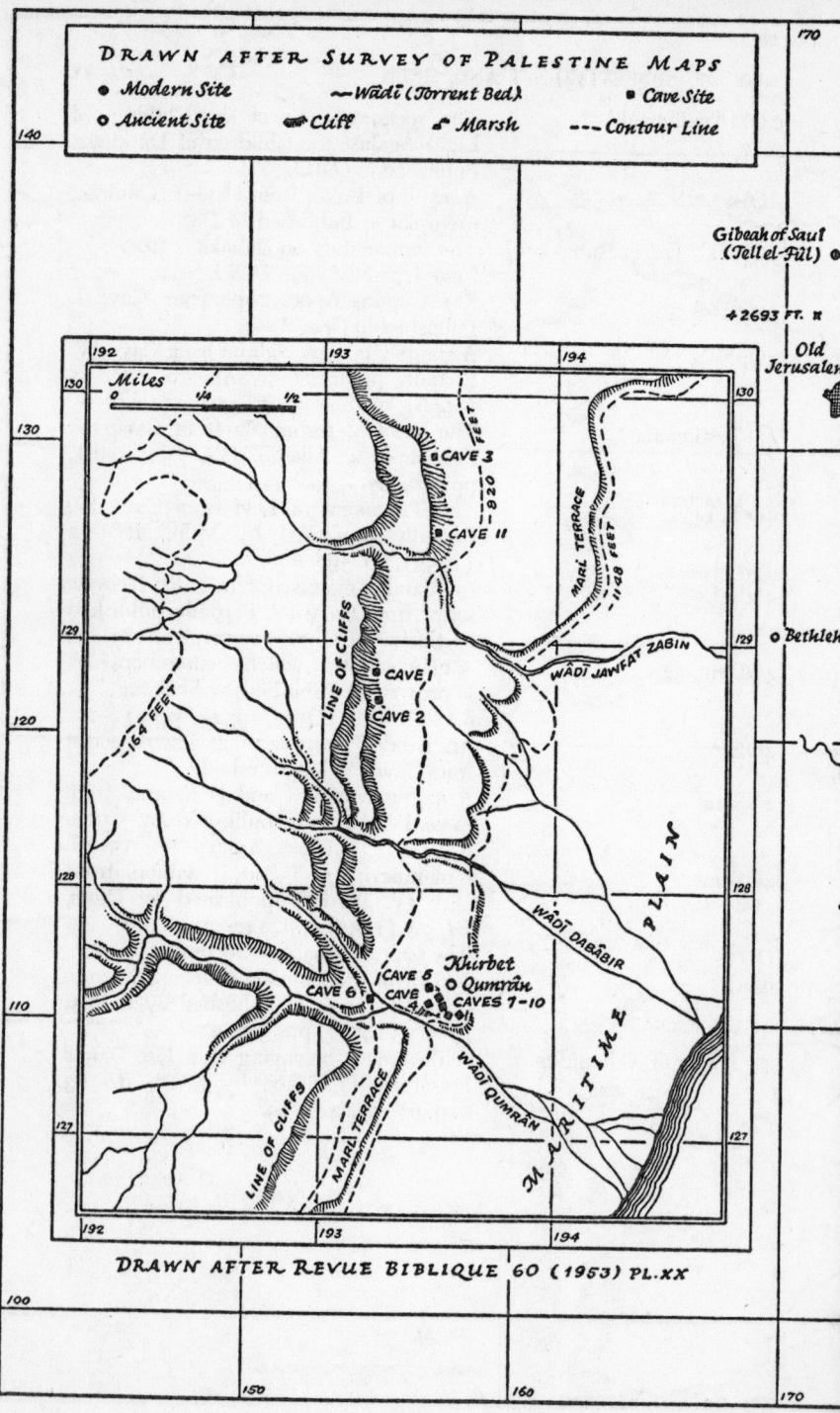

DRAWN AFTER SURVEY OF PALESTINE MAPS
- Modern Site — Wādī (Torrent Bed) • Cave Site
○ Ancient Site ⌇ Cliff ⚲ Marsh --- Contour Line

Gibeah of Saul (Tell el-Fūl) ○

↟ 2693 FT.

Old Jerusalem

Miles
0   ¼   ½

CAVE 3
820 FEET
CAVE 11

MARL TERRACE
1128 FEET

○ Bethlehem

LINE OF CLIFFS

CAVE 1
CAVE 2

WĀDĪ JAWFAT ZABIN

164 FEET

WĀDĪ DABŪBIR

M A R I T I M E   P L A I N

Khirbet Qumrān
CAVE 5
CAVE 6   CAVE 4
CAVES 7–10

WĀDĪ QUMRĀN

LINE OF CLIFFS

MARL TERRACE

DRAWN AFTER REVUE BIBLIQUE 60 (1953) PL. XX

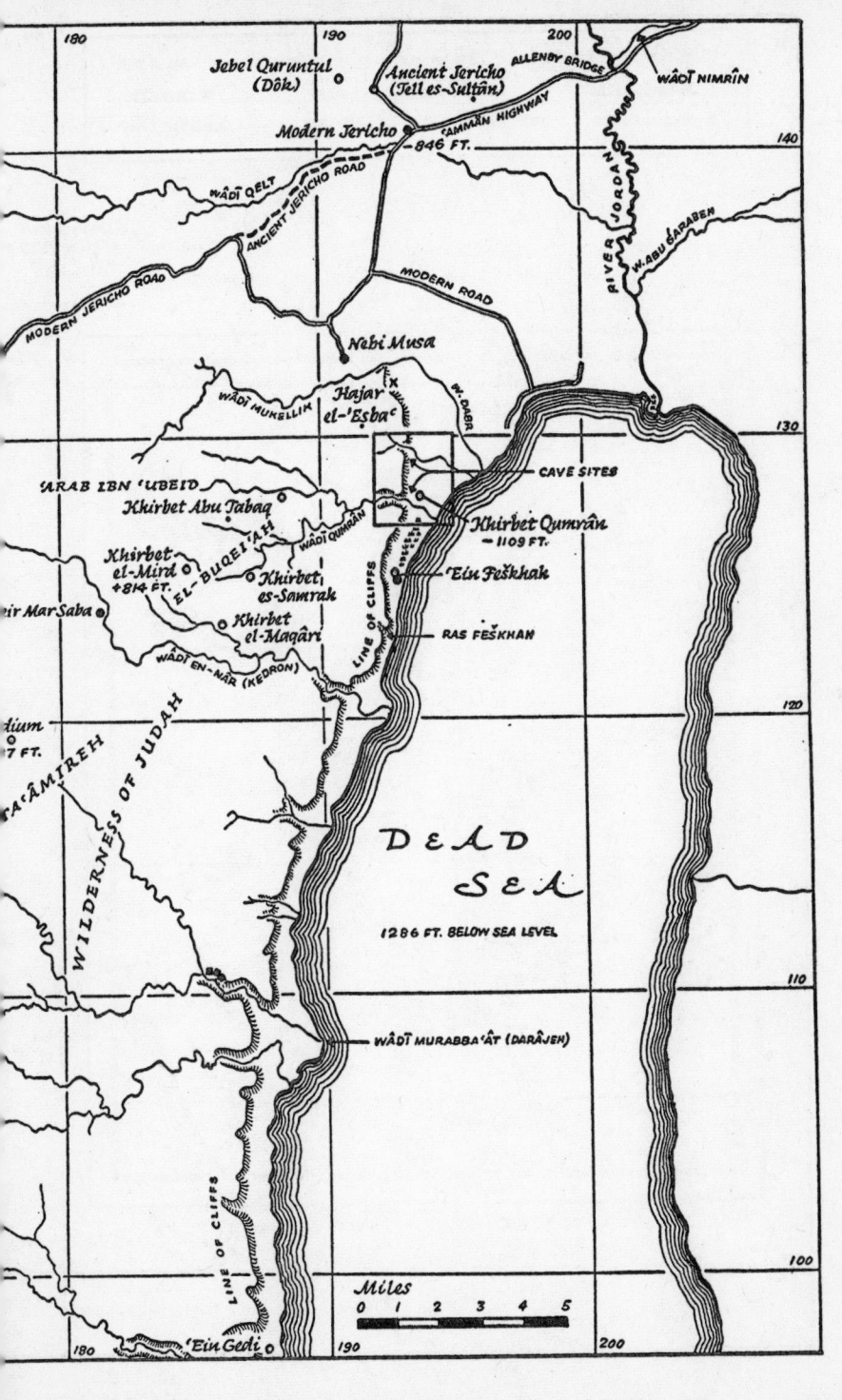

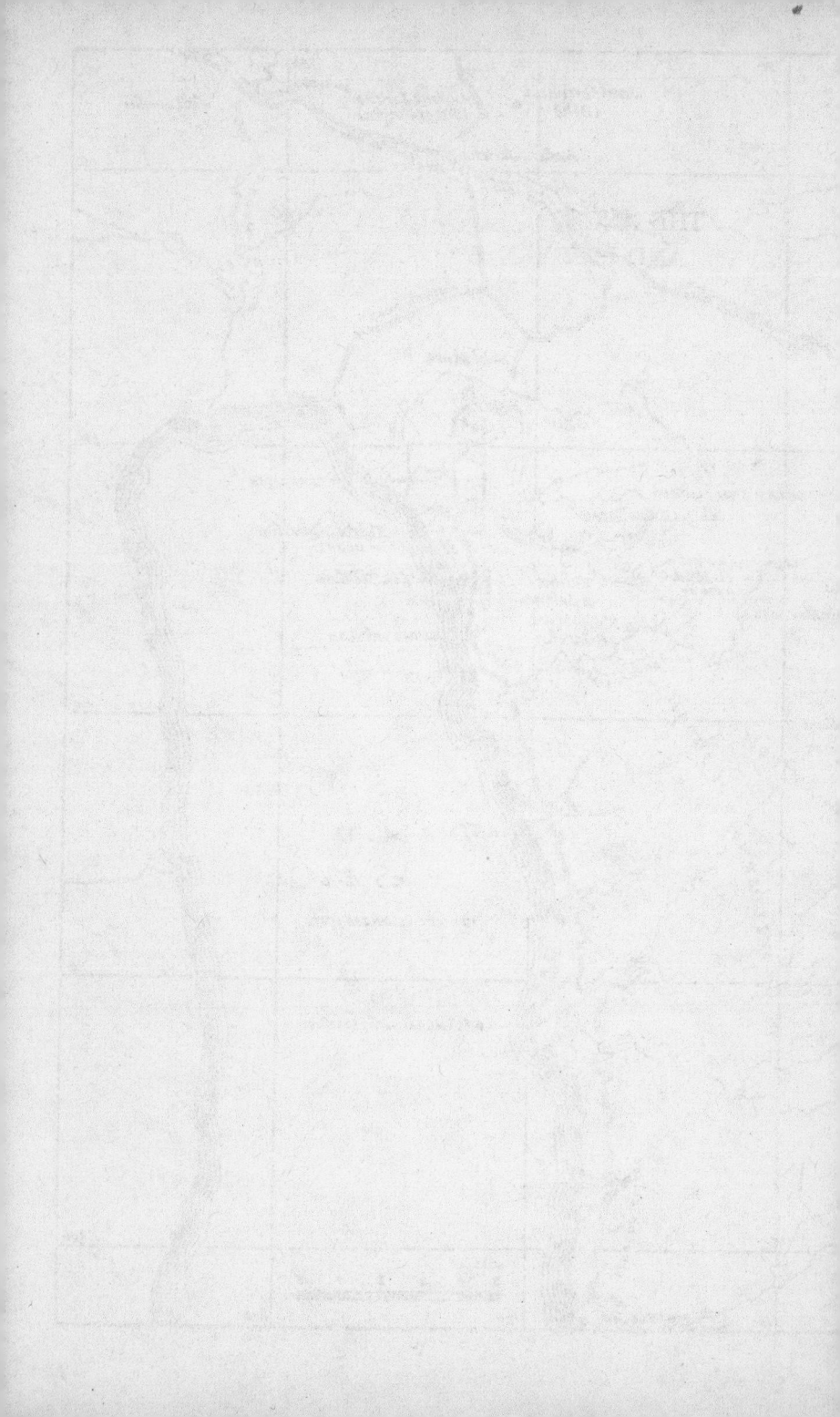

THE ANCIENT LIBRARY OF QUMRAN
AND MODERN BIBLICAL STUDIES

CHAPTER I

Discovery of an Ancient Library

TEN YEARS AGO seven antique rolls of leather were found by shepherds in the Judaean wilderness near the northwestern shore of the Dead Sea. This discovery set off a series of manuscript finds which are without precedent in the history of modern archaeology. Since the first cave and its manuscripts were found, the lonely precincts of the desert have been invaded successfully again and again by seekers of leather and papyrus treasure. A competition has developed between clandestine Bedouin diggers and accredited archaeologists, with laurels going frequently to the scientists, more often to the ignorant but patient shepherds.

The most important as well as the best known finds have come from caves in the vicinity of Wâdî Qumrân, a gorge cut by winter torrents through the cliffs which border the Dead Sea, some seven or eight miles south of modern Jericho. But other districts in the Judaean wasteland have yielded precious antiquities as by-products of the intense search. Groups of documents, scarcely less interesting than those of Qumrân, have been dug out of the gargantuan caves of the Wâdî Murabba'ât, which lies about twelve miles southwest of Qumrân; others have come from an unknown place—known precisely only to Bedouin—further south along the Dead Sea; yet another group has been found in the ruins of Khirbet Mird (ancient Hyrcania) situated on a peak inland from Qumrân in the western flank of the Judaean Buqê'.

Eleven caves clustered about ruins on the Wâdī Qumrân have now produced manuscripts or manuscript fragments. These include the cave of the initial discovery in 1947 (Qumrân I), and the most recent find, a cave discovered in January 1956 (Qumrân XI). Of the Qumrân caves, only Caves I and XI have produced relatively intact manuscripts. The largest single cache, however, and probably the most important, was dug from the ancient floor levels of Cave IV found in 1952: tens of thousands of fragments belonging to a corpus of more than three hundred and eighty manuscripts. From the caves of Qumrân alone there are now in the museums of Palestine a total of more than five hundred manuscripts, a few well preserved, most extremely fragmentary, all invaluable. And there is no reason to suppose that the discoveries in this lonely land are at an end.

The task of editing these documents from Qumrân and from other regions in the Judaean desert is no more than well begun. Only the publication of the scrolls of Cave I is near completion, and it is hoped that the groups of documents from Wâdī Murabba'ât, from the "unknown locality," and from the "minor caves" of Qumrân (II, III, V–X) will be ready for their principal publication soon. While some fragments from Cave IV have had preliminary publication, a number of years will pass before the extensive remains from the cave can be fully and definitively published. Not only are there several thousand small scraps from Cave IV yet to be identified, but as recently as the summer of 1956 new lots of large fragments were still being purchased from tribesmen. As for the newly found manuscripts of Cave XI, the work of editing them has not commenced. They lie in the Palestine Archaeological Museum awaiting final arrangements for purchase, still encrusted with the filth from which they were dug.

Even when the majority of these documents from the wilderness of the Dead Sea are published the main labors of research will not be done. Scholars will be occupied for decades in the tedious studies required to assimilate adequately the knowledge available in these new sources, and to relate this new learning to biblical and ancillary disciplines.

1. *The First Cave*

The story of the first cave has been obscured by time and legend. This circumstance, it must be confessed, is due less to the faulty memories of the native discoverers than to the fervid imagination of Western writers. Even so, while a full history of the find may never be reconstructed, certain essential facts are well established, partly by cross-examination of tribesmen and their middlemen, partly by subsequent events.[1]

In the spring of the year 1947 two shepherd lads were grazing their mixed flocks of sheep and goats along the foot of the crumbling cliffs that line the Dead Sea in the vicinity of Qumrân. There was nothing unusual about their being in this terrain. The few clans of their tribe, the Ta'âmireh, that still live in "houses of hair" following flocks, customarily use the bubbling springs of Feshkhah immediately south of Qumrân as a watering place, and often in the spring, when the desert turns green for a brief few weeks, may be found in these wild pastures.[2]

1 The most authoritative account—as well as one of the briefest—is that given by G. Lankester Harding in *Qumrân Cave I, Discoveries in the Judaean Desert I [DJD I]*, by D. Barthélemy, O.P., J.T. Milik, *et al.* (Oxford, 1955), pp. 1–7; cf. "The Dead Sea Scrolls," *PEQ* 81 (1949), pp. 112–16.

2 The writer, engaged in explorations in the Judaean wilderness to the west of Khirbet Qumrân, has come by chance upon an encampment of the Ta'âmireh clan involved in the discoveries. Actually the traditional range of the Ta'âmireh lies mostly south of the Wâdī–Nâr. The region of 'En Feshkhah and Qumrân is disputed with the 'Arab

According to their account, one of their animals strayed. In searching for it, one of the shepherds, Muhammed ed-Dîb by name, casually threw a stone into a small, circular opening in the cliff face. Instead of the expected smack of rock against rock, he heard a shattering sound. He was frightened and fled. Later, presumably when the fear of *jinn* or hyenas finally gave way to the lure of buried gold, he and his companion Ahmed Muhammed returned and crept into the cave and found decaying rolls of leather in one of a number of strange elongated jars embedded in the floor of the cave. These were the original "Dead Sea Scrolls."

In the year between the Bedouin discovery and the first press releases announcing the discovery to the world, there was confusion, blundering, and intrigue, as is associated often, unfortunately, with spectacular, chance finds. At least one, and probably several clandestine excavations ravaged the cave site; additional materials came to light; there is evidence that a considerable amount of precious material was destroyed in the process. The details of this phase of the vicissitudes of the scrolls of Cave I are most difficult to establish. In any case, after some of the scrolls (three, according to Ta'âmireh claims) had passed about in the tents of clansmen, they were brought to Bethlehem for sale and fell into the hands of antiquities dealers. At some point they were joined with a portion of the manuscript materials from clandestine excavations. Ultimately one lot came into the possession of the Syrian Orthodox Metropolitan of Jerusalem, a Syrian cobbler

ibn 'Ubêd. However, one of the old burying grounds of the 'Arab et-Ta'âmireh is immediately north of the cave area near Hajar el-'Asba'. (Cf. Cross and Milik, 'Explorations in the Judaean Buqê'ah," *BASOR* 142 [April 1956], pp. 5–17; especially p. 5, n.1). For a tribal history of the Ta'âmireh, see B. Couroyer, "Histoire d'une tribu semi-nomade de Palestine," *RB* 58 (1951), pp. 75–91.

It is to be noted that the Ta'âmireh were not without experience in archaeological matters before the manuscript discoveries. M. R. Neuville, the late French prehistorian, used these tribesmen in his excavation of caves in Ta'âmireh country; and tribal traditions reflect pride in these caves and their antiquities.

of Bethlehem acting as broker;[3] another was purchased by the late E. L. Sukenik for the Hebrew University.[4]

The metropolitan, Athanasius Yeshue Samuel, upon acquiring his lot of manuscripts, was anxious to have them authenticated, or to be more precise, perhaps, evaluated. A series of

3 One Khalil Iskander Shahin, better known as Kando. It is rather evident that Kando, a henchman named George Isaiah, and probably representatives of the Syrian monastery in Jerusalem were responsible for at least one of the clandestine forays on the cave. However this may be, Kando since has won the trust, not only of the Ta'âmireh, but also of antiquities officials handling purchase of newer Bedouin finds, and so has become the regular middleman for virtually all transactions in scroll materials. Such a person was necessary to both sides. Theoretically the manuscripts acquired by clandestine excavations could be confiscated by the Department of Antiquities. In fact it was necessary to establish a standard but indirect procedure for purchasing the precious leather. Otherwise the materials would have been smuggled and scattered, broken up and held for higher and higher prices, or, worst of all, destroyed in the face of threatened seizure. Fixed prices by centimeter of inscribed surface were agreed upon early with the Bedouin, and a fixed commission for Kando. All sides have kept faith, with the result that the manuscripts have flowed into the Palestine Museum with a minimum of loss to the scientific world, and at a minimum cost.

4 Accounts of the early history of the scrolls as told by principals may be found in the following: M. Burrows, *The Dead Sea Scrolls* (New York, 1955), pp. 3–28; E. L. Sukenik, *'wṣr hmgylwt hgnwzwt* (Jerusalem, 1954) (*OMG*), pp. 13–20; A. Y. Samuel, "The Purchase of the Dead Sea Scrolls," *BA* 12 (1949), pp. 26–31; John C. Trever, "The Discovery of the Scrolls," *BA* 11 (1948), pp. 46–68. The enormous secondary literature on the early discoveries is recorded by H. H. Rowley, *The Zadokite Fragments and the Dead Sea Scrolls* (Oxford, 1952), pp. 3–6. Newer developments have wholly antiquated the early discussion, though it retains some human interest. To these may be added the account of J. M. Allegro, *The Dead Sea Scrolls* (Penguin Books), 1956, pp. 15–34. It may be noted that while Allegro's account draws on interviews with the principals, his account, like others, is at best a reconstruction. Many discrepancies remain. For example, we still are not sure which scrolls came from the shepherd find, which from Syrian (illegal) excavations. And the precise fashion in which Sukenik's lot arrived in his possession is thoroughly obscure. We know only that they were purchased from a Muslim dealer of Bethlehem (not directly, at least, from Kando), through a well-known Jerusalem dealer in antiquities.

persons, including reputable scholars, was consulted and given opportunity to examine them. No one, however, who was competent in Hebrew paleography saw the scrolls. The episodes which mark this interlude are quite amusing in retrospect but are best forgotten, perhaps, in kindness to the scholars who failed.

The Syrian scrolls finally were brought to the American School of Oriental Research in February 1948, nearly a year after their discovery. Their antiquity and value were then recognized by a young scholar of the school, John C. Trever, who, together with William Brownlee, began first studies of the lot and systematically photographed it. Some prints of sections of one scroll, the great Isaiah scroll, were immediately dispatched to the distinguished orientalist, W. F. Albright, a leading authority in matters of Jewish paleography. He quickly replied, confirming Trever's judgments of the scrolls, congratulating him on "the greatest discovery of modern times." In the meantime, the Director of the American School, Professor Millar Burrows, had returned after an absence in Iraq to find his staff absorbed with the old leather rolls. He also convinced himself of the extreme age and importance of the new finds, and on April 11, 1948, made the first announcement of the discovery of the manuscripts to the press of the world.[5] Two weeks later (on April 26), Professor Sukenik announced the existence of the Hebrew University collection.

In point of fact, Sukenik had recognized the scrolls for what they were before the metropolitan approached the American School with his collection. In late November, Sukenik was shown fragments in a Jerusalem antiquities shop. His familiarity with Hebrew inscriptions of the period had prepared him as few were prepared for the discovery. He relates, however, that he could scarcely believe what his

5 Cf. G. Ernest Wright, "A Phenomenal Discovery," *BA* 11 (1948), pp. 21–23; W. F. Albright, "Notes from the President's Desk," *BASOR* 110 (April 1948), pp. 2–3.

knowledge and senses told him was true![6] His delay in announcing the discoveries was occasioned, no doubt, by his reluctance to alert Bedouin and their middlemen to the value of their finds before as much material as possible had been acquired by scientists. The Hebrew University lot was acquired in purchases in November and December 1947. In December, Sukenik also learned of the Syrian collection, and during the following month attempted to arrange its purchase through one Anton Kiraz, a member of the Syrian Orthodox community. Actually, the St. Mark's scrolls came into Sukenik's hands for some days, but negotiations were broken off, presumably after the Syrian monks had approached the scholars of the American School.[7]

Ultimately the four scrolls belonging to the Syrian monastery were smuggled to America by the metropolitan, and after the publication of three of them by the American Schools of Oriental Research in 1950 and 1951, were purchased through indirect channels for the Hebrew University in the summer of 1954. Professor Sukenik's negotiations were thus completed more than six years later; and scrolls which would have sold for a few hundred dollars in 1948 brought a reported $250,000 in 1954.[8]

Arab-Israeli fighting began so to disturb Palestine in the spring of 1948 that attempts to locate and excavate the site of the extraordinary finds were frustrated. With the war that followed the end of the British mandate in May 1948 communications were cut between the scholars who knew of the finds and the antiquities officials resident in Palestine (now

6 Cf. the excerpts from Sukenik's diary, *OMG*, p. 20.

7 The account related by the metropolitan differs at this point from that of Sukenik. Samuel maintains that the scrolls were shown to Sukenik by Kiraz after they had been taken to the American school and photographed. However, the precise dates given by Sukenik, presumably drawn from his diary, are evidently to be followed in reconstructing the sequence of events.

8 Actually the purchase—worked out by Yigael Yadin, Sukenik's son—was not announced until February of 1955.

Arab Jordan). Indeed, Mr. G. Lankester Harding, the Director of the Department of Antiquities of Jordan, learned of the discoveries only upon reading the April 1948 issue of the *Bulletin of the American Schools of Oriental Research,* which reached him in Ammân in November 1948! As soon as arrangements could be made, Arab legionnaires were dispatched to comb the cliffs of the Dead Sea in search of the cave. After only two or three days' search, in late January 1949, whitish debris which had cascaded down a ravine in the cliffside revealed the position of the cave to Captain (now Colonel) Akkash el-Zebn. It lay about .6 mile (1 kilometer) north of Wâdî Qumrân, low in the six- or seven-hundred-foot cordon of cliffs, at a point just over a mile distant from the shore of the Dead Sea.[9]

Scientific excavations were carried out successfully (February 15–March 5, 1949), and fragments belonging to about seventy documents, including fragments of two of the original seven manuscripts, were found.[10] However, the fragments recovered by the archaeologists were taken from Bedouin debris, and from more or less disturbed levels in the cave, so that none was impressive in size. Nevertheless, the provenience of the purchased lots was established, and sufficient archaeological data were recovered to date the context of the scrolls roughly, confirming earlier paleographical results.[11]

9 The cave is located at map co-ordinate 193.3:128.9. Owing to a *lapsus calami,* the position is wrongly given in *DJD I.* Cf. Cross, "Qumrân Cave I," *JBL* 75 (1956), p. 121, and the references in n. 2.

10 Bits of 1QM and 1QH were discovered in controlled excavations. In addition lots from clandestine digs were later purchased from Kando and included extensive portions of the Rule of the Community (1QS), smaller bits of the Hebrew University Isaiah (1QIsa^b), and of the Genesis Apocryphon (1Q20).

11 *DJD I,* pp. 6–38. Cf. Harding, "The Dead Sea Scrolls"; R. de Vaux, "La grotte des manuscrits hébreux," *RB* 56 (1949), pp. 586–609; O. R. Sellers, "Excavation of the 'Manuscript Cave,'" *BASOR* 114 (April 1949), pp. 5–9.

2. New Treasures from the Wilderness

The fantastic episode seemed closed. For nearly two years the desert was left undisturbed. It was generally assumed that by a stroke of fortune an isolated cache had been found. Apparently it occurred to few scholars that Cave I was other than a chance hiding place, or storage place, chosen by some odd but happy quirk of an ancient mind. The discovery was unique; to the sophisticated, the odds against parallel discoveries seemed staggering. The Ta'âmireh clansmen, however, having made a successful debut in the archaeological field, were inclined to make a vocation of it. They ranged the sterile wastes of the Judaean desert, peering into caves, scratching in their floors, oblivious to passing months, patient and undiscouraged by persistent failure. Their range lands were rich only in caves and they proposed to exploit them.

In the fall of 1951 the Bedouin made new discoveries in caves far to the southwest of the first cave, somewhere in the heart of the Judaean badlands. Scholars were alerted to the find when documents of a new order—unrelated to the Qumrân finds—were offered for sale in Jerusalem. Investigation was made; in fact the caves of the Wâdī Murabba'ât which produced the finds were actually visited; but the search was inconclusive, and only later was the site of the new discoveries surely confirmed. Meanwhile it was supposed that a small find had been made and exhausted.[12]

In November and December of 1951, G. Lankester Harding, Director of Antiquities, and R. P. Roland de Vaux, Director of the École Biblique et Archéologique Française in Jerusalem, proposed to make soundings at the ancient ruins to the south of Cave I on the Wâdī Qumrân. The ruin was by no means unknown. De Saulcy in the nineteenth century had

12 See R. de Vaux, "Les grottes de Murabba'ât et leur documents," *RB* 60 (1953), pp. 245–75; especially p. 245.

identified it as biblical Gomorrah; and soberer scientists in
the modern period of archaeology had noted evidence of its
Roman date.[13] The excavations at Cave I had brought the
curious ruin to immediate attention, and speculation as to its
possible connection with the people who deposited the scrolls
made its systematic excavation desirable.[14]

Excavations in 1951 initiated a series of five campaigns,
the most recent in the spring of 1956.[15] The first soundings at
Khirbet Qumrân yielded enough evidence to permit the
tentative suggestion that the site was an ancient community-
center of the Essenes,[16] one of the major religious parties in
Judaism, who, together with the Pharisees and Sadducees,
competed for the loyalty of Jews in late pre-Christian and
early Christian times. Already the internal evidence of certain
of the sectarian manuscripts had led scholars to assign them an

13 De Vaux lists the older published materials relating to Khirbet
Qumrân in his article, "Fouille au Khirbet Qumrân," *RB* 60 (1953),
p. 89, notes 1–8; unpublished material is available in the files of
the Palestine Archaeological Museum.

14 De Vaux and Harding made surface explorations and dug two
tombs at Khirbet Qumrân in 1949. However, they were disinclined to
see any connection between the cave and the ruin. See De Vaux, *op. cit.*,
p. 89, and "La grotte des manuscrits hébreux," *RB* 56 (1949), 586, n.1.
These scholars were not satisfied, however, with the superficial character of their examination of the site; moreover, other scholars were
clamoring for further study of the site (see P. Kahle, *Die hebräischen
Handschriften aus der Höhle,* [Stuttgart, 1951], pp. 59 f.).

15 See De Vaux, "Fouille au Khirbet Qumrân," *RB* 60 (1953),
pp. 83–106; Harding, "Khirbet Qumrân and Wady Muraba'at," *PEQ*
84 (1952), pp. 104–9; De Vaux, "Fouille au Khirbet Qumrân. Rapport
préliminaire sur la deuxième campagne," *RB* 61 (1954), pp. 206–36;
"Chronique archéologique: Khirbet Qumrân," *RB* 61 (1954), pp. 567 f.;
RB 63 (1956), pp. 73 f.; and especially, "Fouilles de Khirbet Qumrân.
Rapport préliminaire sur les 3e, 4e et 5e campagnes," *RB* 63 (1956),
pp. 533–77. Cf. E. Vogt, "Effossiones in Hirbet Qumrân," *Biblica* 36
(1955), pp. 562–64 (with diagram of the ruins); J. A. Kelso, "The
Archaeology of Qumran," *JBL* 74 (1955), pp. 141–46; A. Parrot, "Les
manuscrits de la Mer Morte: le point de vue archéologique," *RHPR*
35 (1955), pp. 61–67; etc.

16 See De Vaux, "Fouille au Khirbet Qumrân," p. 105.

Essene authorship.[17] Slowly a new pattern began to emerge: the scrolls belonged to an ancient people who occupied the caves north and south of Khirbet Qumrân, and the ruin was precisely the Essene desert retreat remarked by the Roman historian Pliny.[18] However, in late 1951 this construction of the origin of the scrolls and the character of the site on the Wâdī Qumrân was yet to be established securely.

Concurrently, at the end of November 1951 a new large lot of documents was presented for sale at the École Biblique. It became clear, now, that the Ta'âmireh had continued their enterprise in the caves of the wilderness, and that their finds were of major importance. Père de Vaux entered directly into conversations with representatives of the Ta'âmireh, both to negotiate purchase and to seek information about the locality of the new series of caves. If unusual wit was needed to bargain successfully with the Bedouin for their precious manuscripts, one can only speculate on the adroitness required to educe the secret of the source of their treasure. Père de Vaux was equal to the task. At a visit of the tribesmen, when a rather high price was suggested for a fragment, De Vaux was openly, if not ostentatiously, horrified. The Bedouin then spoke eloquently of their "operations," the gargantuan caverns in which they worked, forty or fifty strong, for days and weeks, to recover the pieces presented for sale. When De Vaux appeared dubious about the details of their tale they energetically defended the account of their hardships, and argued (rhetorically) that if he would come and see, he would find them vindicated. Père de Vaux was not one to turn down even an oblique invitation. He would go! But, he hastened to remark, was there not danger from the police? Less energetically, no doubt, they allayed any fears of the police De Vaux might have entertained. They had sentinels posted

17 See especially A. Dupont-Sommer, *Aperçus préliminaires sur les Manuscrits de la Mer Morte* (Paris, 1950), pp. 105–17.

18 Pliny, *Naturalis historia*, V, xv, 73. Cf. *Dio apud Synesium* 39 (ed. Migne).

in the hills. If police appeared in the neighborhood, signals flashed through the wilderness and the workmen vanished into "the caverns of the rock and the clefts of the crags." De Vaux was reassured, and had a helpful suggestion to make as well. Perhaps he could get permission from the Department of Antiquities for the journey, so that neither he nor his guides need go to prison if caught. The Bedouin agreed that this was a capital idea. So he added another suggestion. Perhaps he could prevail on the Director of Antiquities himself to accompany them. The Bedouins indicated that they would be highly honored.

The expedition could not be launched until after the season of excavations at Khirbet Qumrân; but in late January a party set out including Harding and De Vaux, an Arab foreman, a police escort (!), and the Bedouin guides. A trip by truck into the edge of the wilderness, and a three-hour march farther brought them into the Wâdī Murabba'ât, a portion of the Wâdī Darâjeh. They came upon the site of the caves at a point about twelve miles southwest of the Qumrân caves, about twelve miles southeast of Bethlehem, in a landscape comparable to that ascribed to the moon. They were in a gorge whose vertical sides cut more than six hundred feet into the desolate mountains, about three miles short of its mouth in the Dead Sea. The caves were in the north face, about two hundred feet above the floor of the *wâdī* bed.

The first glimpse of the caves assured the party that they had come to the right place. A stream of Bedouin were fleeing the caves; De Vaux counted no less than thirty-four clandestine diggers slipping out! Four caves were found. Two of them contained inscribed material and evidence of ancient occupation. Each of the latter two attains a length of more more than one hundred fifty feet, one of them (Cave II) dividing into two long galleries which plunge deep into the cliff. The Bedouin proved Père de Vaux's skepticism ill-founded—to his delight—and while their description of the magnificence of the caves had been mildly exaggerated, their account of the hardships of working at the site had been under-stated. The excavations which followed were perhaps the most testing and arduous ever undertaken in Palestine.[19]

Scientific excavations were undertaken in the caves of Wâdī Murabba'ât from January 21 to March 3, 1952. Occupation levels and documentary materials of several periods were discovered. The caves had been the hiding places for guerillas, refugees, and brigand bands through the long troubled history of Palestine. There were evidences of men who had huddled in the caves three millennia before David hid from Saul's jealous wrath in the caves of this same hinterland. In the days of the Hyksos and the kings of Judah, in the era of the Jewish revolts against Rome and the Arab conquest, desperate men found shelter in the caverns of Murabba'ât and left behind bits of pottery and tools, and in the later periods scraps of their "papers" and books.[20]

Although the documents of the library of Qumrân are to be discussed following the narrative of the series of discoveries, perhaps it is best to describe the literary remains of unrelated discoveries in the context of our story.

Of considerable interest among written materials from Murabba'ât[21] is the earliest papyrus in Hebrew ever found in

19 The description of De Vaux's negotiations is told in his article, "Les grottes de Murabba'at et leur documents," *RB* 60 (1953), pp. 245–48. For the full color of the events leading to the discovery of the caves, however, one needs to hear the story from his own lips. Both Harding ("Khirbet Qumran and Wady Muraba'at," *PEQ* 84 [1952], pp. 104–9) and De Vaux (*op. cit.*, pp. 249–75) give vivid, detailed descriptions of the work in the caves. Cf. Allegro, *The Dead Sea Scrolls*, pp. 166–79.

20 That is, Chalcolithic, Middle Bronze II, Iron II, Roman, and Arab levels appeared superimposed in excavation.

21 For a partial catalogue of the texts, see the articles cited in n. 19. Several texts have been given preliminary publication: De Vaux, "Quelques textes hébreux de Murabba'at," *RB* 60 (1953), pp. 268–75; Milik, "Une lettre de Siméon Bar Kokheba," *ibid.*, pp. 276–94. For recent literature on the last-mentioned text, see Cross, "La lettre de Siméon Bar Kosba," *RB* 63 (1956), pp. 45–48; to which is to be added S. Yeivin, *'Atiqot* I (1955), pp. 95–108. The reports of the excavation

Palestine. Unfortunately, it is not a literary text; rather it is a list of names and numbers written in the script of the seventh century B.C.[22] Moreover, the piece is a palimpsest. The underwriting is dim, but appears to be a letter of roughly the same date. More important, no doubt, are a series of texts of the late first and early second centuries A.D. from a cache belonging, apparently, to remnants of the army of Simon bar Kokheba, the "pseudo-Messiah" who led the second Jewish revolt against Rome (A.D. 132–35). They include Greek, Aramaic, and Hebrew documents, among them dated letters and contracts, as well as a few biblical fragments.

Actually, the most important of the Murabba'ât finds, a magnificent scroll of the Minor Prophets from the second century A.D., came to light early in 1955. The preserved portion of the manuscript extends from the middle of Joel to the beginning of Zechariah, including (in traditional order) Amos, Obadiah, Jonah, Micah, Nahum, Habakkuk, Zephaniah, and Haggai. Four columns are almost perfectly preserved.[23]

While the archaeologists busied themselves in the Wâdī Murabba'ât in the early part of 1952, the Ta'âmireh, forced away from their new set of caves, took advantage of the absence of scientists from Qumrân to begin searches and soundings in the original area of discovery. In February 1952 the tribesmen found the fragmentary remains of manuscripts in a new cave hard by Cave I, no more than a few hundred yards to the south of it. Cave II, Qumrân, was not an impres-

in the Wâdī Murabba'ât, together with the publication of the texts, compose the second volume of *Discoveries in the Judaean Desert* (forthcoming).

22 Abbé Milik, who is to publish the text, prefers an eighth-century date (oral communication). The script is an unusual cursive; perhaps we should await publication and detailed paleographical analysis before committing ourselves too closely to a dating. One thing is clear, however, the script is archaic, not archaizing, and therefore is not to be compared with the paleo-Hebrew series of Qumrân.

23 The MS, found by *bedu*, purportedly comes from a fifth Murabba-'ât cave a kilometer or so east of the four investigated in 1952. As we shall see, the text of the Murabba'ât manuscript of the Twelve Prophets,

sive find.[24] However, the find was enough to bring the archaeologists—too late—out of the Wâdī Murabba'ât in a frantic
effort to keep up with the chain of discoveries.

With evidence now that more than one cave in the area of
Qumrân held pre-Christian manuscripts, and the growing
realization that the manuscripts actually derived from a community with its center at Khirbet Qumrân, the various archaeological schools in Jerusalem were galvanized. They mounted
an expedition to explore all the caves of the high rocky cliffs
north and south of Khirbet Qumrân on a line some five miles
long. The exploration was carried out during the month of
March 1952.[25] Teams of archaeologists, with foremen and
the obliging Ta'âmireh in their pay, clambered over the dizzy-
ing heights, systematically combing the cliffs. The excitement of the search turned aging scientists into a new breed
of archaeological mountain goats. Soundings were made in
more than two hundred caves. In twenty-five the pottery
recovered proved to come from the same potteries[26] which
had served the building complex at Khirbet Qumrân and
Cave I. Moreover, evidence was detected of tents and lean-tos
adjacent to clefts or caves containing domestic pottery of
the period, giving indication of an extensive occupation radi-
ating out from the communal buildings at Qumrân. However,

like that of the more fragmentary biblical material, is virtually identical
with the Masoretic consonantal tradition. See further in Chap. 4.

24 M. Baillet gives a full catalogue of its contents in "Le travail
d'édition des manuscrits de Qumrân," RB 73 (1956), p. 54. (This
article has now appeared in English translation, "Editing the Manuscript Fragments from Qumran," BA 19 [1956], pp. 75–96; Baillet's
account is on p. 81.)

25 See De Vaux, "Exploration de la région de Qumrân," RB 60
(1953), pp. 540–56; W. L. Reed, "The Qumrân Caves Expedition
of March, 1952," BASOR 135 (October, 1954), pp. 8–13.

26 That is, the pottery was not merely that common to the late
Hellenistic and early Roman period (first century B.C.–first century
A.D.); its paste, form, and decoration were sufficiently homogeneous to
suggest a common place of manufacture. As we shall see, this common
pottery is almost certainly the elaborate installation found in the excavations of the community center.

only one new cave produced inscribed materials. This was
Cave III, found on March 14, 1952. Its most spectacular treasure was dug out nearly a week later (the doorway of the cave
had collapsed in antiquity), the so-called "Copper Scrolls."

The "Copper Scrolls" are actually a single work, preserved
in two oxidized rolls of beaten copper. After a delay in which
experiments were made to discover a way in which the rolls
could be opened and deciphered, they were cut into small
strips at the Manchester College of Technology. The first announcement of their contents was made on June 1, 1956.[27]

The unique find had caused considerable speculation in the
interim between its discovery and decipherment. Hints of the
contents of the document had been gained by examination of
its exterior where reverse impressions of letters showed
through, thanks to the force of the engraver's hammer. It was
inscribed in Hebrew, more or less in the format of a leather or
papyrus scroll. Evidently it had to do with treasures and their
hiding places.[28]

Lost scrolls of high antiquity containing secrets of hidden
hoards of gold and silver: here was a subject to stir the imagination! One can excuse the soberest scientist being bitten by
the Gold Bug. But, as is virtually inevitable in the case of
legends of treasure, on full examination the Copper Document
proved disappointing.

The twelve columns of writing on the strips of copper list
some sixty treasures. The gold and silver, not to mention other
precious stuffs, come to more than two hundred tons of precious metal according to a minimal calculation. The specifi-
cations of the hiding places of the treasures are also given in
each case. Both the fabulous amounts of the treasures, and the
vague or traditional character of their hiding places are suffi-

27 The scrolls are scheduled to be published in the third volume of
Discoveries in the Judaean Desert along with other materials from the
"minor caves." Meanwhile, a provisional report on their opening and
contents may be found in J. T. Milik's article, "The Copper Document
from Cave III, Qumran," *BA* 19 (1956), pp. 60–64.

28 See n. 29.

cient evidence of the folkloristic character of the document. In any case, none of the decipherers of the Copper Document has come into sudden wealth—or has even invested in a compass and spade.

Presumably the strange text records the priestly or royal treasures which popular imagination assigned to old Israel, and supposed had survived in caches distributed over Palestine.[29] In some respects, indeed, the chief interest of the

29 On the Copper Document, K. G. Kuhn's provisional study, "Les rouleaux de cuivre de Qumrân," *RB* 61 (1954), pp. 193–205, is still useful. It is a bold and discerning attempt to reconstruct its text from what could be read in reverse on the outside of the rolls. However, his natural supposition that the treasures were actual Essene hoards buried in the neighborhood of Qumrân has proved untenable.

Mr. John Allegro's recent statements supporting the original form of the Kuhn hypothesis (*The Dead Sea Scrolls*, pp. 181–84) are, to the writer, quite bewildering. To be sure, the document is difficult, and a number of ambiguities are as yet unsolved. The points which are clear, however, can in no fashion be fitted into the picture drawn earlier by Kuhn: the size and type of the treasure, the vague or traditional places of concealment (coupled with precise measurements!), the vulgar dialect in which it is written, and the clumsiness of the scribe.

Professor Kuhn, himself, in an article published since the opening of the document (". . . Bericht über neue Qumranfunde und über die Offnung der Kupferrollen," *TLZ* 1956 cols. 541–46), proposes an alternate suggestion that the rolls may contain a record of real treasures, presumably those of the Herodian Temple destroyed in A.D. 70, and that this record may have been put into the hands of the Essenes for safekeeping.

Though it is clear from Josephus' notices that the Temple treasures were burned or taken by the Romans, at least in considerable part, as Kuhn observes, it is not impossible that some treasures were secretly hidden.

I am in agreement that the treasures probably are meant to be national and/or temple treasures of Israel. But I am dubious that even the temple of Herod could have mustered such glittering heaps of gold and silver, much less that such amounts escaped the greedy besiegers. Moreover, in this hypothesis, the treasures would necessarily have been smuggled out and hidden in the early days of the Revolt, and the lists transmitted to Qumrân before the latter's demise early in the Revolt (A.D. 68). Perhaps this is possible; in any case it must be admitted that the date of the Copper Scroll—scarcely earlier than the middle of the first century A.D.—raises no objection.

A more serious objection comes when one recognizes that under

text—now that it is open—is in the proto-Mishnaic dialect in which it is written.

The attrition of heat, malaria, and simple fatigue brought the expedition to a halt at the end of March. It had succeeded in investigating most of the natural caves of the limestone

such a hypothesis we must assume that temple officials gave a list to the counter-priesthood at Qumrân, whose open contempt for their orthodox brethren in Jerusalem can scarcely have been unilateral. This dilemma is avoided if the document was made up after Zealot forces took control of the temple, but in this case we are in chronological difficulties again.

Again, I cannot believe that the document in hand was in any sense official. Too much has been made (by the writer as well as others) of the costliness of copper. The scribe appears unskilled. Even taking into account the awkward material in which he worked, he cannot be compared with the facile scribes of Qumrân. And the notion of a priestly official having a record of treasure made up in copper and hidden against the future in a remote cave seems overly dramatic.

I should prefer to propose, tentatively to be sure, that we have to do with traditional, i.e., fabulous treasures, perhaps of the temple of Solomon. Such would "appropriately" be hidden in the monument of Absalom, the cairn of Achan, and in Mount Gerizim (of the Samaritans!). And it is just possible to imagine a priestly hermit of Qumrân taking such folkloristic traditions seriously enough to preserve them in copper. Mr. J. Strugnell has called my attention to II Baruch 6:7–10 in this connection. Professor Stendahl has reminded me of the curious tale of "holy vessels" hidden (by Moses according to Josephus' text) in Mount Gerizim, told in the days of Pilate (*Antiq.* XVIII, 85–87).

It may be observed in this connection that Cave III, like most of the "minor caves," should not be thought of as a "hiding place," much less a *genîzāh* for Essene documents. Rather the minor caves are to be designated as repositories for members of the Essene community who lived in the cliffs. Presumably the remnants from the minor caves constitute the remains of scrolls in private use, most of them no doubt copied at the Qumrân center, and "lent out from the main library," so to speak. The Copper Document, like other texts from this and other caves, was left behind lying openly on the ancient floor, presumably at the time of the Roman attack of A.D. 68. Cave IV, with its massive remains of nearly 400 MSS, and possibly Cave I, with some seventy documents, at least three of which were in a jar, are to be treated as exceptions. Cave I may have been a hiding place, sought out when the settlement appeared doomed; Cave IV almost certainly contained the remnants of the great collection originally housed in the community center only a stone's throw distant from its opening.

cliffs. On the other hand, it had ignored the artificial caves and clefts in the marl terrace at the foot of the cliffs.[30] Time and funds were short, and logical Western minds, noting that the caves which had yielded manuscripts all were located in the upper level, concluded that exploration of the marl caves was to no purpose. So the archaeologists retired from the desert of Qumrân. The Bedouin continued the search. Being less logical, and perhaps less energetic, they attacked the marl terrace supporting Khirbet Qumrân. In the late summer of 1952 they discovered a cave two hundred yards or less from the site of the Essene center and, some feet beneath the modern floor of the cave, came upon the matted and decayed remains of manuscripts. They had struck the main lode: Qumrân Cave IV.

The clandestine diggings of the Ta'âmireh were halted, fortunately, before the contents of the cave were exhausted.[31] In the month of September (22–29) 1952 controlled excavations replaced Bedouin efforts and met with good finds in the remaining untouched levels of the cave. To be sure, the lion's share fell to the clansmen; but Harding, De Vaux, and their co-workers succeeded in recovering fragments belonging to

30 The marl caves (Caves IV–X) are clearly the work of human hands in ancient times. No doubt they made handy living quarters immediately adjacent to the communal buildings, which, to judge from the function of the architectural details, made little provision for the living accommodations of the large community at Qumrân. It is not impossible that the caves were originally cut for tombs for the Iron II (ninth–sixth century B.C.) settlement which underlies the Essene structures. Despite search, no Iron Age tombs have come to light. Against this it must be said that no Iron Age deposits have been found in the floor levels of the marl caves, an extraordinary circumstance even if the caves had been thoroughly cleaned and expanded in Hellenistic-Roman times.

31 According to reports, the well-organized Ta'âmireh had teams working in shifts to hasten their exploitation of the cave. At least one new entrance was opened into the cave. More than a meter of debris appears to have been removed in the process of their diggings. But so well had they learned their new trade that few scraps remained in their dumps.

more than a hundred manuscripts, including pieces of most of the chief manuscripts of the cave. Obviously this circumstance has proved important in establishing beyond doubt the provenience of lots of Cave IV fragments bought from Bedouin over the following five years.[32]

Caves V and VI were found in conjunction with the discovery of Cave IV. Cave VI, situated near the waterfall of Wâdī Qumrân, low in the rocky face where in geological times the marl terrace was cut away by the cascade, was discovered by Ta'âmireh in the late summer. Cave V was discovered by scientists during the excavations in Cave IV; it is located immediately north of Cave IV in the marly terrace. Both V and VI contained significant but minor finds.

The summer of 1952 brought as by-products of the desert search other series of manuscript discoveries in precincts of the wilderness remote from Qumrân. The most significant of these is a cave or caves discovered by the Ta'âmireh in a locality which has never been precisely fixed; though it seems clear enough that it lies to the south of Murabba'ât in one of the *wâdīs* that empty into the Dead Sea. These documents of undesignated provenience made their appearance in Jerusalem in July 1952 and were bought up in several purchases in the month following. Like Murabba'ât, the bulk of them

32 Among the scientifically excavated materials deep in undisturbed soil were such odd items as Septuagint fragments, phylacteries, paleo-Hebrew materials, cursive bits of Exodus, as well as the usual Qumrân run of Hebrew and Aramaic documents on papyrus and leather. The writer had the opportunity to begin his labors on the scrolls by examining and doing preliminary identification of the excavated materials before they were combined with the great mass of purchased fragments. I was struck with the fact that the relatively small quantity of fragments from the deepest levels of the cave nevertheless represented a fair cross section of the whole deposit in the cave, which suggests, among other things, that deterioration of the manuscripts must have begun even before time sealed the manuscripts in the stratified soil, and that the manuscripts may have been in great disorder when originally abandoned in the cave. The paucity of sherds in the cave certainly indicates that the scrolls of Cave IV were not left stored away in jars.

must be attributed to the era between the Jewish revolts against Rome.[33] The most important text for our purposes, no doubt, is a manuscript of the Minor Prophets in Greek, a lost recension of the Septuagint, the old Greek version of the third-second centuries B.C. When combined with three "standard" Septuagint manuscripts from Cave IV, Qumrân,[34] this newly found recension will place textual critics in a much improved position to reconstruct the early history of the text of the Septuagint.[35] [36]

33 Several of the texts of the find have been published together with brief notices of the find as a whole: Barthélemy, "Redécouverte d'un chaînon manquant de l'histoire de la Septante," *RB* 60 (1953), pp. 18–29; J. Starcky, "Un contrat nabatéen sur papyrus," *RB* 61 (1954), pp. 161–81; J. T. Milik, "Un contrat juif de l'an 134 après J.-C.," *RB* (1954), pp. 182–90.

34 Qumrân IV has produced leather fragments of two MSS of the LXX—one of Leviticus, the other of Numbers. A third MS, represented by papyrus fragments, is a second copy of Leviticus. These documents are probably to be dated in the first century B.C. paleographically; in any case, none can be later than the early first century of our era. There is no doubt that they belong to the common LXX tradition. This is noteworthy in as much as they derive from a pre-Christian Jewish community in Palestine. Otherwise only two fragmentary papyri of comparable age are known, both of Egyptian provenience. I am indebted to Patrick W. Skehan for permitting me to read in manuscript his treatment of the Qumrân LXX fragments published in *Actes du 2e Congrès international pour l'étude de l'Ancien Testament, Strasbourg, 1956*.

35 In addition to Barthélemy's preliminary publication (see n. 33), cf. Vogt, "Fragmenta Prophetarum minorum deserti Iuda," *Biblica* 34 (1953), pp. 423–26; J. W. Wevers, "Septuaginta-Forschungen I," *TR* 22 (1954), pp. 136–38; K. Stendahl, *The School of St. Matthew* (Copenhagen, 1954), pp. 177–80; Cross, "The Manuscripts of the Dead Sea Caves," *BA* 17 (1954), pp. 12 f.; P. Kahle, ". . . Die im August 1952 entdeckte Lederrolle mit dem griechischen Text der kleinen Propheten und das Problem der Septuaginta," *TLZ* 79 (1954), pp. 82–94; P. Katz, "Septuagintal Studies in the Mid-Century," in *The Background of the New Testament and its Eschatalogy*, W. D. Davies and D. Daube, eds. (Cambridge, 1956), pp. 206–8.

36 Mention also may be made at this point in our narrative of the late Byzantine and early Arabic finds from the cisterns of Khirbet Mird (ancient Hyrcania) by Bedouin in the summer of 1952. For references

Quiet descended upon the desert for nearly three years, save for the seasonal excavations at the site of Khirbet Qumrân. Then, in the spring of 1955 came a new cycle of finds.[37] During the fourth campaign at Qumrân four additional productive caves were located and exploited: VII–X. Like Caves IV and V, these latter were found in the marl terrace adjacent to the settlement. Unlike Cave IV, they had collapsed in ancient times as a result of erosion along the ravines which make up the complex of the Wâdī Qumrân. Only a handful of fragments was recovered from all of these caves combined, enough to prove, only, that manuscripts had once been deposited in them. Most of the treasures had washed with the winter torrents into the sea.[37a]

Finally, or perhaps we should say most recently, the ubiquitous tribesmen detected another cave not far from Cave III, well over a mile to the north of the ruin.[38] Its entrance was collapsed, but crevices remained open through which hosts of bats fluttered at dusk and dawn. By Herculean efforts the cave was opened and excavated by the finders. Their labors were thorough; when archaeologists pitched their tents on the plain below and halted the unauthorized digging, little more than Iron Age and Chalcolithic levels remained untouched, sealed

to the discoveries and the subsequent expedition of the Mission Archéologique Belge de Louvain in February–April 1953, see Milik, "Un inscription et une lettre en araméen christo–palestinien," *RB* 60 (1953), pp. 526–39, especially pp. 526 f.; De Vaux, "Fouille au Khirbet Qumrân," *ibid.*, p. 85; and Cross, "The Manuscripts of the Dead Sea Caves," p. 12.

37 For the discovery in the Wâdī Murabba'ât in early 1955, see n. 23.

37a See provisionally, De Vaux, "Fouilles de Khirbet Qumrân . . . 3ᵉ, 4ᵉ et 5ᵉ campagnes," pp. 572 f. Of especial interest are some papyrus bits of the Greek Epistle of Jeremiah from Cave VII.

38 Cave III lies at map co-ordinates 193.5:129.8 (cave no. 8 of the exploration map [*RB* 60, 1953, Pl. XX opposite p. 560]). No co-ordinates are published for Cave XI; however, the cave lies low in the *falaise*, well to the north of Cave I, and slightly south of Cave III.

in millennial deposits of bat guano. Two virtually complete scrolls were taken by Taʿâmireh, and significant fragments of at least five other works by Taʿâmireh and archaeologists. Cave XI thus rivals Caves I and IV in importance.

3. A Catalogue of the Library of Qumrân

We shall be concerned here chiefly with the great collection from Cave IV. Cave I texts are now almost completely published and relatively well known; those of Cave XI have received only the most cursory examination, and, while in the possession of the Palestine Archaeological Museum, are not yet purchased. The remaining "minor caves" have produced each only some few ill-preserved fragments, and aside from the Copper Document discussed at some length above, can be relegated to footnotes.[39]

From Cave I came the seven manuscripts of the original shepherd find. These are the great Isaiah scroll (1QIsaᵃ), a commentary (*péšer*) on Habakkuk (1QpHab), and the Rule of the Community (1QS), all three published by the American Schools of Oriental Research in 1950–51.[40] Another group

39 A full catalogue of the texts of Caves II, III, V, and VI may be found in "Le travail d'édition des manuscrits de Qumrân," pp. 54–56 ("Editing the Manuscript Fragments from Qumrân," pp. 81–83). Texts from the minor caves which have received preliminary publication may be found in the following articles: R. de Vaux, "Exploration de la région de Qumrân," pp. 555–57 and Pl. XXIVb; M. Baillet, "Fragments araméens de Qumrân 2. Description de la Jérusalem Nouvelle," *RB* 62 (1955), pp. 222–45; "Fragments du document de Damas: Qumrân, grotte 6," *RB* 63 (1956), pp. 513–23.

40 Burrows, Trever, Brownlee, eds., *The Dead Sea Scrolls of St. Mark's Monastery;* Vol. I, *The Isaiah Manuscript and the Habakkuk Commentary* (New Haven, 1950); Vol. II: 2, *Plates and Transcription of the Manual of Discipline* (New Haven, 1951).

The literature on these scrolls is now quite extensive. For bibliography the reader is referred to the excellent listings of H. H. Rowley, *The Zadokite Fragments and the Dead Sea Scrolls* (Oxford, 1952), pp. 89–125; and M. Burrows, *The Dead Sea Scrolls* (New York, 1955),

of three, published in 1954 by Hebrew University scholars, includes a second, fragmentary copy of Isaiah (1QIsa^b); a sectarian collection of thanksgiving psalms (*hôdāyôt;* 1QH);[41] and an extraordinary document called the Order of the War Between the Children of Light and the Children of Darkness

pp. 419–35. More recent items may be found in the *Elenchus Bibliographicus Biblicus* published yearly by *Biblica* under the heading "Manuscripta Deserti Juda" (1954: pp. 58°–62°; 1955: pp. 46°–50°; 1956: 42°–47°), as well as under biblical books: Isaias, Prophetae Minores, etc.

For translations of the Habakkuk Commentary, the non-specialist is directed to the translations in English of Burrows, *The Dead Sea Scrolls,* pp. 365–70; Gaster, *The Dead Sea Scriptures* (Anchor Books, Garden City, New York, 1956). The most comprehensive study (with text and translation) is that of Elliger, *Studien zum Habakuk-Kommentar vom Toten Meer* (Tübingen, 1953), on which cf. the review article of Dupont-Sommer, "Quelques remarques sur le *Commentaire d'Habacuc,* à propos d'un livre récent," *VT* 5 (1955), pp. 113–29.

For translations of the Rule of the Community (the so-called Manual of Discipline) in English, the reader is directed to Burrows, Gaster, and W. H. Brownlee, *The Dead Sea Manual of Discipline (Supplementary Studies* 10–12 of the *BASOR*) (New Haven, 1951). A vocalized Hebrew text has been published by A. M. Habermann, '*dh w'dwt* (Jerusalem, 1952), pp. 62–88; and by R. Marcus, "On the Text of the Qumran Manual of Discipline, I–IX," *JNES* XVI (1957), pp. 24–38.

41 Sukenik and Avigad, *OMG.* For bibliographical resources, see n. 40. The best of the older translations of 1QH is that of G. S. Glanzman, "Sectarian Psalms from the Dead Sea," *Theological Studies* 13 (1952), pp. 487–524. Among the better English translations are those of Burrows and Gaster cited above, and Baumgarten and Mansoor, "Studies in the New *Hodayot* (Thanksgiving Hymns), I–III," *JBL* 74 (1955), pp. 115–24; pp. 188–95; *JBL* 75 (1956), pp. 107–13. J. Licht (cf. "The Doctrine of the Thanksgiving Scroll," *IEJ* 6 [1956], pp. 1–13; 89–101) has announced a substantial monograph (in Hebrew) on the *hôdāyôt.*

On the special problems raised by the psalm in *OMG* Pl. 37, ll.1–18, see J. V. Chamberlain, "Another Qumran Thanksgiving Psalm," *JNES* 14 (1955), pp. 32–41; "Further Elucidation of a Messianic Thanksgiving Psalm from Qumran," *ibid.,* pp. 181 f.; A. Dupont-Sommer, "La mère du Messie et la mère de l'Aspic dans un hymne de Qoumrân," *RHR* 147 (1955), pp. 174–88; L. H. Silberman, "Language and Structure in the *Hodayot* (1QH3)," *JBL* 75 (1956), pp. 96–106; Mowinckel, "Some Remarks on *Hodayot* 39.5–20," *ibid.,* pp. 265–76, especially p. 276.

(1QM).[42] The seventh of these scrolls recently has had preliminary publication under the title *A Genesis Apocryphon*.[43] It is an elaboration of Genesis in Aramaic, and will prove most useful as a basis for linguistic analyses of the Aramaic of Palestine in a little-known era. To these seven are to be added the seventy fragmentary manuscripts, biblical, apocryphal, apocalyptic, liturgical, published in 1955 in the first volume of *Discoveries in the Judaean Desert*.[44]

Detailed descriptions of the scrolls from Cave XI are yet to be published.[45] The best preserved of these materials is a magnificent scroll which contains, in the portion which has been opened, certain of the canonical psalms. It appears to be the Book of Psalms relatively intact. I suspect that only the Isaiah scroll (1QIsa^a) will prove to be in a better state of preservation among the biblical texts from Qumrân. There is a second biblical text, a copy of Leviticus in a late, paleo-Hebrew script,[46] which is only slightly less well preserved.

42 The best and most thorough treatment of 1QM is that of Y. Yadin, *mgylt mlḥmt bny 'wr bbny ḥwšk mmgylwt mdbr yhwdh* (Jerusalem, 1955). An English translation is to appear shortly. The non-specialist is referred to the translations of Burrows and Gaster already cited, and to J. Van der Ploeg, "La Règle de la guerre," *VT* 5 (1955), pp. 373–420, perhaps the best of the several French translations which have appeared.

43 Edited by N. Avigad and Y. Yadin (Jerusalem, 1956). The roll has been called the Apocalypse of Lamech mistakenly, since a preliminary identification was made on the basis of a few scraps which had broken off before the badly preserved scroll was opened. Cf. Trever "Identification of the Aramaic Fourth Scroll from 'Ain Feshkha," *BASOR* 115 (October 1949), pp. 8–10; *DJD I*, pp. 86.; and *BA* 19 (1956), pp. 22–24.

44 Among the several longer reviews and review articles dealing with *DJD I*, see especially F. M. Cross, "Qumran Cave I," *JBL* 75 (1956), pp. 121–25; J. Hempel, "Randbemerkungen zu Qumran I," *ZAW* 67 (1955), pp. 131–39; H. M. Orlinsky, *Jewish Social Studies* 18 (1956), pp. 217–20; E. Vogt, *Biblica* 37 (1956), pp. 231–35.

45 Announcement of the details of the discovery, and preliminary description of the texts, is scheduled before the time of the appearance of these lectures. The writer's remarks here are based on superficial examination of the material in the summer of 1956.

46 This script, sometimes incorrectly called "Phoenician," or

Among only four of five non-biblical works so far tentatively
identified are two of interest: a fragmentary copy of the
"Description of the New Jerusalem,"[47] and a lost Targum of
Job. The latter is of particular interest because since it ap-
pears to be the Targum condemned by the Rabbi Gamaliel I
(Paul's alleged teacher, cf. Acts 22:3), and among the earliest
Targums committed to writing.[48]

From Cave IV have come tens of thousands of fragments,
as we have remarked, and the collection is unrivaled in its
size and import. It seems clear that the great library once
housed in the Essene community center was abandoned in
Cave IV; in its texts we find a cross section of the literature of
sectarian Judaism at the end of the pre-Christian era.

Unlike the several scrolls of Caves I and XI which are
preserved in good condition, with only minor lacunae, the
manuscripts of Cave IV are in an advanced state of decay.
Many fragments are so brittle or friable that they can scarcely
be touched with a camel's-hair brush. Most are warped, crinkled, or shrunken, crusted with soil chemicals, blackened
by moisture and age. The problems of cleaning, flattening,
identifying, and piecing them together are formidable.[49]

The fragments when they are purchased from tribesmen
generally come in boxes; cigarette boxes, film boxes, or shoe
boxes, depending on the size of the fragments. The precious

"Samaritan," derives from the old pre-exilic Hebrew script. Apparently
it survived as a book hand and enjoyed a renascence in the period of
Maccabean nationalism and archaism. In any case, at Qumrân it appears
in documents contemporary with the Jewish hand, a derivative of the
official Aramaic cursive of the late Persian Empire. The Samaritan is
a descendant of this paleo-Hebrew script of the Hasmonaean period.

47 Cf. *DJD I*, p. 134; "Le travail d'édition . . ." pp. 55 f.; Baillet, *RB*
62 (1955), pp. 222–45.

48 Talmud Babl., Shabbat 115a; Talm. Jer., Shabbat 16a; The addition at the end of the Septuagint to Job may be quoted from this Targum.

49 Cf. Père Benoit's description of the process of editing the fragments in "Le travail d'édition . . ." pp. 52 ff. ("Editing the Manuscript
Fragments . . ." pp. 79 ff.)

leather and papyrus is delicately handled by rough Bedouin hands, for the value of the material is all too keenly appreciated. Often cotton wool or tissue paper has been used by Bedouin to separate and protect the scraps of scrolls; and on occasion they have applied bits of gummed paper to pieces which threatened to crack apart or disintegrate. Not since the clandestine digs of Cave I have owners broken up large sheets or columns to sell them piecemeal.

Since 1952 when the cave was found, its myriads of fragments have slowly been gathered into the Palestine Archaeological Museum in Jerusalem. The major share was acquired by a purchase of the government of Jordan from Ta'âmireh, and by the controlled excavations. However, these initial acquisitions by no means exhausted the cave's treasures. After the Department of Antiquities, the Palestine Museum, and other institutions in Jordan had exhausted their financial resources for the purchase of antiquities, the Council of Ministers of Jordan passed legislation permitting reputable foreign institutions to purchase additional lots of manuscripts of Cave IV remaining in Bedouin hands. Such purchases were arranged by the Director of Antiquities, on the condition that scrolls so purchased remain in the Palestine Archaeological Museum for editing, after which they are to be distributed to their owners. Such an arrangement had several advantages. First of all, it prevented loss by destruction or smuggling at the hands of Bedouin; it permitted the fragments to be bought through established official channels at standard prices (about $2.80 per square centimeter of inscribed surface); and more important, it kept the great mass of fragments in one center for editing. Had they been scattered, much of their usefulness would have been destroyed, since obviously much of the joining of fragments into large complexes can be done only with the original leather. Finally donors were to receive in this plan, not the unsorted fragments belonging to the actual lot which their money happened to purchase, but *all* fragments belonging to a group of manuscripts equivalent in size to the amount contributed for purchase.

On this basis lots have been acquired by McGill, Manchester, and Heidelberg universities, the Vatican Library, and, most recently (1956), McCormick Theological Seminary (Chicago).

An international, interconfessional team of eight scholars has been appointed to prepare and publish the manuscripts of Cave IV. From France are two scholars, Fathers D. Barthélemy, O.P., and J. Starcky; from Poland, Father J. T. Milik (now attached to the Centre National de la Recherche Scientifique); from England, Messrs. John Allegro of Manchester and John Strugnell, lately of Jesus College, Oxford; from Germany, Dr. Claus-Hunno Hunzinger of Göttingen; and from America Monsignor Patrick W. Skehan of the Catholic University of America and the writer. The workroom of the Palestine Museum is a veritable Babel of languages. Actually the staff exhibits a remarkably ecumenical spirit. There is a harmony of scientific presuppositions, shared excitement in new discoveries, and a common good humor. Only at night in the café gardens is theology argued.

On arrival at the Palestine Museum, purchased groups of fragments are in unbelievable disorder. Many large, well-preserved fragments come in each lot. But large or small, well or ill preserved, most must be exposed to a process of humidification, cleaned of incrustations and dirt, and repaired or reinforced before being pressed flat between glass plates. Fragments in advanced decay, especially lumps of coagulated layers of leather, require more energy and patience and special techniques, though the same general procedure is followed. Often a fragment will exhibit an area of acute decay and shrinkage in the midst of otherwise pliable leather. The bad spot may draw the entire fragment into a crinkled or scalloped ball, so that the fragment is almost impossible to flatten. The script in such an area of decay may be shrunk to half or less the size of that in good areas. Often such decomposition in sheets of leather has caused splitting and fragmentation, and the problems of fitting into one manuscript healthy, light fragments alongside of wizened and blackened scraps are, to say the least, tedious.

Once the fragments are cleaned and flattened, they must be photographed. Normally all fragments are exposed on infrared plates; it is especially useful in the case of leather materials which have blackened. The infrared does not affect the carbon ink of the documents; it pales out the browns and deep reds of the decaying leather. Often a piece wholly illegible to the naked eye can be read easily on long-exposed plates. Occasionally, especially where the ink is dim or partially gone, ultraviolet photography and special lighting techniques have salvaged texts which seemed hopelessly illegible.

The process of identification and joining goes on apace. When a scholar has worked some years with the scribes of Qumrân they become old friends, and the date of their hands typologically, the personal idiosyncrasies of their scripts, and the various manuscripts which they prepared become so well known that they are recognized at a glance. Nevertheless, fragments belonging to a given work must be specifically identified, and joins with other fragments sought out. A single fragment may require many hours of study before it receives exact identification and is placed in a slowly growing column of a manuscript. Moreover, the action of soil and moisture, not to mention generations of ancient worms, has frayed or distorted the edges of fragments in such a fashion that joins are not obvious. This is the ultimate in jigsaw puzzles.

Biblical fragments are most quickly separated and identified. Usually they have a standard format and are written in an elegant book hand; scribal treatment of non-canonical works is rarely as careful or fine. More than that, the text is well known, and small combinations of words or even letters are readily discovered in a concordance. Rarely, biblical texts are sufficiently at variance with the traditional text that they escape immediate identification; in the case of certain of the historical books a concordance to the Septuagint is more efficient in making specific identification of fragments belonging to a recognized manuscript.

Non-biblical fragments are sorted into groups and reconstructed with much greater effort. In the case of published manuscripts of other caves a complete concordance has been prepared by the staff to facilitate identification. Certain other texts are known in Greek, Latin, and Ethiopic versions and can with patience be identified by passage and put together. Texts which are wholly unknown must be reconstructed simply by discovering mechanical joins until the structure and development of the work are discerned.

Beginning in 1953, long tables filled with plates of unknown fragments were placed at one end of the museum workroom; a few tables at the other end were reserved for identified fragments. In the summer of 1956 the workroom held long tables of identified material, some twenty-odd plates only remaining of unidentified material. Meanwhile each fragment and its photograph have been studied many times by each of the staff, so often that the shape, script, and verbiage of the fragment become filed away in the memory against the moment when suddenly its place appears on a manuscript being reconstructed.

All this is preliminary work. The tasks of paleographical analysis, transcription, textual study or translation, as the case may be, and interpretation then follow before the editor is ready to publish his completed manuscript groups.

A sketch of the contents of Cave IV may be helpful in the discussions to follow. At the end of four years' labor 382 manuscripts have been identified from this cave. The number can change. A few thousands of fragments are awaiting initial identification. New lots are still being bought from Bedouin, the latest in July 1956. Most of the material from new lots and the plates of unidentified fragments belongs, however, to known documents and presently will be fitted in place in gaping lacunae. Of the manuscripts identified thus far, about one hundred, slightly more than one fourth of the total, are biblical. All of the books of the Hebrew canon are now extant, with the exception of the Book of Esther.[50]

The best-preserved manuscript of the biblical lot, and in some ways the most important biblical document of all the finds, is a manuscript of Samuel designated 4QSam[a].[51] The secret of its relatively good state of preservation is a backing of papyrus applied in antiquity, perhaps a half century or so after it was copied.[52] As expected, both books of Samuel were copied on a single roll. A total of forty-seven of the fifty-seven columns of the original manuscript is preserved in fragmentary form. II Samuel is the better preserved; some pieces of each of its twenty-four columns are extant, and the disposition of its columns can be reconstructed rather closely. The best-preserved columns are the first, especially 2–5 (II Sam. 2–5). On the other hand, Chapters 15–21 are represented only by a few small fragments. Of thirty-three columns originally belonging to I Samuel, columns 12, 16, 18–24, and 28 are missing. After column 12 the calculation of the columns is by no means certain, save in isolated cases. Columns 2, 3, and 6 are the best preserved of I Samuel. However, in no part of Sam-

---

50 See Cross, "A Report on the Biblical Fragments of Cave Four in Wâdî Qumrân," *BASOR* 141 (February 1956), pp. 9–13; "Le travail d'édition . . ." pp. 56–58.

51 Fragments of this MS recovered in the controlled excavations of Cave IV by Harding and De Vaux have been given preliminary publication in Cross, "A New Qumran Biblical Fragment Related to the Original Hebrew Underlying the Septuagint." *BASOR* 132 (December 1953), pp. 15–26; cf. the corrections to the reconstruction in Cross, "The Oldest Manuscripts from Qumran," *JBL* 74 (1955), p. 165, n. 40.

52 This is deduced from two factors: (1) The scroll was reinforced in places with leather even before the papyrus backing was applied, suggesting the scroll was considerably worn; and (2) the papyrus is inscribed (unfortunately on the side which was gummed to the leather), and while no extensive parts can be read, the script appears somewhat later than that of the leather roll.

uel, at least for the present, do we have a complete or nearly complete column.[53]

The importance of this exemplar of Samuel lies less in its bulk than in the unusual text it records. As we shall see, it belongs to a textual family known to us hitherto only in the Septuagint.[54] Even more extraordinary, in passages where Samuel and Chronicles overlap, this manuscript often preserves a text much closer to the text of Samuel used by the author of Chronicles than to the traditional text of Samuel surviving from the Middle Ages.

At the other extreme is the single copy of the Book of Chronicles from Qumrân. It is found on a three-inch strip of leather. Parts of six lines, two columns, are preserved; but worms have gorged themselves on Holy Writ. The result is leather lace with only four complete words legible.

A fairly extensive group of fragments belong to a late (Herodian) manuscript of Numbers (4QNum[b]); its text is of great interest, taking a middle position between the Old Samaritan and the Old Greek. The roll is unique in being decorated by its scribe with red ink. Headings of sections are inscribed in red; the ink is still bright enough to read easily with the naked eye; the infrared film of the photographer, however, is blind to the rubrication, and certain technical problems are thereby raised. If infrared plates are used, the black ink is visible, the red invisible. If color film is used, the reverse is true. Presumably the problem will be solved in publication by use of filters and double printing.

Three very old documents have been found in Cave IV. Presumably they are master scrolls, imported into Qumrân at the founding of the community. They include an old copy

53 There are some sixteen plates of large quarto size filled with fragments of this manuscript, and it is always possible that with new accessions, it will be enlarged.

54 The affinities of 4QSam[a] with the tradition of the Septuagint are somewhat closer than even the published fragments might lead one to expect, to judge from the very ample cross section of its text now in process of being edited.

of Samuel, preserved in only a handful of fragments;[55] a patched and worn section of Jeremiah, red and translucent with age (4QJer[a]); and a copy of Exodus (4QEx[f]) of which only a column and a few tatters are extant. The last-mentioned was studied for the first time in the summer of 1956. Its condition is such that decipherment was successful only with the aid of both infrared and ultraviolet photographs, and by *étude par transparence,* reading by a strong light projected *through* the leather.[56]

The archaic Samuel scroll can date scarcely later than 200 B.C. A date in the last quarter of the third century is preferable.[57] The Jeremiah is probably slightly later. The archaic Exodus has not been subjected to detailed paleographical analysis; moreover, its script belongs to a proto-cursive type less well known than the formal or book hand. Nevertheless it appears to be no later than the old Samuel fragments and probably is earlier.

One copy of Daniel is inscribed in the script of the late second century B.C.; in some ways its antiquity is more striking than that of the oldest manuscripts from Qumrân, since it is no more than about a half century younger than the autograph of Daniel. It is thus closer to the original edition of a biblical work than any biblical manuscript in existence, unless it be the Rylands Fragment of John from the first half of the second century A.D.

A special category among the biblical documents is a group written in paleo-Hebrew script.[58] These include five Pentateuchal manuscripts and some fragments of Job. Especially

55 Published by the writer, "The Oldest Manuscripts from Qumran." A sample of the script of the Jeremiah scroll (see below) is given in Fig. 2 of this article. Since publication of the archaic Samuel (4QSam[b]), a number of small fragments have been added.

56 The technique proved quite useful also in deciphering blackened portions of 1QSa (see Barthélemy, *DJD I, ad loc.*).

57 Cf. the extended paleographical discussion in "The Oldest Manuscripts from Qumran," pp. 147–65.

58 See n. 46.

interesting is a superb specimen of Exodus which presents a text type related to the Samaritan recension of Exodus.[59]

The biblical scrolls from Qumrân span in date about three centuries. A few archaic specimens carry us back to the end of the third century, as we have seen. The heavy majority, however, date in the first century B.C. and in the first Christian century, the series terminating with the death of the community center in A.D. 68.[60]

The most popular books among the sectarians, to judge from the number of copies preserved in Cave IV, are Deuteronomy, 14 MSS; Isaiah, 12 MSS; and Psalms, 10 MSS. There are also eight copies of the Book of the Twelve Prophets. None is complete. We cannot always be sure that all twelve of the Minor Prophets were copied on a given roll. There can be no doubt, however, that this was the standard practice at Qumrân, as in the case of the great Minor Prophets scroll of the second century A.D. from Murabba'ât.

Another large portion of Cave IV documents belongs to the category of Apocryphal and Pseudepigraphical works in both Hebrew and Aramaic: Tobit, Jubilees,[61] The Psalms of Joshua, pseudo-Jeremianic works, Testaments of Levi and Naphtali,[62] sources of the later Testaments of the Twelve Patriarchs, Enoch, and an apocryphal Daniel literature[63] are examples.

There is another lot of specifically sectarian works, though

59 See P. W. Skehan, "Exodus in the Samaritan Recension from Qumran," *JBL* 74 (1955), pp. 182–87.

60 Specifically sectarian scrolls (as distinguished from non-biblical in general) are much more restricted in date, the earliest dating to the late second century B.C.; cf. the writer's remarks, "The Oldest MSS from Qumran," p. 164, n. 35.

61 From Cave II came a few fragments of Ecclesiasticus (Ben Sira).

62 See J. T. Milik, "Le Testament de Lévi en araméen. Fragment de la grotte 4 de Qumrân," *RB* 62 (1955), pp. 398–406. The Testament of Naphtali is unpublished, and only recently identified.

63 Cf. J. T. Milik, " 'Prière de Nabonide' et autres écrits d'un cycle de Daniel," *RB* 63 (1956), pp. 407–15.

this category overlaps with the former. In this group fall the recensions of the Rule of the Community, best known from Cave I; the Damascus Document known otherwise from the old Karaite synagogue of Cairo;[64] and various books too numerous to list in detail, containing laws, liturgies, prayers, beatitudes, blessings, hymns, and wisdom of the Essenes.[65]

There are the biblical "commentaries," including works on Psalms, Hosea, Isaiah, and Nahum[66] (cf. Micah, Zephaniah, Psalms, and Habakkuk from Cave I[67]). The commentary on Nahum is remarkable because of its direct allusions to known historical figures, the first such allusions among the many published documents from Qumrân.[68]

Among the curiosities of Cave IV are several documents in a cryptic script. When they were discovered we felt certain we had in hand at last the famous secrets of the Essenes. One of the fragments provided a clue to the script. The three of us in Jerusalem at the time set up a competition in decipherment. We worked unsuccessfully until lunch time and strolled home busily discussing decipherment techniques, about which we knew little. After lunch two of us arrived back promptly at the museum. Abbé Milik was late. Allegro and I discussed the ethics of starting before he arrived, and, of course, proceeded

64 The best editions are those of Rabin, *The Zadokite Documents* (Oxford, 1954); and L. Rost, *Die Damaskusschrift* (Berlin, 1933). Photographs of the document are published by S. Zeitlin, *The Zadokite Fragments* [*JQR* Monograph Series 1] (Philadelphia, 1952).

65 For a relatively complete catalogue of these documents, together with brief descriptive notices, see the reports in "Le travail d'èdition des fragments . . ." pp. 56–67; "Editing the Manuscript Fragments. . ." pp. 88–96.

66 Cf. J. M. Allegro, "A Newly Discovered Fragment of a Commentary on Psalm XXXVII from Qumrân," *PEQ* 1954, pp. 69–75; "Further Messianic References in Qumran Literature," *JBL* 75 (1956), pp. 174–87; and "Further Light on the History of the Qumran Sect," *ibid.*, pp. 89–95.

67 Cf. *DJD I*, pp. 77–82.

68 Another document, as yet unpublished, also has references to historical persons of the Hasmonaean era, by name. The fragmentary work is in process of study by Abbé Milik.

without him. Some minutes later Milik arrived, drew from his pocket a photograph of the fragments, and announced that he had deciphered the script during lunch.

Secrets are usually more exciting before they are found out. The contents of the cryptic documents, in any case, are not startling, but belong to well-known categories of literature at Qumrân.[69] One document contains astronomical observations related to the astronomical section of Enoch (Part III); another is named the "Exposition [midraš] of the Book of Moses."

Finally, there is a series of calendrical works found in Cave IV, relating to the zodiac, to the calculation of the feast days, and the courses of the priests (mišmārôt). Already the calendar materials found in published works have enabled scholars to solve a number of long-standing problems related to the solar calendar used in Jubilees and Enoch;[70] now it appears that this calendar was at home among the Essenes at Qumrân, and that it is reflected in certain of the primitive Christian traditions in the Gospels.[71]

69 This script is labeled "A" by Milik; another related (cursive) cryptic script, as yet undeciphered, also appears in Cave IV. Allegro is to edit a further curiosity, a document in which the cryptic, Jewish, paleo-Hebrew, and Greek scripts are intermingled. If for no other reason, the document is important as an aid to the paleographer.

70 With the publication of the mišmārôt MSS by Milik, promised for an early issue of RB in 1957, the details of the Qumrân calendar will be clarified. The counsels of caution in the late Professor Obermann's paper, "Calendaric Elements in the Dead Sea Scrolls," JBL 75 (1956), pp. 285–96, no longer have any justification.

71 For the discussion of the calendar of Qumrân, its relations to the calendrical data of Jubilees, Enoch, and the Passover of the Gospels, see D. Barthélemy, "Notes en Marge de publications récentes sur les manuscrits de Qumran," RB 59 (1952), pp. 187–218, especially pp. 200 ff.; A. Jaubert, "Le calendrier des Jubilés et de la secte de Qumrân. Ses origines bibliques," VT 3 (1953), pp. 250–64; J. Morgenstern, "The Calendar of the Book of Jubilees; Its Origin and Its Character," VT 5 (1955), pp. 34–76; Jaubert, "La date de la dernière Cène," RHR 146 (1954), pp. 140–73; cf. Vogt, "Antiquum kalendarium sacerdotale," Biblica 36 (1955), pp. 403–8; "Dies ultimae coenae Domini," ibid., pp. 408–13; J. T. Milik, Dix ans de découvertes dans le Désert de Juda [Les Editions du Cerf] (Paris, 1957), pp. 70–74.

CHAPTER II

The Essenes, the People
of the Scrolls

THERE IS NOW sufficient evidence, to be supplemented as publication of the scrolls and reports of excavations in the vicinity of Qumrân continue, to identify the people of the scrolls definitively with the Essenes[1]. The community at Qum-

1 The common derivation from *ḥasên*, *ḥasayyâ*, the standard East Aramaic equivalent of Hebrew *ḥasîdîm*, "pious," is thoroughly suitable. This etymology has indirect support from Philo, who in two passages connects the name with Greek ὁσιότης "piety," "holiness" (*Quod omnis probus liber sit*, XII, 75 [cf. XIII, 91]; *Hypothetica, apud Eusebius, Praep. evang.* VIII, 11., cf. Josephus, *War* II, 119).

Attempts to provide an alternative etymology have failed, including that of A. Dupont-Sommer, *The Jewish Sect of Qumran and the Essenes* [=*Nouveaux aperçus sur les Manuscrits de la Mer Morte, Paris, 1953*] (London, 1954), p. 63. The latter attempts to connect Hebrew *ʿēṣâ*, "deliberative council," "party," with Ἐσσαῖοι Ἐσσηνοί. He ignores the problem of middle steps in the derivation, how *ʿēṣâ* (root *yʿṣ*) would be turned into an adjective in Hebrew, yielding an equivalent of the Greek gentilic, or, if he attempts to go directly from *ʿēṣâ* to the Greek, how it is that the noun is taken and made into a plural gentilic which had no Hebrew equivalent. Even if the linguistic development were transparent, one would still ask how *ʿēṣâ*, rather than *yáḥad*, the sect's own characteristic name for its "communion," came to be used as an appellation.

The attempt to derive from a putative *ʾāsayyâ*, "healers," and to connect this with the Egyptian θεραπευταί breaks down in several directions:

rân was an Essene settlement.[2] In the discussion to follow we
wish to trace the process of historical synthesis, the combination of data dug up by the spade, culled from classical
writers, and sifted out of the scrolls themselves, by which the
ancient Essenes have been resurrected. The reconstruction
of the history and life of the Essenes is a tedious task; but the
product of these historical labors is well worth the effort.
These little-known Essenes have proved to be exceedingly
important for our understanding of early Judaism and Christianity, supplying a lost chapter in the development and
transmission of the Judaeo-Christian heritage.

1. An Essene Community in the Wilderness

The ruins of the Essene community center lie on a marly
terrace between limestone cliffs and the maritime plain at the
point where the torrent bed of the Wâdī Qumrân cuts its deep
gorge through to the Dead Sea. The site is called a *khirbeh,*
"ruin," by the Arabs; and, presumably, from its location on the
Wâdī Qumrân it receives the full designation *Khirbet
Qumrân.*[3] Its older, biblical name has not been known until

(1) the transcription *ess-* suggests *has-,* not *'ās-;* (2) "healers" is scarcely
suitable as an appellation; and (3) as observed by Schürer among
others (*Geschichte des jüdischen Volkes im Zeitalter Jesu Christi*
[*Geschichte*³], 3. Aufl., II, pp. 559–60), the Alexandrian sect is always
termed θεραπευταὶ θεοῦ "servants, or worshipers of God," not "phy-
sicians."

2 Among the most recent discussions of the identification, see R.
Marcus, "The Qumran Scrolls and Early Judaism," *Biblical Research* 1
(1956), pp. 9–47; B. J. Roberts, "Qumrân Scrolls and the Essenes,"
NTS 3 (1956), pp. 58–65; F. M. Cross, "The Dead Sea Scrolls," in
Interpreter's Bible XII (New York-Nashville, 1957), pp. 657 f.,
especially n. 69 and the literature there cited; and J. T. Milik in his
volume, *Dix ans de découvertes dans le Désert de Juda* (hereafter
Découvertes), Chap. III.

3 The etymology of the name Qumrân remains obscure. The attempt
to derive it from κάλαμος (from the Byzantine name of this district)
involves too many linguistic shifts to be convincing (see J. T. Milik,

recently; but thanks to new data, including remains of Israelite constructions of the ninth to the sixth century, we may confidently identify it as the biblical '*îr ham-mélaḥ*, "City of (the Sea of) Salt," one of a series of fortress towns in the desert province of the Judaean kings, listed in Joshua 15.[4]

The site had been designated a Roman fort by Dalman and Avi-Yonah, who had done surface explorations in the area, previous to the scroll finds.[5] Harding and De Vaux in 1949 re-examined the site, dug two tombs in the cemetery of some

RB 60 [1953], p. 538, n. 8). Probably it must be derived from an Arabic root *qmr*. In the simple stem, the active (*qamara*) means "to gamble," the stative (*qamira*) "to be white," "to be moonlit" (or "to be in the moonlight"). H. Michaud ("A propos du nom de Qumrân," *RHPR* 35 [1955], pp. 68–74) derives from the stative root a putative °*qâmir*, pl. *qumrân*, and translates "*veilleurs (au clair de lune)*"; but normally in Arabic the *qâtil* form of a stem *qatila* is stative in meaning, viz. "being white, moonlit." Moreover, the form *qutlân* may be the plural of a variety of singulars including '*aqtal*, used of colors; hence '*aqmar*, pl. *qumrân* is a more plausible combination if *qumrân* is to be explained as a plural. But in fact, we can get no certainty from a morphological analysis of the name. In Syrian Arabic *qumrân* may reflect older Arabic *qamrân* or *qimrân* (as well as *qumrân*), by the regular assimilation of the vowel to the bilabial. The form may be a common adjectival pattern (frequent in proper names), or an infinitive (cf. Brockelmann, *Grundriss d. vergl. Gramm. d. sem. Sprachen* I, §§ 210–17; Wright-de Goeje, *A Grammar of the Arabic Language* I, § 304, XIX, 6).

There is little likelihood that any memory of the Essene community was transmitted into Arab times; to be sure, the local tribesmen are quite aware that these ruins belong to the days of the *jâhiliyyah*; but this knowledge (as they explain) rests on the non-Muslim orientation of the tombs in the vicinity.

4 See most recently, F. M. Cross and G. E. Wright, "The Boundary and Province Lists of the Kingdom of Judah," *JBL* 75 (1956), pp. 202–26, especially 223 f.; and Cross and J. T. Milik, "Explorations in the Judaean Buqê'ah," *BASOR* 142 (April 1956), pp. 5–17, especially, p. 16, n. 27. Cf. R. de Vaux, "Fouilles de Khirbet Qumrân. Rapport préliminaire sur les 3ᵉ, 4ᵉ, et 5ᵉ campagnes," *RB* 63 (1956), pp. 535 f. (hereafter, *Rapport III*), and Milik and Cross, *RB* 63 (1956), pp. 74 ff. The identification of Khirbet Qumrân with biblical '*Ir ham-mélaḥ* goes back to M. Noth, *Das Buch Josua* (Tübingen, 1938), p. 72.

5 See above p. 10, n. 13.

twelve hundred[6] tombs adjacent to the ruin, but found insufficient evidence to connect the site with the cave a kilometer north. However, they were not wholly satisfied with the then current description of the site. It was certainly of the Hellenistic-Roman period, at least on the surface; but if it were a military outpost, what could be made of the extensive, adjacent cemetery? The tombs themselves were of a type unknown at the time, but certainly not Muslim.

In 1951 there were new reasons to re-examine the ruin. Debate over the date of the scrolls raised anew the possible connection of the ruin with the scrolls, and there were demands that it be dug. Again, study of the sectarian literature of Cave I had created a plausible hypothesis that the scrolls derived from Essene circles, and it was well known that Pliny placed their settlement somewhere below Jericho, above 'Ain Geddi, near the shore of the Dead Sea; this description admirably fitted the location of Khirbet Qumrân.[7]

The first campaign was launched on November 24, 1951, and continued until December 12. It was a small series of soundings; nevertheless, the excavators found sufficient evidence to date the ruin roughly to the beginning of the Christian era, to suggest that it was neither military nor private, but communal in character, a conclusion reinforced by the contemporary cemetery; the pottery of the site proved to be identical with that of Cave I and suggested, at least, a direct link between the people who once inhabited the settlement, and the cave deposit. Père de Vaux suggested, on the basis of his spadework, that it was most reasonable to conclude that the people of the scrolls were indeed Essenes and, further, that Khirbet Qumrân was the Essene retreat in the wilderness alluded to in the classical sources.[8]

6 The figure includes the tombs of the two small cemeteries north and south of the main cemetery of some one thousand tombs. See *Rapport III*, p. 569–72.

7 See above, pp. 10 f., n. 14, 17, 18.

8 *Rapport I, RB* 60 (1953), pp. 103–6.

In the winter of 1951, however, this construction of the facts, while thoroughly plausible, was by no means securely established. Obviously, major excavations at Khirbet Qumrân were called for. Now five compaigns at the site are completed, the second in the spring of 1953, and the remaining three in successive spring seasons, the latest in the spring of 1956.[9] A sixth campaign is projected in the region of 'Ên Feškhah, a little less than two miles to the south of Khirbet Qumrân, where new Essene installations were detected in 1956.[10]

Meanwhile the exploration of the caves north and south of Khirbet Qumrân, in March 1952, together with subsequent cave discoveries, quite shifted the perspective.

Khirbet Qumrân proved to be the hub of a Hellenistic-Roman occupation spreading nearly two miles north along the cliffs, and some two miles south to the agricultural complex at 'Ên Feškhah. The people of this broad settlement lived in caves, tents, and solid constructions, but shared pottery made in a common kiln, read common biblical and sectarian scrolls, operated a common irrigation system,[11] and, as we shall see, depended on common stores of food and water furnished by the installations of the community center.

The caves yielding manuscripts and identical pottery also radiate out from the center northward and southward. Five of the productive caves, including that containing the remains of an enormous library (Cave IV), lie cut into the south edge of the terrace supporting the settlement, hardly more than a stone's throw from the central building complex.

9 Full bibliography is given above, p. 10, n. 15.

10 Political troubles in the Near East may delay exploitation of the 'En Feškhah ruins. The soundings in 1956, in any case, indicate that the establishment north of the spring is a large one. See *Rapport III*, pp. 576 f. On the biblical name of 'En Feškhah, see W. R. Farmer, "The Geography of Ezekiel's River of Life," *BA* 19 (1956), pp. 17–22.

11 See *Rapport III*, pp. 575 f. De Vaux's suggestions that the irrigation works are Iron Age constructions, re-used by the Essenes, is almost certainly correct, to judge from parallel Iron Age irrigation works in the Buqê'.

Finally, explorations to the south toward 'Ain Geddi and westward into the Judaean Buqê', the biblical valley of 'Akôr,[12] have failed to locate other evidence of anciently occupied sites which flourished in the heyday of the Essenes. There appears to be no site which can furnish a rival claim as the Essene retreat. If the people of the scrolls were not the Essenes, they were a similar sect, living in the same center, in the same era.

The history of the community which dwelt at Qumrân can be reconstructed generally, out of the ruins and artifacts uncovered in the five seasons of excavation. Three periods of occupation are marked off by two major destructions within the occupational history of the site. The character of the life of the settlement's occupants in each period may be read in the architectural function of the structures built, as well as determined by their contents; and the dates of the periods are certified by the coins, pottery, and other artifacts sealed in undisturbed strata.

The Essene settlement was built on the shattered foundations of an Israelite fortress which had lain deserted since the sixth century B.C. The first major period (Level I) consists of two phases, (a) the brief temporary installations which were replaced by (b) the elaborate central buildings which fix the permanent lines of the Essene settlement. Period Ia consists in large measure of archaeological bits and tatters found covered by or built into the subsequent main building phase: some lines of walls, a cistern or two (one a re-used Iron Age cistern), two pottery kilns underneath a Period Ib cistern. It cannot be reconstructed in detail, and its date and duration are difficult to fix with precision.

The exact date of the foundation of the settlement is, of course, a datum we should very much like established, for it bears directly on problems of Essene history within the sectarian scrolls. We can at least set limits between which the

12 This identification was suggested first by M. Noth, ZDPV 71 (1955), pp. 42–55.

beginning of constructions at Qumrân must fall. Copper coins are one excellent clue for establishing the date of strata. At Qumrân, after five seasons, the series of copper coins recovered begins in the reign of John Hyrcanus I (134–104 B.C.) [fifteen coins identified to date], mounts sharply in the reign of Alexander Jannaeus (103–76 B.C.) [eighty-six examples], and then declines in the remaining days of the Hasmonaean era (76–37 B.C.) [six examples].[13]

How is this coin index to be used? Two principles operate in opposite directions. On the one hand, coins circulate for some period of time. The appearance of a considerable number of Hyrcanus coins does not necessarily require us to fix the foundation of the community in his reign; certainly we cannot go lower, however, than the early reign of Jannaeus for the beginning of the settlement. The coins of Jannaeus are much too numerous. Indeed it is highly probable that the *main* building phase of Period I commenced no later than the reign of Alexander Jannaeus.

On the other hand, the foundations of settlements are notoriously difficult to date archaeologically, for some years pass before a litter of debris, coins included, accumulates and this circumstance is exaggerated in the present instance, since the first phase (Ia) is small, and underwent extensive rebuilding and the establishment of a larger community before many years had passed. It is not improbable, therefore, that the foundation of the community dates well before the reign of Jannaeus, though we can scarcely go earlier than the beginning of Hyrcanus' reign or the end of Simon's reign. The absence of Seleucid coppers of pre-Hyrcanus date becomes increasingly difficult to explain with each year one mounts before Hyrcanus' accession. It becomes decisive evidence against any dating of beginnings at Qumrân more than a half dozen years before Hyrcanus, since Seleucid coppers did not

13 A silver coin or two (Antiochus Sidetes, 138–129 B.C.) carries us back into the end of Simon's reign. However, silver coins are notoriously misleading in attempting to establish a *terminus ante quem.*

cease to circulate on the day Hyrcanus began to mint coppers, even among nationalist Jews.

The first major period of communal occupation prospered and grew until Herodian times. Then the community center was destroyed by earthquake early in Herod's reign; a crevasse opened through the center of the community buildings, and the eastern side of the complex dropped some fifty centimeters below the western with the shifting of the ground on which the buildings were founded. Archaeological evidence combines with historical notices in Josephus to indicate that the cataclysm in question was the great earthquake of 31 B.C. in which some thirty thousand men of Judaea died.[14]

Reoccupation of the site was not immediate. It appears to have lain abandoned during the remainder of Herod's reign (37–4 B.C.). The second period of occupation began with the repairing and partial rebuilding of the old settlement during the early years of Herod's successor, Archelaus (4 B.C.–A.D. 6), to judge chiefly from the evidence of coins.[15] The fundamental plan of the site was not changed, and the function of most of the installations was not altered. There can be no doubt that the same community which had abandoned the site resettled it.

The desert settlement continued to thrive, without apparent interruption, through the years of Jesus' ministry and the

14 De Vaux, *Rapport II, RB* 61 (1954), pp. 231 ff.; Josephus, *War* I, 370–72; *Antiq.* XV, 121–47.

15 Archaeological data suggest a gap. Coins of Herod are proportionately few (5 coins) in relation to the length of his reign. A treasure of 558 silver coins hidden in three jars was found below the floor level of Period II in locus 120, above the debris of Ib. Most are of Tyrian stamp, tetradrachms, spanning in date the first century B.C., the latest according to Seyrig and De Vaux falling between the years 9/8 B.C. and 1 B.C./A.D. 1. Presumably the coins were buried at the time of the rebuilding of the site—whether by some one holding out wealth from the common treasury on entrance to the community (cf. Acts 5: 1–6), or by an embezzling "bishop" (i.e. *mĕbaqqēr* or *pāqîd*). De Vaux's alternate hypothesis, that the hoard belongs to the era of abandonment, seems less likely (*Rapport III*, pp. 568 f.).

turbulent days of the Roman procurators in Judaea, until the dark days of the first Jewish revolt against Rome (A.D. 66–70). The community buildings of Qumrân were destroyed under armed attack during the Jewish Revolt. The walls of Period II are mined through; the building ruins were sealed in layers of ash from a great conflagration; and in the blackened debris of the main fortification are the telltale iron arrowheads used by the Roman legionaries.

Actually we can reconstruct in some detail the occasion of the end of the settlement.[16] The last caches of coins from Period II date from the second and (a few) the third year of the First Revolt. Above these in the levels of Period III are some nine coins of Caesarea, three of Dura (near Caesarea) minted in the year 67/68, as well as later coins. We know from Josephus that Vespasian rested his forces, including the Fifth, Tenth, and Fifteenth Legions, in Caesarea in the summer of 67 after the first phase of his Galilean campaign.[17] The Fifth

16 We do not know the extent to which the Essenes engaged in the war with Rome. Certainly the sect was girded to take up arms in the final Holy War as we know from the liturgy of the apocalyptic war (1QM, 4QM), as well as from hints of military organization (after the pattern of the priestly prescriptions for the battle camp in the desert [Numbers]) in earlier works. Philo's remarks about their refusal to traffic in the weapons of war (*Quod omnis probus liber sit* XII, 78) simply reveal the other face of apocalypticism, its quietism vis-à-vis the present world. The sect refused to soil its holiness in secular violence and the seeking of worldly gain. However, the war against Rome may have lent itself to interpretation among the Essenes as the beginning of the final Holy War; certainly in other circles of Judaism apocalyptic fanaticism motivated the suicidal revolt. At all events, the Essene retreat at Qumrân was defended to the end, presumably by some Essene stalwarts. And from Josephus we learn of a certain John the Essene, appointed general of Jewish forces in northwest Judaea in the early stages of the First Revolt (*War* II, 566; III, 11).

Milik (*Découvertes,* Appendice) suggests Zealot influence in the War scroll and in the late Essene movement; the evidence he calls upon, however, can be sufficiently explained by the apocalypticism of the sect—early and late. On the other hand, compare Hippolytus, *Refutatio omnium haeresium,* IX, 26.

17 Josephus, *War* III, 409, 412; cf. *III*, 65; De Vaux *Rapport II,* pp. 232 f.

and Fifteenth Legions wintered in Caesarea, the Tenth in Scythopolis (Bethshan).[18] In the early spring of 68 Vespasian took up his campaign to reduce Judaea and Peraea. The Tenth Legion (*Fretensis*) under Trajan, father of the future emperor, crossed Jordan into Peraea; Vespasian marched eastward from Caesarea, striking first south, then north, reducing Judaea. In June, A.D. 68, Vespasian led his troops from the pass at Shechem (later Neapolis) down into Jericho, where he was

18 Josephus' evidence on the place of wintering of the Tenth Legion, is, on first look, confused. In *War* III, 412, he seems to say that the Fifteenth Legion was sent to Scythopolis, two legions (apparently the Fifth and Tenth) were quartered in Caesarea. However, in *War* IV, 87, we are told that in the fall of 67 the Tenth Legion was sent to Scythopolis while Vespasian returned to Caesarea with the other two legions (apparently the Fifth and Fifteenth). The latter text seems confirmed by Josephus, *War* IV, 450, where it is said explicitly that Trajan, commander of the Tenth Legion (cf. *War* III, 289) joins Vespasian's forces only after the latter comes to Jericho. Evidently the text of *War* III, 412, which reads τὸ δέκατον δὲ καὶ πέμπτον εἰς Σκυθόπολιν, ". . . and the Fifteenth to Scythopolis," must be corrected, πέμπτον "Fifth" to πεμπτόν "sent," "dispatched"; ". . . and the Tenth dispatched to Scythopolis." Then our evidence is unequivocal, and De Vaux's treatment of the movements of the Tenth Legion is to be corrected accordingly (see *Rapport II*, pp. 232, 3).

Mr. John Strugnell, in discussing the above problem with the writer, has suggested two further points to support or nuance the solution I have proposed. One may argue also that since Titus is in command of one legion (cf. Suetonius, *Titus* IV, 3), and had his winter headquarters in Caesarea, the case is substantiated for the Fifteenth wintering in Caesarea, the Tenth in Scythopolis. We know that the Fifth under command of Cerealius stayed in Caesarea (*War* III, 310), and that Titus took command of the Fifteenth in Alexandria (III, 8, 64, 65; on III, 8, see the edition of Thackeray [Loeb, II], p. 576, n. 2). Unless there was a shift of command of which we have no indication, therefore, it appears that Trajan and the Tenth Legion are left at Scythopolis. (cf. Schürer, *Geschichte*[3] I, p. 610, n. 31.)

Mr. Strugnell suggests secondly that in the amended text III, 412, τὸ δέκατον δὲ καὶ πεμπτὸν εἰς Σκυθόπολιν, the καί is anomalous and suggests that ΚΑΙΠΕΜΠΤΟΝ is a corruption of ΚΑΤΑΠΕΜΠΤΟΝ, owing to a misreading of abbreviations of καί and κατα–. Examples in the *Antiq.* of the textual confusion of κατά and καί may be found at XVIII, 327 (ed. Niese, p. 199, l. 27), and XX, 268 (p. 320, l. 20). The text would then read, ". . . and the Tenth send down (from headquarters in Caesarea) to Scythopolis."

joined by the forces of Trajan come from Peraea. Most of the population fled before the Romans; in any case Vespasian subjugated Jericho, leaving troops behind to garrison the territory. In an interesting aside Josephus tells us that Vespasian investigated the Dead Sea and tested its strange powers of buoyancy by throwing bound prisoners into the sea to see if they would sink or float.[19]

The center at Qumrân was destroyed, no doubt, by a contingent of Vespasian's troops in the early summer of 68. The coins from the coastal cities dated 67/68, including an (undated) coin of Ascalon stamped with the Roman numeral X, countermark of the paymaster of the Tenth Legion, are grim confirmation.

Whether the Essenes in whole or in part fled their settlement with the approach of the Romans, or were trapped in Qumrân and slaughtered, we cannot know with certainty.[20] At all events the Essenes were prevented from carrying away their manuscripts, with the result that their library, abandoned in nearby caves, survived. Ironically, had the community survived, the manuscripts no doubt would have perished.

The third period of Khirbet Qumrân belongs to a Roman garrison, presumably a forward post to protect Jericho against the centers of guerrilla resistance southward in the desert of Judah. The soldiers sliced up some of the common rooms of the main building of the complex into barracks, utilizing only the most easily fortified portion of this building, leaving the remainder of the site in ruins. The elaborate water system of the earlier settlement, not being required by the small com-

19 Josephus, *War* IV, 451; 476, 7; cf. De Vaux, *Rapport II*, p. 233.

20 See n. 16 above. There is some likelihood that the Essenes, at least in part, put up resistance. Certainly someone resisted the Romans, using Qumrân as a bastion. And Josephus has special occasion to underline Roman persecution and torture of the Essenes during the Revolt (*War* II, 152). Finally, had they abandoned Qumrân completely, prior to the imminent threat of Roman troops, they no doubt would have removed their MSS with them. The caves immediately surrounding the center, especially Cave IV, can under no circumstances be described as carefully chosen hiding places.

pany, was by-passed by a crude canal dug helter-skelter through Period II installations[21] to connect with a single cistern in the southeast. The post was maintained for some few years, being abandoned toward the end of the first century. Save for squatters in the time of the second Jewish revolt (A.D. 132–35), the site was not again occupied until archaeologists pitched their tents alongside the ruin in 1951.

The communal life of the Essenes is vividly reflected in their settlement at Khirbet Qumrân. In the first main period of their settlement (Ib) they built an imposing central building, originally square in shape, 37.5 meters (about 124 feet) to the side. To the west, alongside a deep ravine, is a smaller building complex, no doubt the earliest of the substantial structures of the Essene community. Later in the period the constructions were extended to the south of both the western complex and the main building. The eastern side of the central complex is defended by a long line of wall which branches at a slight angle from the northeast side of the central building, forming a triangular area immediately southeast of the central building; the defense wall continues south of the buildings, however, to the precipitous bank of the *wâdī*, sealing off the settlement's exposed flank.[22]

In the northwest quadrant of the main building was a fortified tower to lend security to the community. Their isolated location in the desert, within striking distance of razzias from the southern desert, required such defenses. In the northeastern quadrant were a large community kitchen and storage

21 The Roman canal cuts through the SW corner of loc. 77, cuts the walls of loc. 86. The destruction of 86/89, the "pantry" of the great common room of the community (77) is dated by De Vaux to the end of Period Ib; Milik has suggested that the locus, with its more than 1080 pieces of "tableware," was not sealed in debris until the Roman conquest, since the hall, loc. 77, continued in use; and an inscribed bowl from 86/89 seems clearly to be dated paleographically to the first century A.D.

22 No amount of descriptive detail can call up an adequate picture of the community center. The reader is directed to the superb plans drawn by Père Coüasnon, *Rapport III*, Pl. III (see end-paper plan).

magazines; in the southeastern a cistern (abandoned after a crevasse caused by the earthquake split it from end to end!), and facilities for washing. The quadrant to the southwest contains rooms for small convocations, study, and, perhaps, for the community's records. The function of one room in particular, is clear and significant. A long central chamber in this quadrant, measuring 13×4 meters (about 43×13 feet), contained in the debris of the second period, a narrow plaster table, about 5 meters (about 16½ feet) in length, as well as two other shorter tables. Associated was a low bench of equal length. Both originally had been built as permanent fixtures, the table fixed into the plaster floor of its room, the bench into the wall alongside. These are the appurtenances of the ancient scriptorium of the community.[23] Mingled in the debris were also two inkpots, one still containing traces of dried ink.

In the scriptorium many of the scrolls must have been penned, almost certainly those copied by scribes whose work turns up repeatedly on scrolls from several caves. It is not unlikely, moreover, that the library of the community found in Cave IV nearby was normally housed in this quadrant of the main building.

To the west and south of the central building is the maze of water channels and cisterns which connects to an aqueduct, still well preserved, which led water from a dam at the foot of the waterfall of the Wâdī Qumrân. Seven major cisterns, and at least six small pools, settling basins, baths, or the like, have been cleared. While all may not have been in use at the same time, it is nevertheless an astonishingly large water system and is capable of serving a substantial community through the long arid seasons normal to this part of Palestine.

The elaborate water system of Qumrân, especially the step cisterns, has produced much fanciful speculation. To those acquainted with Essene habits of baptism, but unacquainted

23 See *Rapport II*, p. 212. In addition a plaster hand basin was recovered in the debris, apparently used in lustrations practiced in connection with inscribing biblical texts.

with cistern types in Roman Palestine, the pools seem admirably designed for bathing rites. Unfortunately the pools are typical examples of water reservoirs well known from other sites.[24] On the other hand, two or three small pools are probably baths, including the shallow pool at the entrance way to the settlement. One suspects, however, that the demands of the community for water to be used for drinking and other mundane purposes, as well as water for the ordinary rites of maintaining ritual purity, stressed especially in the priestly practices of the Essenes, is sufficient explanation for the size of the water system. Probably the ritual baptisms called for the living waters of the Jordan not far distant; possibly the waters of 'Ēn Feškhah nearby would have sufficed. In any case, we do not believe they immersed themselves in their drinking water.

On the south side of the central building is a great hall, 22×4.5 meters ($72\frac{1}{2} \times 15$ feet). Its floor and walls were plastered. Plaster pillars supported a roof, probably of thatched palm. However, the pillars are found in the eastern extremity of the hall only, and in an annex on the southwestern end of the building. This asymmetrical plan is explained by a round, stone pavement at the western end of the hall, the podium of a reader, expositor, or presiding officer. This hall is clearly the main assembly hall of the community.

There is evidence also that in this room the Essenes gathered to celebrate their sacred common meals. This is suggested first of all by arrangements for washing the hall, including a side canal from the aqueduct to lead water to the hall, and planned drainage.[25] Striking confirmation comes from finds in the annex on the southwest corner of the hall, which has proved to be the pantry for the commons. In this room, sealed in by the debris of the Roman destruction,[26] more than 1080

24 See A. Parrot, *RHPR* 35 (1955), pp. 61–67; De Vaux, *Rapport III*, pp. 539–40.

25 *Rapport III*, p. 542.

26 See n. 21 above.

pieces of pottery were uncovered by the excavators: plates and bowls, serving dishes, water decanters, wine flasks, and drinking cups, the "tableware" of the community.

The western quarter, after the completion of the main building in Period Ib, was used chiefly for storage and domestic industries. Two heavy mills of basalt were discovered in position; silos for storing grain, the communal bakery, and what appears to have been a forge were among the other installations uncovered.

The community pottery works was uncovered in the triangle on the southeast of the main building, and proved to be one of the best-preserved establishments of its kind ever found in Palestine. It includes a pit, water outlet, and a walled plaster platform for kneading, cleaning, and drying clay; a platform, presumably for the potter's wheel; a great kiln for baking large pots, another for small vessels.

With the further excavations at ʿÊn Feškhah, in the large enclosure and buildings which remain scarcely touched by the soundings of 1956, we should learn a great deal more of the daily life of the Essenes of Qumrân, particularly if the structures prove to be an agricultural adjunct to the main settlement, as now appears most likely.[27]

One rather curious find calls for special mention. In many open areas of the settlement, especially in the court to the north of the western quarter, and in the esplanade to the south of the settlement, the excavators came upon burials of animal bones. The condition of the bones certified that the animals had been slaughtered and eaten: sheep, goats, cattle. The burials were not a means of sanitary garbage disposal. The burials are inside the community enclosure; the bones were neatly placed in jars, or between large sherds of jars, and were carefully buried individually in a large number of deposits. Certainly the bones are the remains of the sacramental feasts of the community. They raise acutely, moreover, the question as to whether the Essenes carried on a

27 *Rapport III*, pp. 576 f.

sacrificial cultus at Qumrân, a question to which we shall return.

All these details dredged up by spade and trowel admirably illustrate the life of the community of which we read in classical texts dealing with the Essenes and in the scrolls themselves.

2. The Old Sources and the New Scrolls

We have seen that as Khirbet Qumrân has revealed its communal facilities—its enormous water system, its scriptorium, and banquet hall; its common workshops, stores, and agricultural adjuncts; and indeed, its network of caves for the living and tombs for the dead—the possibility that it could be identified with anything other than the Essene "city in the wilderness" described by Pliny and Dio Chrysostomus,[28] has become increasingly remote. Similarly, fresh analyses of the classical sources, especially Josephus, in the light of the expanding literature from Qumrân have shown that there are few discrepancies between the accounts of the Essenes in the sources and the sectarian literature of Qumrân which are not easily explained by the exterior view or Hellenizing tendency of the classical writer.[29] And we may say further that most of the discrepancies commonly observed by scholars during the early controversy over the identity of the sect of Qumrân exist, not between the sources and the texts, but between former scholarly interpretations of the sources and the texts.

28 Pliny, *Naturalis historia* V, xv, 73; *Dio apud Synesium,* 39 (ed. Migne).

29 Attention may be called to B. J. Roberts' apt statement, "The Qumrân Scrolls and the Essenes," *NTS* 3 (1956), p. 58; "Whereas previously one argued for or against the identity according to the extent of disagreement between the scrolls and the sources, the scrolls now become the yardstick by which Philo and Josephus are measured." Cf. R. Marcus, "The Qumrân Scrolls and Early Judaism," *Biblical Research* I (1956), pp. 28–31.

Our chief older sources for the life and practice of the Essenes are Philo Judaeus and Flavius Josephus, to which may be added the short notice of Pliny the Elder.[30] The various accounts of the Essenes in the Church Fathers depend wholly on these sources and consequently are of no independent value. An exception, in probability, is the extended passage in the *Refutatio omnium haeresium* of Hippolytus.[31] While on the whole it reproduces the information given by Josephus in *The Jewish War*, exhibiting identical wording regularly, as well as taking up subject matter in the same order, the passage adds and subtracts in detail and occasionally contradicts Josephus. With the control afforded by new data from the scrolls, we can now show that in some instances the special readings of Hippolytus may be authentic and, in a few cases, may be superior to Josephus. It would seem to follow that Hippolytus and Josephus (and perhaps Philo as well) drew on a common written source.[32]

While Josephus regularly describes the Essenes as one of the three orders ($\tau \acute{a} \gamma \mu a \tau a$) of the Jews, along with the Pharisees and Sadducees, we must recognize, as Schürer has observed, that in the case of the Essenes we deal with a sect which in structure differs radically from the two main branches of Judaism.[33]

30 Philo, *Quod omnis probus liber sit* XII–XIII (75–91), quoted in full by Eusebius, *Praep. evang.* VIII, 12; *Hypothetica* (*Apologia pro Iudaeis*), quoted by Eusebius, *Praep. evang.* VIII, 11 (cf. Loeb edition, XI, 437–43); Josephus, *War* II, 119–61; cf. I, 78; II, 567; III, 11; V, 145; *Antiq.* XIII, 171–73; XV, 371–79 (x, 4–5); XVIII, 18–22 (i, 5). For the older secondary literature on the Essenes, see Bauer, "Essener," in Pauly-Wissowa, *Real-Encyclop. d. kl. Altertumswiss.* Supplementband IV, cols. 386–430.

31 *Refutatio omnium haeresium* (ed. Wendland) IX, 18–28.

32 See most recently, M. Black, "The Account of the Essenes in Hippolytus and Josephus," *The Background of the New Testament and its Eschatology*, eds. W. D. Davies and D. Daube (Cambridge, 1956), pp. 172–75.

33 *Geschichte*[3] II, p. 559. Ralph Marcus has called the Essenes "gnosticizing Pharisees" (*op. cit.*, pp. 25–40), and Saul Lieberman, es-

The older sources stress that the Essenes separated themselves physically from other Jews, and in so far as possible eschewed all contact with non-Essenes.[34] The separatist tendency of the sectaries is not fully explained in our sources, but

pecially, has underlined the parallels between the societies (*ḥăbûrôt*) of the Pharisees and the Essene communities ("The Discipline in the so-called Dead Sea Manual of Discipline," *JBL* 71 [1952], pp. 199–206). Such parallels are expected in groups which almost certainly have common roots in the Hasidic movement of the Maccabean age. As a priestly movement, they also have some features in common with the Sadducees (cf. R. North, "The Qumrân 'Sadducees,'" *CBQ* 17 [1955], pp. 164–88). These parallels indicate at most, however, that the Essenes were more deeply rooted in the Judaism of the second century B.C. than scholars had supposed on the basis of reconstructions of Philo and Josephus. That which places a gulf between the Essenes and the main stream of Judaism is their apocalypticism, or more precisely, their formation of apocalyptic communities. In no case can the Pharisees, much less the Sadducees, be called apocalyptists, and by no stretch of the imagination can their associations be said to be the *Sitz im Leben* of an apocalyptic literature.

The only plausible ground for hesitation in making a definite identification of the Qumrân sect with the Essenes—once the date and the provenience of the scrolls were established and the life of the Qumrân community was reconstructed—has been the argument that since Palestine "swarmed" with obscure sects in the first century B.C., one must exercise caution in assigning our sect to a known group. This argument has only apparent relevance to our problem. When the Damascus Document alone was known, one could well suppose that an obscure or unknown sect was responsible for its composition. Now that an extensive library is known, the perspective is quite changed. The Qumrân sect was not a small, ephemeral group. Its substantial community at Qumrân persisted some two centuries or more. Morever, it was not restricted to Qumrân, but, as we know from its documents, counted its camps and settlements in the villages of Judah. Its own sectarian literature is enormous, and of profound and direct influence on Jewish Christian and Christian movements of the first century A.D. and later.

The enumeration of various minor divisions and ephemeral groups which allegedly proliferated in Judaism is no longer pertinent, therefore, to our discussion. Our task is to identify a major sect in Judaism. And to suppose that a major group in Judaism in this period went unnoticed in our sources is simply incredible. The people of the scrolls belonged to the Essene party.

34 See Philo, *Quod omn. prob. lib. sit*, 76; and especially Hippolytus, IX, 26.

one is led to believe that it is to be attributed to the desire to attain moral perfection as well as ritual purity by dissociation from the corruption of the world. This and other apparently ascetic or alien motives in a Jewish "party" confused earlier scholars.

The Qumrân texts emphasize no less the obligation of the sectarian to avoid all pollution by the children of darkness. The Qumrân community retreated into the desert "to separate themselves from the abode of perverse men."[35] The motivation of the group, partially obscured in Philo and Josephus by Greek thought forms, proves to root profoundly in older Judaism, specifically in the priestly laws of ritual purity coupled with a thoroughgoing apocalypticism.[35a] To be sure, the

35 1QS 8:12–13; cf. 5:13–20; 9:3–11, 12–21, especially 19–20; etc.

35a The term "apocalypticism" or "the apocalyptic" will be used frequently. Perhaps it will be useful at the outset to delineate its main motives.

The apocalyptic movement may be succinctly described as the late Jewish attempt to revive Old Testament doctrines of history. In a world filled with a rich mixture of ideas, many of Hellenistic, Iranian, and ancient oriental origin, the apocalyptic impulse to recapture the old prophetic understanding of the history of salvation results in fact in the creation of a new theology of history obsessed with "last things." Prophecy became eschatology.

Apocalypticism sees world history in the grip of warring forces, God and Satan, the spirits of truth and error, light and darkness. The struggle of God with man, and of man with sin, evil, and death becomes objectified into a cosmic struggle. The world, captive to evil powers and principalities which have been given authority in the era of divine wrath, can be freed only by the divine might. But the day of God's salvation and judgment dawns. The old age has moved to its allotted end and the age of consummation is at hand, the age of the vindication of the elect and the redemption of the world. Current events signal the approach of the end. The final war, Armageddon, has begun. The Messiah is about to appear "bringing a sword." The Satanic forces, now brought to bay, break out in a final, defiant convulsion, manifest in the persecutions, temptations and tribulations of the faithful. In short, the apocalypticist lives in a world in which the sovereignty of God is the sole hope of salvation, and in the earnestness of his faith and the vividness of his hope he is certain that God is about to act. The faithful will be given the gift of salvation.

Such apocalyptic themes find their way into various forms of liter-

community isolates itself to achieve a form of perfection and shuns contact with temptation, living in rigorous simplicity. Their retreat, however, is to be understood, not in a framework of nature-spirit dualism of Greek type, but in the ethical or "spirit-spirit" dualism of apocalypticism. They go into the desert for a season, to be born again as the New Israel, to enter into the New Covenant of the last days.[36] They await in the desert the Second Exodus (or Conquest), "preparing the way of the Lord," disciplining themselves by the rule of the ancient Wars of Yahweh to be ready to fight the final war of God.

Our old sources are thus confirmed but also supplemented by the new. And the Essenes prove to be an apocalyptic community, a *Heilsgemeinshaft*, imitating the ancient desert sojourn of Mosaic times in anticipation of the dawning Kingdom of God.[36a] They are priestly apocalyptists, not true ascetics.

ature, as we shall see. Characteristic, however, as the term "apocalyptic" makes evident, is the apocalypse, a book of revelations of things to come in the last days. Daniel and Revelation are canonical examples; the Enoch literature and the Testaments of the Twelve Patriarchs are non-canonical representatives of the genre.

The apocalyptic literature is featured by fantastic visions, calculation of times, and veiled references to contemporary history. The mythological imagery and astrological motives of the ancient Near East, including dualistic themes from Iran, strongly color the language of visions and can be recognized in the speculations about angels and spirits, and preoccupation with calendrical observations. Myths of creation are turned to the use of eschatology, to point to the struggle issuing in the "new creation." The national Messiah of Israel, a "historical" savior, is transformed into a transhistorical warrior (and ultimately into a cosmic redeemer). Yet with all these transcendental and mythological elements, the main impulse of the apocalyptic is the Old Testament understanding of the history of salvation. The diverse borrowings are wholly informed by the Judaic spirit.

36 Cf. *CD* 4:2–4; 6:18–19; 8:21; and especially 1Q34 bis II, 5–8 (*DJD I*, p. 154).

36a In the War scroll (1QM), the camp of the Sons of Light (i.e., the sectarians, Israel-in-truth) is ordered precisely after the prescriptions for the priestly arrangement of the Mosaic camp of the desert in

We are not to think of the Essenes as a community restricted to the desert of the Dead Sea. Philo reports that they lived in villages and in many-membered "communities," ὅμιλοι.[37] The latter term suggests that Philo, like Pliny, knew of independent associations like the principal Essene center at Qumrân, called in the texts the *yáḥad*.[38] Josephus no doubt distorts the situation in stating broadly that they settled in large numbers in every town.[39] But he agrees with Philo in numbering the Essenes at four thousand.[40]

Our new scrolls as well make abundantly evident that the community of the desert by no means exhausted the membership of the sect, and laws are laid down to govern the "community," *yáḥad*, the "camps" *maḥănôt*, and the "congregation," *ʿēdāh*. The last-named term is clear. It applies to the totality of the camps, that is, (sectarian) Israel.[41] The precise range of meaning of the first two terms is not as clear.

The term *yáḥad*, "community" seems to apply to the community par excellence; i.e., the principal settlement in the desert. The Qumrân settlement is probably unique, not only in being the original "exile in the desert," the home of the

---

Num. 2:1–5:4; 10:17–28; etc. (1QM 3:12–4:11). The law of the camp (Num. 5:1–4) is kept (1QM 7:3–7). The victory of God in the final war is compared with the first Exodus (1QM 11:8). The typology of the Mosaic camp lies close to the surface in *CD* (20:26 quotes Deut. 2:14 of the Mosaic camp) and 1QS and 1QSa. The typology of the second Exodus appears in the use of Is. 40 (1QS 8:12–14) and Ezek. 20 (1QS 6:2 *mgwryhm:* cf. Ezek. 20:38; 1QM 1:3 *mdbr h'mym:* cf. Ezek. 20:35), etc.

37 *Hypothetica* XI, I.

38 R. Marcus goes so far as to suggest that the term ὅμιλος in Philo is a direct translation of *yáḥad*, "Philo, Josephus and the Dead Sea Yahad," *JBL* 71 (1952), pp. 207–9. Rather, I think, the term refers to the "camps," *maḥănôt*, and is not an attempt at direct translation. See n. 43 below.

39 *War* II, 124.

40 *Quod omn. prob. lib. sit,* 75; *Antiq.* XVIII, 20.

41 *CD* 14:3–6, 10–12. Cf. 1QM 3:13; 4:9.

founder of the sect, but also in following a celibate rule.[42] It is possible, but not probable, I think, that more than one community could be termed the *yáḥad*. In the Damascus Document, for example, the term *yáḥad* seems to be used only of the old community, the "Community" of the founder, while the term "camp" is regularly used of the various settlements, the units of the inclusive *'ēdāh*, "congregation."[43]

"Community," *yáḥad*, is also used more generally, especially in the Rule of the Community (IQS), of the "community of God," especially with eschatological overtones: Israel of the New Covenant.[44]

42 See 1QS 1:1, 12, 16; 3:2; 5:1, 2, 7–8; 6:18, 21, 22; 7:6, 20, 24; 8:11, 12, 16–17, 19; 9:2, 19. On the place of celibacy in the sect, see below.

43 On the use of *yáḥad* in *CD*, see 20:1, 14, 32. Both the term "camp" and *'ēdāh* belong to the priestly terminology of the desert organization of Israel (cf. Num., *passim*). So too the "Prince of the Congregation," *neśî' há'ēdāh*, is taken from priestly and Ezekielian contexts to apply to the Davidic Messiah (Ezek. 34:24; 37:25).

Contrary to the impression given by Gaster (*The Dead Sea Scriptures* [Garden City, New York, 1956], pp. 327 f.), the term *yáḥad* is not used in the plural in any of our texts. On the other hand, "camps" is frequent, and certainly is a unit organizationally in *CD*. The standard quorum of ten applies to the "camp," *CD* 12:22–13:3. In 1QS 6: 2–8 one may recognize in prescriptions for a quorum of ten, etc., provision for more than a single *yáḥad*. I think that in fact, however, in the development of Essenism, the term *maḥănēh* replaced *yáḥad* for all but the desert settlement.

Gaster also attributes to Marcus the opinion that Philo's term κοινωνία is a translation of *yáḥad*. Actually, I believe, Marcus only connected Philo's ὅμιλος with *yáḥad*. Gaster's instinct is correct, however, for Philo's frequent use of κοινωνία of the sect, especially in such passages as *Hypothetica* 11, 1, certainly reflects Essene usage. Cf. 11, 14–17; *Quod omn. prob. lib. sit*, 85, etc.

44 See 1QS 2:22, 24, 26; 3:11–12; and especially 5:5–6 and 9:3–11. The translation "community" is poor in English, since it permits secular connotations or the wide English usage to blur its narrow meaning. The normal theological overtones are made explicit in such phrases as *byḥd 'l, byḥd 'mtw, lyḥd qwdš, bryt hyḥd, lbryt yḥd 'wlmym, lyḥd bryt 'wlm*.

Often, of course, the term *yáḥad* means simply "fellowship," "com-

There are hints that at least some of the "camps" were secular, and following "the order of the earth," entered into marriage contracts.[45]

There is finally an order of the "cities of Israel"; whether this rule is to be sharply distinguished from the rule of the camps is doubtful.[46]

munion," and in combination, "communal" as in such an expression as "communal council." ('*ăṣat hay-yáḥad*).

45 See, for example, *CD* 7:6–8 (19:3–5); cf. *War* II, 160–161.

46 There is no hint in the classical sources of Essenes dwelling outside Palestine. This raises the vexed problem of the meaning of the term "land of Damascus" in *CD*. In the expositional portion of *CD*, the expression appears in 7:14–20, an apocalyptic reinterpretation of Amos 5:26–27, along with the phrases, "the repentant of Israel who went out from the land of Judah and sojourned in the land of Damascus" (6:5); ". . . those who entered the New Covenant in the land of Damascus" (6:19); and "all the men who entered into the New Covenant in the land of Damascus" (8:21–19:33/34). Many scholars have taken the "land of Damascus" literally to apply to a place of sojourn of at least one order of Essenes, and some have supposed that *CD* preserves the order of the Damascene communities. Cf. the carefully worked-out views of M. H. Segal, "The Hababkkuk 'Commentary' and the Damascus Fragments," *JBL* 70 (1951), pp. 131–47; and J. T. Milik, *Découvertes*, Chap. III. R. de Vaux has suggested that the exodus to Damascus, if literal, may fall in the archaeological gap at Qumrân during the reign of Herod (*Rapport II*, pp. 235 f.). De Vaux himself is quite tentative. The view has been taken up by others and argued more strongly (cf. C. T. Fritsch, "Herod the Great and the Qumran Community," *JBL* 74 [1955], pp. 173–81).

I believe we are now in a position to dispense with De Vaux's suggestion. An unpublished copy of *CD* from 4Q cannot be dated later than the Hasmonaean period, and is almost certainly pre-Roman. Composition of *CD*, in any case, must be pushed back into the late second century B.C., or better, perhaps, the early first century B.C. This dating should have been evident already on the basis of internal data. For example, the Kittî'îm, normally the Romans in the Qumrân scrolls composed late (the *pešārîm* and 1QM; see below), play no role in *CD*.

I am increasingly inclined to those views (a shift from my earlier published opinion) which hold that the "land of Damascus" is the "prophetic name" applied to the desert of Qumrân. As the Essenes interpreted the Prophets (and Law for that matter) in apocalyptic fashion, they discovered esoteric titles for themselves, for their contemporaries, for their place of sojourn preceding the end, etc., all alluded to in the biblical materials. "The land of Damascus," the place of exile in Amos 5:25–27 is understood eschatologically, and is evidently such an esoteric designation, parallel to the "desert of the peoples," another "prophetic name" of their place of retreat taken from Ezek. 20:35 (1QM I, 2–3).

A number of arguments can be called upon to support this view. First of all, there can be no doubt that CD was popular at Qumrân, surviving not only in seven MSS in the main library (4Q) but also appearing in private collections (6Q; cf. M. Baillet, "Fragments du document de Damas. Qumrân, grotte 6," RB 63 [1956], pp. 513–523). The number of appearances is higher than that of Pentateuchal MSS (except Deuteronomy) or of Jeremiah and Ezekiel, for example, so that it is difficult to suppose that the work is not "at home" in Qumrân. If the Damascus sojourn is to be understood literally, the entire community must have taken part. In no case can CD be the document of a splinter Essene order condemned by the main group (pace Segal). Again, it may be noted that the Damascus references are only in expositional material, not in the "rules." In the latter sections of the work (which at Qumrân is a single work, contrary to the theory of Rabin), the legislation applies to the "cities of Israel" (12:19), an awkward designation for "Damascene camps," and references to the "city of the sanctuary" (12:1–2), and provision for carrying out sacrifices (12:19 ff.; etc.) suggest either that the sectarians of CD were near to Jerusalem, or had an independent sacrificial cultus (see below).

Finally, the texts in the expository passages are most easily understood if "Damascus" is the "revealed" name for the desert settlements of the Essenes. The "Damascus" references are often in combination with allusions to the formative period of the sect when the "repentant of Israel" (cf. the "repentant of the desert") went out and "entered the New Covenant." The laws of the "men of the Community" (yáḥad) and "Righteous Teacher" (20:27–34) or "Teacher of the yáḥad" (19:34–20:1) are the stipulations of the covenant which was "established in the land of Damascus" (cf. 20:12). Again, the Star, the priestly Messiah of 7:18, associated in this context with the Scepter, the royal Messiah, is said to be coming to "Damascus" (hab-bâ' dammḗseq). The problems raised are formidable under any principle of interpretation, but they are insurmountable, I think, if "Damascus" is not taken as referring to the desert retreat in the wilderness of Qumrân.

There are, to be sure, slight differences between certain laws of the yáḥad in 1QS and the "camps" or "cities" of CD. These are explained most easily, I think, not by positing a different, Damascene Essenism, but by (1) recognizing that the various "orders" (sĕrākîm), in 1QS, 1QSa, and CD apply, among other things, to groups within the one congregation which follow slightly differing rules; and by (2) allowing for evolution in the sect, especially in the formative phase. CD is almost certainly a later composition than 1QS.

Philo, Josephus, and the Qumrân writings all speak vividly and repetitiously of the intimate fellowship and sense of community cultivated among the Essenes. Philo more than once comments on "their indescribable community" ($\kappa o\iota\nu\omega\nu\iota\alpha$)[47] and speaks specifically of their shared treasury, quarters, and clothing, as well as their common meals.[48] Josephus, similarly, is impressed with their common life, their self-appointed poverty and community of goods,[49] and describes their communal meals in considerable detail.

From the Qumrân texts we learn both of the motivation for the communism of the sectarians and of the detailed prescriptions governing communal use of property. "All who dedicate themselves to the truth of God shall bring all their knowledge and strength and wealth into the Community of God. . .";[50] "communally they shall eat and communally they shall bless and communally they shall take counsel . . .";[51] "this is the rule of the men of the Community . . . that they separate from the congregation of the men of perversion and become a community in doctrine and property."[52]

Without anticipating too much of what is to be said in a later chapter, we may observe here that the fully communal existence of the Essenes, as in the primitive Church, is a concomitant of an intense preoccupation with the qualities of life to be realized in the dawning New Age: unity (through the Spirit), brotherhood, love of one's fellow, the breakdown of the disparity between the (wicked) rich and the (oppressed) poor. Jesus in his first Beatitude paraphrases, or rather gives an eschatological interpretation to Psalm 37:9(–29). "The meek shall inherit the earth" is understood in the sense, "the

---

47 *Quod omn. prob. lib. sit*, §§ 84, 91.
48 Ibid.,§§ 86–91; *Hypothetica* 11, 4–13.
49 *War* II, 122–27.
50 1QS 1:11–12; cf. *CD* 13:1.
51 1QS 6:1–3; cf. 6:17–23; 9:7–8; etc.
52 1QS 5:1–2.

poor shall inherit the Kingdom of God." The Qumrân sectaries fully anticipate Jesus' interpretation in their commentary on Psalm 37, explaining that the "meek who shall inherit the earth" are the "Congregation of the Poor" (i.e., themselves) who will inherit the New Jerusalem, while the wicked of the nations and Israel will be destroyed forever.[53] And their practice of giving their goods to the "Poor" is directly alluded to in this setting.[54] Thus the practice of a communal economy among the people of the "New Covenant" is prompted by their conception of the coming "economy of God."

Central in the community life of the Essenes is their communion meal.[55] Josephus describes their practice in considerable detail, underlining the mystery and sacredness of the meal. Baths precede the meal. In special garments they enter a private hall. All uninitiated are prohibited entrance. In Josephus' words, "they proceed to their dining room as to some

---

53 Cf. Lk. 6:20 (Mt. 5:3, 5); and 4QpPs. 37 (Allegro, "A Newly-Discovered Fragment of a Commentary on Psalm XXXVII from Qumrân," *PEQ* 1954, pp. 69–75) I:8–10; II: 1–2; and especially II: 10–11. It should be noted—to avoid misunderstanding—that the Kingdom-to-come is in the (transfigured) earth, not in "heaven," both in the Jewish and early Christian understanding. "Heaven" in the phrase "Kingdom of Heaven" is, of course, simply a circumlocution for "God," a device now documented in the scrolls as well as other Jewish literature.

54 See Gaster's translation of 4QpPs. 37 A:II, 8–13 (*Dead Sea Scriptures*, p. 260).

55 K. G. Kuhn in an article, "The Lord's Supper and the Communal Meal at Qumrân" (an expansion of his older article, "Uber den ursprünglichen Sinn des Abendmahles und sein Verhältniss zu den Gemeinschaftsmahlen der Sektenschrift," *ET* 10 [1950/1951], pp. 508–27) now published in *The Scrolls and the New Testament*, edited by Krister Stendahl (New York, 1957), pp. 65–93, has made detailed comparison of Josephus' account and the passages of the Rule of the Community and Congregation (1QS 6:4–6; 1QSa II, 11–22). His study is important for revealing the peculiarity of Essene practice over against other Jewish meals.

holy precinct."[56] They take their seats in silence. None partakes of food prepared by priests[57] until "the priest" says a blessing.[58] These meals are daily, at midday and in the evening.

These notices parallel the legislation and rubrics for the meal in the Qumrân *Rule*. For example, the Rule of the Community states, "the novitiate shall not touch the banquet[59] of the Many until his completion of a second year among the men of the Community."[60] Both in Josephus and the Rule, the novitiate, after a first year within the community,[61] is permitted to draw nearer to its communal life, but admission to the common meal is the final step, taken only after the full two-year term of the novitiate.

The full significance of the common meal of the Essenes becomes clear in the rubrics preserved in the so-called Rule of the Congregation.[62] The heading of the section reads, "This is the rule for the whole congregation of Israel in the end of

56 *War* II, 129.

57 *Antiq.* XVIII, 22.

58 On the order of the blessings in Essene, Pharisaic, and Christian meals, see Kuhn, *op. cit.*

59 The Hebrew term is *mšqh*, which like biblical *mšth* is the festal meal which includes wine. More frequently the term *ṭhrh*, literally "purity" is used of the ritual purity of the inner community, including the food of the meals. But to judge from certain passages (e.g., 7:19–20), the *ṭhrh* extends to matters of purity beyond the food of the cultic meals.

60 1QS 6:20–21.

61 *War* II, 138. Josephus adds to the two-year novitiate an additional year outside the community as "postulant." Milik has argued that this datum may be harmonized with the two-year novitiate of 1QS, the candidate passing through three stages in his approach to full membership. I am rather inclined to the view that Josephus here errs in interpreting his source. His first year is equivalent to the first degree of 1QS, and the two-year period of testing is equivalent to the (one year) second degree of 1QS. The failure of Josephus to distinguish between the last two years suggests that he had conflated a first degree and a two-year total into a three-year period (*War* II, 137–42).

62 1QSa II, 11–22; cf. 1QS 6:4–6.

days . . ."; i.e., for the eschatological community.[63] Here are
excerpts of the order itself:[64]

> [This is (the order) of the ses]sion of the "Men of the Name
> who are [invited] to the Feast"[65] for the communal council[66]
> when [God] sends[67] the Messiah[68] to be with them[69]:

63 1QSa I, 1. It must be borne in mind, at all times, that the
"apocalyptic community" was at once the future congregation of the
elect and the "present" sect whose life was conceived as a foreshadow-
ing of the New Age. To fail to grasp fully this eschatological ethos of
the sect can only lead to misinterpretation of its texts. For this reason
Gaster's translation of the text in question (*Dead Sea Scriptures*, pp.
307–10) is flat and distorted. J. Van der Ploeg's study, "The Meals of
the Essenes," *JSS* II (1957), pp. 163–75, must be criticized on similar
grounds. Cf. R. E. Brown, "The Messianism of Qumrân," *CBQ* 19
(1957), pp. 78 f.; and Krister Stendahl, "The Scrolls and the New
Testament, an Introduction and Perspective," in *The Scrolls and the
New Testament*, pp. 1–17.

64 Cf. Cross, "Qumrân Cave I," *JBL* 75 (1956), pp. 124 f.

65 The phrase is taken from Num. 16:2 and typologically rein-
terpreted. Its precise meaning is not clear. The term translated "feast"
(*mw'd*) means "appointed time," and regularly in our texts means a
"set feast," or, better, "cultic" convocation.

66 *'ăṣat hay-yáḥad*. This is frequently used in the technical sense
"full-fledged members of the community."

67 Reading *ywly<k>* for *ywlyd* in the text. Cf. Cross, "Qumrân
Cave I," p. 124, n. 8. Gaster's remarks on this reading and his suggested
emendation must be rejected categorically (*Dead Sea Scriptures*, p.
279). In the first place, the understanding of the text as a liturgical
anticipation of an eschatological (Messianic) meal in no way depends
on the reading. In the second place, the first three letters are clear
beyond cavil. The ink is not faint; the leather is blackened, and photo-
graphing is made difficult. Those who have had access to the original—
and no one is happy with the reading—have without exception agreed
that *ywlyd/k* is paleographically fixed. If we have *ywlyd* (or *ywlyk*,
J. T. Milik's emendation), followed by a subject which must fit in a
space of two letters (the following *'t* is preserved only in the top of an
aleph), the restoration of the editor's (*'l*) is difficult to avoid.
To be sure the restoration suggested here is not certain; rather it is
awkward. But Gaster's restoration is wrong.

68 *I.e.*, the royal Messiah. Cf. Cross, "Qumrân Cave I," p. 124,
n. 9.

69 The phrase is parenthetical. No doubt in the assemblies of the
Essenes the lay head and the priestly head of the community (the

[The Priest][70] shall enter [at][71] the head of all the congregation of Israel and all the fa[thers of] the Aaronids . . . and they shall sit be[fore him each] according to his rank.

Next the [Messi]ah of Israel [shall enter], and the heads of the thou[sands of Israel] shall sit before him [ea]ch according to his rank . . .

[And][72] they shall sit before the (two) of them, each according to his rank . . .

W[hen th]ey solemnly meet together [at a tab]le of communion[73] [or to drink the w]ine, and the common table is arranged[and the] wine [is mixed] for drinking, one [shall not stretch out] his hand to the first portion of the bread or [of the wine] before the priest; for [he shall b]less the first portion of the bread and the wi[ne and shall stretch out] his hand to the bread first of all. Nex[t] the Messiah of Israel shall [str]etch out his hand to the bread. [Next]all the congregation of the Community [shall give tha]nks (and partake), each according to his rank.

And they shall act according to this prescription whenever (the meal) [is arr]anged, when as many as ten solemnly meet together.

The common meal of the Essenes is hereby set forth as a liturgical anticipation of the Messianic banquet. This is clear on the one hand from the roles of the Priest and the Messiah of Israel in the protocol. But it is especially clear

types of the Messiahs to come) stood in the stead of the Messiahs of Aaron and Israel.

70 Restoring *hkwhn* as in l. 19.

71 Restoring *[b]rw'š*. See Cross, "Qumrân Cave I," p. 124, n. 7.

72 Restoring *[w]yšbw*.

73 Text: *[lšl]ḥn yḥd*. The translation "communion" is technically correct, though it may carry too many connotations in English. Cf. the next line, where I translate *hšwlḥn hyḥd*, "the common table," which errs in the other direction since "common" carries too few religious connotations.

when the final rubric (ll. 21–22) is compared with the elaborate protocol. That is, in the "taking of seats" at the meal, the whole of (true) Israel is arranged before the two Messianic figures, the priestly class before the Priest, the laity before the Messiah; in the rubric, however, we are told that this prescription is to be carried out *whenever* the meal is arranged, when as many as *ten men* meet together. Obviously this applies to the current practice of the sect.[74]

The motif of the banquet already appears in the Old Testament in passages which lend themselves to apocalyptic exegesis, and in eschatological dress reappears in the intertestamental and especially New Testament literature. Perhaps the most important of the Old Testament passages is Is. 25: 6–8, which reads:

On the mountain the Lord of Hosts shall prepare
    for all peoples
A banquet of rich food, a banquet of old wine;
Fat and marrowy viands, old and refined wine.
On this mountain he shall swallow up
The veil (of mourning) which enwraps all peoples,
The mantle (of grief) which covers all the nations.
He shall swallow up Death forever;
[He] shall wipe tears from every face;
His people's reproach he shall remove from the whole earth.
For the Lord hath spoken.

The familiar passage Is. 55: 1–5 also received interpretation, rightly or wrongly, as the banquet of David *redivivus*.[75] And a whole kaleidoscope of ideas, the streaming of the nations

---

74 It would not be surprising if in the gathering of all the camps for the annual festival of covenant renewal at Pentecost, one finds the *Sitz im Leben* of the elaborate protocol. For the annual ceremony of the (New) Covenant, see 1QS I, 1–II, 12, etc.; J. T. Milik has established the date of the festival by a combination of an unpublished text with Jubilees 6:17 (*Découvertes*, Chap. IV).

75 So in Rev. 22:17; cf. Ezekiel 44:3.

to the exalted mountain of Zion,[76] the feeding of the flocks (the children of Israel) on the "height of Israel,"[77] the healing and nourishing river issuing from the New Temple on its "very high mountain,"[78] were woven into an apocalyptic fabric.[79] By Hellenistic and Roman times the eschatological banquet and its associated themes became frequent in apocalyptic writing, and are amazingly frequent in the New Testament.[80] It comes as no surprise, therefore, to discover these motives were at home among the Essenes.[81]

76 Cf. Is. 2:2–4 (Mic. 4:1–4), Ps. 74:12–17, especially v. 14, and Is. 60. For use of the latter passage at Qumrân, see 1QM 12:10–18 which may be, as Milik and others have suggested, a Messianic hymn.

77 Cf. Ezek. 34:14–16.

78 Cf. Ezek. 40:2; 47:1–12.

79 A full discussion of the theme, "the Banquet of Salvation on the World Mountain" is given in the third chapter of J. Jeremias' volume, *Jesu Mission für die Völker* [*Franz Delitzsch–Vorlesungen* 1953] (Stuttgart, 1956).

80 In the New Testament, see especially Mt. 8:11 f.=Lk. 13:28 f; Rev. 19:9; Lk. 14:15–24 (cf. Mt. 22:1–14); Lk. 22:30. Cf. I Enoch 62:14. Specifically Eucharistic passages utilizing the themes of the Messianic banquet will be dealt with below in another connection.

81 Another example in the Qumrân literature, hitherto missed, is found in 4QpPs. 37 II, 10–11. It appears that 37:11 is taken by the expositor as alluding to the eschatological banquet. In any case, the phrase *hr mrwm yśr'l* is pregnant with eschatological meaning, recalling the theme, "banquet on the holy mountain." The phrase is found in Ezek. 20:40 (a favorite Essene passage for typological exegesis) parallel to *bhr qdšy*. Perhaps we should reconstruct . . . *hr mrwm yśr['l bhr] qwdšw yt'ngw* . . . The expression also appears in Ezek. 34: 14–16, another passage which played an important role in eschatological symbolism. Again the term *yt'ngw*, "take exquisite delight," "make merry," is associated with the language of the eschatological meal. Note its use in the key passage Is. 55:2 as well as in Ps. 37:11.

We noted above parallels between Jesus' interpretation of Psalm 37 in eschatological terms in the first Beatitude (Lk. 6:20 and parallel), and that of the Essene 4QpPs. 37. The "poor" are to inherit the Kingdom in the New Age. We should observe at this point also that in the second Beatitude, Jesus seems to continue his exposition of Psalm 37, alluding, like 4QpPs. 37, to the eschatological banquet: "Blessed are ye that hunger for ye shall be filled." (Lk. 6:21.)

The classical sources on the Essenes, because of their apologetic purposes and Hellenizing tendencies, largely conceal the apocalyptic overtones of Essene thought. Nevertheless there are hints of this theological pattern in all our sources.

Josephus, for example, describes the Essenes as the most "fatalistic" of the sects in Judaism.[82] Translated from the Greek frame of reference, this characterization points to the predestinarian doctrine typical of apocalyptic thought. In a world captive to the powers of darkness, salvation is the gift of God to His elect, achieved by His new creation. In the section of the Rule of the Community dealing with the doctrine of the Two Spirits[83] (to which the sons of light and darkness are allotted from creation), we find a rigorous predestinarian formulation which teeters on the edge of determinism.[84] And even as the predestinarian doctrine of the Essenes recalls the (milder) Pauline doctrine, so a sectarian doctrine of "justification by grace" appears in their writings as a corollary of predestination, adumbrating the classical Pauline statement of salvation by faith.[85]

Josephus also takes note of the esoteric nature of their teachings,[86] their interest in angels,[87] their thorough knowledge of the sayings of the prophets[88] and "the writings of the ancients,"[89] and their practice of prophecy.[90] Each of these characteristics of the sect's doctrine and practice, especially

82 *Antiq.* XIII, 172. The term $\epsilon\iota\mu\alpha\rho\mu\acute{\epsilon}\nu\eta$ is used.

83 1QS 3:13–4:26.

84 See the excellent discussion of Kuhn, "$\pi\epsilon\iota\rho\alpha\sigma\mu\acute{o}\varsigma$—$\acute{\alpha}\mu\alpha\rho\tau\acute{\iota}\alpha$—$\sigma\acute{\alpha}\rho\xi$ im Neuen Testament und die damit zusammenhängenden Vorstellungen." *ZTK* 49 (1952), pp. 200–22.

85 On the scrolls and "justification," see the excellent article of S. E. Johnson, "Paul and the Manual of Discipline," *HTR* 48 (1955), pp. 157–65.

86 *War* II, 141.

87 *War* II, 142.

88 *War* II, 159.

89 *War* II, 136.

90 *War* II, 159; cf. *War* I, 78; II, 113: *Antiq.* XV, 371–79.

the appearance of prophecy among its members, points directly to its apocalyptic structure.

Philo tells us that the Essenes turn their backs upon all philosophy, logical and natural, save that which treats of God and creation, and are much concerned with the ethical branch of philosophy. Translated into another idiom, he is saying that they are interested only in biblical revelation and law. That Philo must be understood so is shown in the succeeding passage where he describes the convocations of the sect in terms strongly reminiscent of the discipline set out in the Rule of the Community.[91] In their convocations, arranged by rank, the sectaries read their Scriptures aloud. One proficient in their interpretation exposits the lection typologically,[92] according to ancient tradition. Philo here records precisely the setting in life of the commentaries of Qumrân.[93] These are collections of typological or apocalyptic expositions of biblical passages, for the most part from the Prophets, the citation of a text alternating with its interpretation. No doubt a body of traditional exegesis developed in the sect, being put down in written form in the so-called commentaries (*pĕšārîm*) of Qumrân.

Hippolytus adds a clear apocalyptic note in attributing to the Essenes a doctrine of world judgment, resurrection of the body (as well as immortality of the soul), eternal punishment of the wicked, and the destruction of the (old) world in a cosmic conflagration. The last-mentioned doctrine is especially distinctive, and is confirmed in the new scrolls.[94]

It is quite impossible within our limits to pursue all of the details in which our classical sources complement and correspond to sources from Qumrân caves. This correspondence

91 Philo, *Quod omn. prob. lib. sit*, 80–82.

92 *Ibid.* 82. We have translated διὰ συμβόλων, "typologically."

93 Cf. 1QS 6:6–13.

94 Hippolytus, *Refutatio* IX, 27: cf. 1QH 3:19–36; Black, *op. cit.*, p. 175. (The same doctrine is attributed to the Pharisees by Hippolytus.)

can be illustrated by citation of details of community organization, offices and trial procedures, or of common practice in
such matters as sanitary regulations,[95] the use of oaths,[96] the
rites of lustration and baptism.[96a] On the one hand we can

95 As we have seen, the sect lives by the rules of "Holy War" associated with the desert era and the Conquest; cf. Josephus, *War* II,
137; 148–49; Deut. 23: 10–14; Num. 5:1–4; 1QM 7:3–7.

96 Josephus, *War* II, 135; *Antiq.* XV, 371; Philo, *Quod omn. prob.
lib. sit*, 84; *CD* 15:1–5; Mt. 5:33–37; 23:16–22; Jas. 5:12.

96a See Josephus, *War* II, 129, 138 (cf. 149, 150; *Antiq.* XVIII,
19). In the Qumrân texts, see especially 1QS 5:8–23. The passage describes the procedure of initiation into full membership (ll.8, 20,
23), including the oath, covenant, baptism, and separation in matters
of goods, labor, food, or even religious discussion. In ll. 10–13, an
instruction is given to have the candidate take upon himself covenant
obligations; there follows a denunciation of those who insincerely enter the covenant. In ll. 13–14 there follows a warning against the
candidate who is baptized without repentance: "[Such a candidate]
shall not enter into the water [and as a result] to come into contact
with the Purity of the holy men: for they are not purified (thereby)
except (*kî 'im*) they repent from their wickedness." In 1QS 2:25–
3:12, there is another list of warnings to him who refuses to enter the
covenant or who does so without faith, obedience, and repentance, in
which the efficacy of the covenant ceremony or any baptism or lustration (even with "seas or rivers!") of itself, *ex opere operato,* is
sharply denied.

Cf. K. Stendahl, "ΑΞΙΟΣ im Lichte der Texte der Qumran-Höhle,"
Nuntius 7 (1952), cols. 53–55; N. A. Dahl, "The Origin of Baptism,"
*Interpretationes ad Vetus Testamentum pertinentes Sigmundo Mo-
winckel septuagenario missae* (Oslo, 1955), pp. 36–51.

M. H. Gottstein in his article, "Anti-Essene Traits in Dead Sea
Scrolls," VT IV (1954), pp. 141–47, has failed to recognize the distinction between the efficacy of baptism in the case of one who is repentant and has a holy spirit (1QS 3:7), *ex opere operante;* and baptism
as an *opus operatum*. Gottstein can show at most that the texts of
Qumrân reject the latter conception of baptism. The Qumrân sectarians
are "baptist," however, both in their general ideas of purity and in the
actual practice of the rites of baptism and lustration. The only question
which remains open is whether or not their rite of baptism on entry into
covenant was annually repeated in the covenant renewal ceremony. 1QS
2:25–3:12 suggests that it was.

C.-H. Hunzinger has identified a papyrus containing directives for a
rite of baptism or purification by water; see previsionally "Le travail
d'édition. . . .," p. 67.

point to verbal reminiscences in Josephus of theological clichés in the Qumrân texts,[97] and on the other hand to the prohibition of spitting in assembly recorded by both Josephus and the Rule of Qumrân.

There are also apparent discrepancies between the Essenes of the classical sources and the people of the scrolls, which require fresh examination.

There is the matter of celibacy. Did the Essenes marry? Philo is unequivocal in stating that they were a celibate order.[99] Josephus says that they shun marriage but do not reject the institution as such. He attributes to them as a motivation the desire to guard themselves "from the wantonness of woman."[100] This seems a convincing enough reason for the practice of celibacy . . . but one suspects it originates, not in Essene theology, but in Josephus' Hellenistic imagination.[101] Elsewhere Josephus records that one order ($\tau \acute{a} \gamma \mu a$) of Essenes did in fact marry, while otherwise keeping to the Essene rule.[102]

The evidence from Qumrân is in part ambiguous. It is

97 For example, in the initiates' oath (*War* II, 139–41), we read ". . . that he must always hate the unrighteous and take the side of the righteous," and "that he must love the truth always and denounce the false." Compare 1QS 1:9–11; 4:23–25, etc.

98 *War* II, 147; 1QS 6:3.

99 *Hypothetica* 11, 14–17. Philo attributes two reasons for their celibacy, its threat to a fully communal life, and the wickedness of woman. In the latter case Philo indulges himself in a diatribe against womankind which tells us more about Philo than about the Essenes.

100 *War* II, 120–21.

101 The late Professor Marcus has observed *à propos* of the Hellenizing distortion of Josephus, "I have long suspected, for example, that Josephus has misled us by presenting the great majority of Essenes as celibates while indicating that only a small group of them practiced marriage for the purpose of procreation. This may actually be a reversal of the true situation or at least a gross exaggeration, since it is difficult to believe that even the most heterodox Jews would have disregarded one of the cardinal and widely accepted principles of Judaism, based on God's first commandment to mankind, 'increase and multiply.' " ("The Qumrân Scrolls and Early Judaism," p. 28.)

102 *War* II, 160–61.

certain that one order within the sectarian community married.[103] In descriptions of the "congregation" (*'ēdāh*), women and children are named.[103a] There is also data, however, which suggests that the Qumrân "community," (*yáḥad*), at least, was largely celibate.[103b] The large central cemetery of Qumrân, containing about one thousand tombs, seems to contain only male burials. In adjuncts to the central cemetery, skeletons of women and children have been found.[104] It is possible that the outlying cemeteries are later in date, and that the older celibate community later became mixed,[105] or we may suppose that within the environs of the desert of Qumrân was an order of married Essenes alongside a larger celibate community.

This area of Essene life can best be understood, not by positing a sect of marrying Essenes alongside a celibate sect, but by recognizing an ambiguous attitude toward marriage integral to the structure of the Essene faith. While a genuine asceticism has no place in Judaism, there are two streams in Judaism which have dualistic tendencies. One of these is an extremely ancient one, rooted in the priestly distinctions between ritual purity and pollution, "physical" holiness and "physical" sin. Certain sexual acts render one unclean so that he may not approach holy things. This is especially vivid in the laws of "Holy War," where all sexual life is suspended, women excluded from the camp, since God's Spirit (or his holy angels) is present in the camp. The second stream is the late developing apocalyptic movement which assimilates certain elements of Persian ethical dualism to the prophetic understanding of history as a drama of divine warfare culmi-

103 See above, n. 45.

103a Cf. 1QSa I:4, 9–10.

103b Professor Herbert May has reminded me of the expression *prwt zr'* in 1QS 4:7, in the list of the blessings of the Spirit in the "world" (*tbl*). Cf. CD 4:21–5:11;7 (=19):6–8.

104 De Vaux, *Rapport III*, pp. 569–72.

105 So Milik, *Découvertes*, Appendice.

nating in the victory of God. In this tradition the "normal life" of the old age is qualified. The faithful live in a crisis which marks the death of the Old World, the birth of the New Creation. It is a time of trial, and therefore of an "abnormal" discipline of the flesh.

At Qumrân these streams come together in a priestly apocalypticism which energizes the dualistic tendencies of both traditions. We have already noted that the rigorous rules of Holy War obtain in the daily regimen of the Qumrân community. Ritual purity is maintained by the community as a whole. The community takes the posture of a priesthood standing in the presence of God.[105a] This disciplined life, moreover, is set in an apocalyptic understanding of history. The trumpet has sounded for God's final Holy War. The men of the Essene community are mustered for battle, rank on rank, poised to march side by side with the "holy ones," the angelic armies of God.[106]

The Essene in his daily life thus girds himself to withstand the final trial, purifies himself to join the holy armies, anticipates the coming conditions in God's inbreaking kingdom. This is the situation which prompts counsels against marriage, at least for some. In the new age he will live eternally in the presence of the holy ones,[107] the angels of God, and even in the very presence of the Holy God. In this new age the righteous live like the angels without need of procreation, and preserve themselves in perpetual "purity" before the throne of God.

The attitude toward marriage in the primitive Church springs from the same theological milieu.[108] In Luke 20: 34–36

105a Cf. 1QSb III; 22–IV, 28; and Ex. 19:6, 15.

106 See especially, 1QM 12:1–5; 6–10.

107 See, for example, 1QS 11:7–8; 1QH 3:19–23; 6:12–14; 7:29–31; and especially 11:10–14; cf. 1QM 7:6; and Col. 1:12.

108 I suspect that certain of the New Testament passages here cited are shaped not merely by *an* apocalypticism, but by priestly, that is, Essene apocalypticism.

is the saying, "The sons of this age marry and are given in marriage; but those who are worthy to have a lot in that new age, and in the resurrection of the dead, neither marry nor are taken in marriage, for they no longer can die, because they, like the angels, are sons of God being sons of the resurrection."[109] Paul's teachings on marriage, that he who marries does well, that he who remains unmarried does better, since "the appointed time has grown very short," are cut from the same theological fabric.[110]

Both in the New Testament and at Qumrân we discover counsels against marriage in *this* decisive moment when *this* world is passing away. In neither community is to be found a theoretical ascetic doctrine of universal validity. Rather we may call Essene (or New Testament) practice an "apocalyptic" asceticism. It is this apocalyptic asceticism which explains the confusing statements of Josephus and clarifies the ambiguities in the data from the texts and cemeteries of Qumrân.

To be sure, the apocalyptic asceticism of the Essenes and early Christianity was unstable. In its first contacts with Greek paganism, especially Platonic forms of thought, the eschatological tension was lost. The precipitate was Docetic and Gnostic asceticism, as well as those more orthodox forms of piety out of which monasticism sprang. In any case we cannot with felicity speak of Qumrân as a "monastery," or of Essene sectaries as "monks."

Before the discovery of the texts of Qumrân, it was generally held, on the basis of passages in Philo and Josephus, that the Essenes rejected sacrifice.[111] Philo, in commenting on their piety, remarks that their "extraordinary devotion to God" is shown "not by sacrificing animals, but by determining to render their own minds holy."[112] This can be taken to mean

109 Cf. Mk. 12:25; Mt. 22:30 (parallels); and Mt. 19:10–12.
110 1 Cor. 7.
111 See, e.g., Schürer, *Geschichte*[3] II, pp. 568 f.
112 *Quod omn. prob. lib. sit*, 75.

that the Essenes repudiated the sacrificial system. It need not be. The conviction that "obedience is better than sacrifice, hearkening (to the voice of the Lord) than the fat of rams" (I Sam. 15:22) is shared by prophet and priest in old Israel, and might have been expressed by a pious Jew of the later period, whatever his party. In other words, Philo's comment would be appropriate if the Essenes (1) rejected the Temple cultus on principle, or (2) insisted only that God's ethical and ritual laws be observed as a prerequisite of valid sacrifices.

The texts of Qumrân leave no doubt that their authors' objections to the cultus of Jerusalem fall under the second alternative.[113] The founder of the sect was a priest, evidently of the legitimate line,[114] and the community was dominated by priests who expected to return to the Temple to reinstitute orthopraxy in the days of the Last War.[115] Meanwhile they assert that the sanctuary is defiled,[116] the reigning priesthood false. Nevertheless they preserve and prepare documents pertaining to the priestly service.[117]

There are two additional data to be considered. Josephus writes, "When the Essenes send their gifts[118] to the Temple,

113 An excellent study of the problem of sacrifice at Qumrân, admirably summarizing the then-known data, is that of J. M. Baumgarten, "Sacrifice and Worship among the Jewish Sectarians of the Dead Sea (Qumrân) Scrolls," *HTR* 46 (1953), pp. 141–59.

114 1QpHab. 2:8; 4QpPs. 37 II, 15. 1QM 17:2–3.

115 1QM 2:1–6. For the role of the future chief priest and priests generally, see 1QM, *passim*; 4QPs. 37 II, 10–11; 4Q Testimonia, 14–20; 1QSb II–V, 19; etc.

On the passage pertaining to sacrifice in 1QS 9:3–6, see J. Carmignac, "L'utilité ou l'inutilité des sacrifices sanglants dans la 'Règle de la Communauté' de Qumrân," *RB* 63 (1956), pp. 524–32 (with postscript by J. T. Milik, p. 532).

116 1QpHab. 12:7–9; 8:8–13; *CD* 20:22–24; cf. 6:11–14; etc.

117 On 4Q *Mišmārôt*, see Chap. I, n. 70; laws pertaining to sacrifice are preserved in *CD* 9:13–14; 11:17–21; 16:13.

118 Greek, $\alpha\nu\alpha\theta\dot{\eta}\mu\alpha\tau\alpha$; Heb. *ḥérem*. Such could be given to the Temple without the donor entering into the cultus or recognizing the legitimacy of the priesthood; the *ḥérem*, unqualified, seems to have been used for repair or ornamentation of the Temple; cf. Lk. 21:5.

they do <not> offer sacrifices owing to a difference in rites of purity which they practice, and therefore being excluded[119] from the common precinct (of the Temple), they offer sacrifices by themselves."[120] On the face of it, this text suggests that the Essenes carried on animal sacrifice privately. Josephus' testimony might simply be dismissed were it not for the appearance at Qumrân of meticulous burials of animal bones.[121] Though it is somewhat difficult to visualize at Qumrân the maintenance of an independent sacrificial cultus by a hyperorthodox sect, I am inclined to think that our evidence now suggests that this was the case.[122]

However the latter question may ultimately be answered,

119 On the meaning of εἰργόμενοι in Josephus, see Marcus, "Pharisees, Essenes, and Gnostics," JBL 73 (1954), p. 158.

120 Antiq. XVIII, 19. εἰς δὲ τὸ ἱερὸν ἀναθήματα στέλλοντες θυσίας <οὐκ> ἐπιτελοῦσι διαφορότητι ἁγνειῶν, ἃς νομίζοιεν καὶ δι᾽ αὐτὸ εἰργόμενοι τοῦ κοινοῦ τεμενίσματος ἐφ᾽ αὑτῶν τὰς θυσίας ἐπιτελοῦσιν. The attempt to read the last phrase "conduct worship separately" (cf. Baumgarten, op. cit., p. 155) while the same expression, in the same sentence is translated "offer sacrifices" seems quite out of the realm of probability. It is better simply to deny the accuracy of Josephus' statement (so Marcus, op. cit., p. 158, n.2) if one cannot bring himself to suppose the Essenes actually conducted separate sacrifices.

121 See above, p. 51 f.; De Vaux, Rapport III, pp. 549 f.

122 Warrant for a sacrificial system may be found in a special interpretation given in CD 3:18–4:4 to Ezek. 44:15 by the sectarian author. The passage of Ezekiel is slightly changed, apparently for sectarian purposes. In any case the sect is identified with "the priests and the Levites and [sic!] the sons of Zadok who kept the office of my sanctuary when the children of Israel went astray from me, they shall bring me fat and blood."

Again, it must be noted that the Essenes did in fact institute and practice an independent calendar of feasts. This is now certain from unpublished documents of Cave IV.

Mr. John Strugnell has suggested to me that a rationale for the establishment of an altar at Qumrân could be derived from the sect's patterning itself after the Mosaic camp of the wilderness, where sacrifice was in fact carried on.

The Essene practice would not be wholly without a parallel of sorts in this period. Onias, the hereditary high priest in the time of Maccabees established a temple and cultus at Leontopolis (Josephus, War I, 31, 33; VII, 422–35).

there can be no doubt that Josephus and the Qumrân manuscripts are in essential agreement as to the sectarian attitude toward sacrifice and the Temple. Similarly other apparent discrepancies melt away when older constructions of the classical authorities are re-examined, and when it is remembered that the theological categories of the Essenes are crudely translated into philosophical categories by both Philo and Josephus in writing for the Greek reader.[123]

In the foregoing discussion we have restricted ourselves to points raised by the older sources and to data from the scrolls which bear directly on the older sources. Hence Philo and Josephus have called the tune. Our purpose has been to show how the older sources and the newer texts are mutually illuminating, how they at each point confirm the identity of the people of the scrolls with the Essenes, how the Essenes emerge

123 Josephus' reference to the morning prayers of the Essenes deserves some comment. His text reads, "They show piety to the Deity in an unusual fashion; before the sun comes up they do not speak of profane affairs, but pray certain traditional prayers to him as if invoking (the sun) to rise" (*War* II, 128). Apparently the antecedent of (εἰς) αὐτόν "him" is τὸν ἥλιον "the sun" rather than τὸ θεῖον, "the Deity"; otherwise the sentence is awkward. On the other hand can we suppose that Josephus really thought the Essenes worshiped the sun? Hippolytus in the parallel passage gives no hint of heterodoxy (*Refutatio* IX, 21). Our manuscripts include a liturgical papyrus containing among other things the sunrise prayer (unpublished; cf. Hunzinger, "Le travail d'édition . . ." p. 67), and in 1QH there is an interesting reference to prayers at specified periods including sunrise (12:4–7). While the sun is determinative in fixing the times of the day and year at Qumrân, so that their calendar is purely solar, there is, of course, no hint of sun worship in these prayers or elsewhere in the Qumrân literature.

Probably Josephus' comment is to be understood as a reference to the unorthodox orientation of the Essene in prayer, facing the rising sun. The Jew normally faced toward the Temple (cf. Dan. 6:10, etc.). Daniélou ("La communauté de Qumrân et l'organisation de l'Eglise ancienne," *RHPR* 35 [1955], p. 108) has noted that early Christian practice follows the Essene custom over against the orthodox. Strugnell has suggested to me that εἰς αὐτόν should be translated "toward it" (the sun), from the usage of the preposition with εὐχάς, supporting Daniélou's interpretation.

KEY TO CHART OF JEWISH SCRIPTS

Line 1. An Aramaic script of the mid-fourth century B.C. From the Louvre papyrus, *CIS* (*Pars secunda*) I:1, Tab. XVII, Nos. 146 A,B. *Line 2.* An archaic manuscript of Samuel from Cave IV, Qumrân (4QSam^b), from the end of the third century B.C. (Cf. Plate 4). *Line 3* An archaic manuscript of Jeremiah (4QJer^a) belonging to about 200 B.C. *Line 4.* A cursive hand from ca. 150–125 B.C. The script is taken from a manuscript of the Minor Prophets (4QXII^a). *Line 5.* The script of the Běnê Ḥēzîr inscription from the end of the first century B.C. *Line 6.* A late hand belonging to a Deuteronomy manuscript (4QDeut^j). The script is to be dated ca. A.D. 50; it is the immediate typological forebear of the standard hand of the second century A.D. and later. All scripts are traced from photographs, with the exception of the Běnê Ḥēzîr inscription. Its forms were traced from a photograph of a new squeeze, and checked by direct photographs. Sigla:1, the letter is broken off at the top;2, final *pe* is not used: °, "final" forms.

from our sources a sect of priestly apocalyptists. The classical sources, however, have sharply limited our picture of the Essenes and their history, and we must now turn to a broader examination of the Qumrân manuscripts themselves to piece together more fragments of their life and history.

CHAPTER III

The Righteous Teacher and Essene Origins

THE LIBRARY FOUND at Qumrân contains no document which can be called properly a historical work. Historiography was not an interest of the sect's authors. Nevertheless, the scrolls, especially the class of documents inexactly called biblical commentaries, contain many allusions to contemporary events, both in the inner history of the sect, and in the political history of Syria-Palestine. Beginning with the publication of the Damascus Document in 1910, and especially with the publication of the Habakkuk Commentary in 1950, scholars have attempted to reconstruct the history of the sect from data found within the scrolls themselves. For the most part these attempts at synthesis have failed, and the number of theories evolved almost equals the number of scholars who have put their hands to the task. In the search for the archvillain of the sect, for example, the "Wicked Priest," scholars have found candidates ranging from pre-Maccabean times down into the Roman era and even later. No Hasmonaean priest-king has been left unturned in his grave.

There is little purpose in reviewing the theories and debate which marked the early discussion of the history of the sect.[1]

1. Surveys of the sundry views held by scholars of the historical

Much of the labor during the early phase of the inquiry consisted of simple guesswork guided by too vague and too few allusions in the extant texts to achieve secure results. That this is true should be evident in the sheer variety of theories spawned in scholars' imaginations. Moreover, much of the early study has fallen to philologians who, following the traditional methods of literary analysis, have failed to train themselves in the relatively new disciplines in the fields of archaeology and especially paleography. The unfortunate result has been that a steady stream of historical studies have been published based on premises excluded by archaeological and paleographical data. On the other hand, many of these prematurely obsolete reconstructions have contained extremely important philological advances and cannot be ignored. Finally, the field has been developing with extreme rapidity. To the veiled allusions of the first published texts have been added now explicit references by name to known historical figures. The analysis of new materials for paleogra-

cadre of the scrolls may be found in the following: M. Burrows, *The Dead Sea Scrolls*, pp. 123–223; K. Elliger, *Studien zum Habakuk-Kommentar vom Toten Meer* (Tübingen, 1953) pp. 226–74; H. H. Rowley, *The Zadokite Fragments and the Dead Sea Scrolls*, pp. 31–61; and G. Vermès, *Les manuscrits du Désert de Juda* (Tournai, 1953), pp. 67–108. Among the recently published reconstructions, see G. Vermès, *loc. cit.*; L. Toombs, "The Early History of the Qumran Sect," *JSS* 1 (1956), pp. 367–81; J. M. Allegro, "Further Light on the History of the Qumrân Sect," *JBL* 75 (1956), pp. 89–95 (cf. *The Dead Sea Scrolls*, pp. 94–100); T. H. Gaster, *The Dead Sea Scriptures*, pp. 24–28; J. T. Milik, *Découvertes*, Chap. III and Appendice; and Cecil Roth, "A Solution to the Mystery of the Scrolls," *Commentary* 24 (1957), pp. 317–24. Reformulations of earlier constructions include the recent studies of I. Rabinowitz, "Reconsideration of 'Damascus' and '390 years' in the 'Damascus' ('Zadokite') Fragments," *JBL* 73 (1954), pp. 11–35; (cf. E. Wiesenberg, "Chronological Data in the Zadokite Fragments," *VT* 5 [1955] pp. 284–308); A. Dupont-Sommer, "Quelques remarques sur le Commentaire d'Habacuc à propos d'un livre récent," *VT* 5 (1955), pp. 113–29; H. H. Rowley, "The Kittim and the Dead Sea Scrolls," *PEQ* 88 (1956), pp. 92–109 (cf. "4QpNahum and the Teacher of Righteousness," *JBL* 75 [1956], 188–93).

phy has made crucial progress in several areas. And with each season of excavation at Qumrân, archaeological controls on the interpretation of the texts become tighter and tighter.

1. Prolegomena to the Study of the Commentaries

At the outset some word must be said concerning the character of source materials in the scrolls with which we must labor in any attempt to work out the details of Essene history. Our sources consist chiefly of expositions of biblical prophecy, or of biblical material reckoned as prophecy by the Essenes. These include (1) commentaries, *pěšārîm*, which expound extended passages or entire biblical books verse by verse; (2) collections of "prophetic" testimonia, sometimes with expository comments appended to each, sometimes without; and (3) historical exposition utilizing a patchwork of biblical citations to interpret in "prophetic" language the meaning and sequence of historical events of the past and future.

The technique of exposition in all these sources grows out of the presuppositions of apocalypticism, and can be rightly understood only within the categories of this special type of eschatological thought. Two major assumptions characterize apocalyptic exegesis. All biblical prophecy is normally taken to have eschatological meaning. The "prophets," Moses as well as Amos, the Psalmist as well as Jeremiah, speak regularly in open or veiled language of the "last days." Their predictions are not to be understood in simple terms of near future or even remote future, but apply to the crisis of the ages, the final times when the historical epoch turns into the transhistorical epoch. Secondly, it must be understood that the apocalyptist understood himself to be living in these days of the final crisis, at the end of days and the beginning of the New Age, so that the events of his own times were recognized as precisely those events forecast by the prophets of old as coming in the last days.[2]

By perusing the Scriptures, the Essenes were able to find detailed descriptions of the events of current history; the central figures of their sect and of their times were hidden in veiled prophetic allusions. The life of their own sect, its origin, purpose, vicissitudes, and glorious destiny all had been laid out in the predictions of the ancients. To be sure, it could be read only by "those who had eyes to see." Essene exegesis was necessarily pneumatic, based on the gift of special eschatological "knowledge." The secrets of the prophets had to be discovered by inspired interpreters.

The tradition of Essene exegesis was initiated directly, no doubt, by the founder of the sect, the so-called "Righteous Teacher" (môrēh haṣ-ṣédeq).[3] It is said of him in the Habakkuk Commentary[4] that he spoke of "all the events which were to come upon the last generation," for "God placed (him) in the [midst of the 'congregation'] to expound all the words of his prophets by whose agency God has related all which is to come upon his people and [his congregation]." In another passage we read,[5] ". . . God has informed (the Righteous Teacher) of all the secrets of the words of his servants the prophets." No doubt the founder himself was heavily indebted to earlier apocalyptic materials, especially to Daniel. At all

2. Cf. K. Elliger, *Studien zum Habakuk-Kommentar vom Toten Meer,* hereafter *SzHK,* pp. 150–64; W. H. Brownlee, "Biblical Interpretation Among the Sectaries of the Dead Sea Scrolls ," *BA* 14 (1951), pp. 54–76. Elliger succinctly summarizes the hermeneutical principles: (1) prophecy is eschatology and (2) the present is the end-time.

3. The title probably includes the ideas of "righteousness" and "legitimacy." However, I cannot agree with those scholars who take ṣédeq to be an objective genitive, "one who teaches righteousness," though, obviously the "Righteous Teacher" teaches righteousness. Cf. T. H. Gaster, *The Dead Sea Scriptures,* p. 5. One may note the parallel title, "righteous or legitimate Messiah," mᵉšíᵃh haṣ-ṣédeq, 4Q Patriarchal Blessings l. 3; šm h'mt, "trustworthy name," 1QpHab. 8:9; etc.

4. 1QpHab. 2:5–10.

5. 1QpHab. 7:4–5.

events, certain set forms of exposition and a traditional body of biblical exposition grew up, stemming from the pattern laid down in the early period. This was transmitted and supplemented, no doubt, in the regular study of scholars of the community, and particularly in the regular sessions of the sect mentioned in our sources, where Scripture was read and systematically expounded by those who had become the experts of the community. In a later era the body of traditional exegesis was put into writing in the commentaries and related documents which have come into our hands.

Such a construction of the literary background of commentary materials is necessary to explain certain features of the works. In the first place, there is a consistent treatment of biblical expressions throughout them,[6] despite the fact that their hermeneutic technique lends itself to extreme subjectivity in dealing with Scripture. The commentaries are based on communal and traditional exposition, therefore, and are not merely the result of individual flights of fancy. In the second place, virtually all commentaries and testimonia[7] appear in manuscripts written in late hands, from the second half of the first century B.C. and the first half of the first century A.D. We have shown elsewhere[8] that there are strong reasons to believe that most of the commentaries are autographs. The argument is quite simple. Biblical works and non-biblical works reappear again and again in the caves, sometimes in as many as ten or fifteen copies of a single work. This duplication (or multiplication) of copies among the various

6. There is, to be sure, an occasional unevenness in treating a "prophetic" expression. For example, the "staff," *mḥqq*, of Gen. 49:10 is differently interpreted in 4Q Patriarchal Blessings and in *CD*. In the former (l.2) it is the royal covenant, i.e., the covenant of David; in *CD* 6:7, the term is equated with *dwrš htwrh*, the priestly office. See below, chap. V, n. 74.

7. An exception is 4Q Testimonia inscribed by the same scribe who prepared 1QS as well as a number of other manuscripts, biblical and non-biblical, found in Qumrân caves. His hand belongs preferably to the first quarter of the first century B.C.

8. "Qumrân Cave I," *JBL* 75 (1956), pp. 123 f.

caves is significantly absent in a single category of literature: the commentaries. In light of the large number of such works now known, especially from Cave IV, it is difficult to avoid the conclusion that such works were rarely if ever copied, and hence are mostly original works. If this conclusion is valid, it has important implications for dating: the date of the script of a commentary will indicate normally its date of written composition. The deduction to be drawn is that a corpus of traditional exegesis was put into writing only toward the end of the sect's life.

These factors suggest, and inductive examination will show, that the commentaries refer to events over a considerable period of history. The allusions to the history of the sect thus cannot all be fitted into the era of its formation. They must be spread out over at least two generations, and probably longer.

Two other comments, both in the nature of warnings, need to be made *à propos* of Essene apocalyptic exegesis. In the nature of the apocalyptic interpretation of history, events are described from within the context of the elect community. The important events in the history of salvation are the events which involve the sect. From the point of view of the critical historian, this means that major political events, Pompey's conquest of Jerusalem, the death of a king, are judged significant according to their direct bearing on the life of the sect, while insignificant events, the rebuke of an Essene leader, the disturbance of a festal celebration, become turning points in world history. In the commentaries the inner history of the sect is bewilderingly mixed with external political events.[9] In the second place, apocalyptic exegesis involves a certain form of typology.[10] A prophet like Moses, a messiah like David,

9. Some attempt has been made on the part of scholars to distinguish between purely historical commentary and purely eschatological, or between commentaries dealing primarily with external history and those dealing primarily with internal history. Such distinctions involve categories foreign to the apocalyptic mind, and can be applied to Essene materials only by forcing and distortion.

10. See Chap. II, n. 46.

a priest like Aaron or Zadok, are expected. There is to be a
new desert sojourn, a new Exodus, a new covenant, a new
gift of "the height of Israel," a new Holy War. Figures bearing titles from prophecy, the Righteous Teacher, the False
Oracle, the Wrathful Lion, and a dozen others appear "in the
last times." Apocalyptic typology often takes an ancient figure
and projects it into the eschatological future. Such typology,
however, never breaks down into allegory, nor even into a
series of types. For example, the "Messiah of Israel" in apocalyptic exegesis can never apply to a series of future Davidic
kings. The "prophet like Moses" does not mean the "continuing prophetic office." The "New Age" never grows old to be
supplanted by a new "New Age." In similar fashion, the
"Righteous Teacher," the "False Oracle," the "Lion of Wrath,"
are not titles designating "offices" to be filled by a series of
appropriate figures. Thus while some of these figures (places,
etc.) may have ancient prototypes, in their eschatological role
they are to appear in the final age . . . finally.[11]

From these rather extended comments on the nature of the
material in our texts, we are led to draw certain methodological conclusions. Theoretically the allusions in biblical commentaries can be utilized in reconstructing the history of the
sect. On the other hand, the elusive character of the data
suggests that we can achieve sound historical results only by
utilizing outside controls to limit the framework within which
our sources operate. Concretely this means that we must approach the problems relating to the historical interpretation
of our texts by first determining the time period set by archaeological data, by paleographical evidence, and by other more

11. For these reasons we cannot accept the proposals of Reicke,
("Die Ta'āmire-Schriften und die Damaskus-Fragmente" ST 2 [1948],
pp. 45–70) and most recently Gaster (*The Dead Sea Scriptures,* pp.
25–28) to apply a systematic typological exegesis. We must attempt to
delineate and adopt the apocalyptic categories of Essene exegesis,
avoiding the pitfalls of various types of "Hellenizing," whether they be
"historicizing," the employing of systematic typology (actually a form
of allegorizing), or the utilizing of late rabbinic forms of exegesis.

objective methods before applying the more subjective techniques of internal criticism.

Paleography, the science of dating documents by typological analysis of their scripts, is perhaps the most precise and objective means of determining the age of a manuscript. As early as 1937 the main lines of the development of Aramaic and Jewish scripts from the fifth century B.C. to the time of the First Revolt were fixed by W. F. Albright's epoch-making study of the Nash Papyrus.[12] In the interval between his programmatic paper and the discovery of the first scrolls of Qumrân the steady increase of epigraphic materials in Aramaic and Hebrew further confirmed his results, so that Jewish paleography had become an established science at the time of the discovery of the scrolls. Immediately upon the publication of the scrolls the specialists in epigraphy and paleography, notably Albright himself, Solomon Birnbaum, Sukenik, and John Trever, fixed the dates of the several scrolls within fairly narrow limits.[13] These dates have since been confirmed by each new development in the field.

The discovery in 1952 of some four hundred fragmentary manuscripts in Cave IV, all dating before A.D. 70, as well as the discovery of documents of the first and second centuries A.D. in the region of Wâdî Murabba'ât, some with date formulae, have made possible rapid new advances in our knowledge of early Jewish paleography and in the precision with which the scrolls can be dated. A typological sequence of scripts including several hundred specimens of Jewish script, a number of them precisely dated on non-paleographic grounds as well as some hundreds of scripts from epigraphic sources, has now been established, extending in time from the

12. "A Biblical Fragment from the Maccabaean Age: the Nash Papyrus," *JBL* 56 (1937), pp. 145–76.

13. For bibliography, see S. A. Birnbaum, *The Qumrân (Dead Sea) Scrolls and Palaeography* [*Supplementary Studies of the ASOR 13–14*] (New Haven, 1952); and F. M. Cross, "The Oldest Manuscripts from Qumrân," *JBL* 74 (1955), pp. 147–72.

late third century B.C. to the late second century of the Christian era.

In 1955 the writer published a first study growing out of his early efforts to systematize the new wealth of data for paleographical analysis.[14] Three major periods within the evolution of the script were defined and dated: (1) Archaic, ca. 200–150 B.C., (2) Hasmonaean, ca. 150–30 B.C. and (3) Herodian, ca. 30 B.C. to A.D. 70. Relative dating within these periods offers no problem, thanks to the extremely swift evolution of the script.[15] Absolute dates are more difficult to fix, especially in the Archaic period. However, manuscripts can be firmly dated in the Hasmonaean and Herodian periods within half centuries, and in the case of certain types of scripts we are able to date to the generation with some degree of probability.[16] Jewish paleography in this period is fast approaching the degree of precision achieved by Greek paleographers in a later era.

The dating of the sectarian manuscripts from Qumrân gives extremely important data for fixing the general framework within which we must look for the setting of Essene origins.

14. "The Oldest Manuscripts from Qumrân," especially pp. 163 ff.

15. The speed of the evolution can be estimated by the fact that in a period of less than *two centuries*, from the early Archaic to the early Herodian period, the evolutionary shifts in the *formal* script are more radical than in the whole of the evolution of the next *millennium*. This means that we can date Qumrân texts within one century with the same typological precision—to make a rough proportion—with which we can date medieval MSS within half a millennium. Morever, the essentially archaizing book hands of the Middle Ages raise special problems for the paleographer which have parallels at Qumrân only in the case of the so-called Paleo-Hebrew script.

16. The dating of a script to a single generation, in the case of individual manuscripts, cannot be converted automatically into an absolute dating. Despite the speed of evolution in this period, allowance must be made for the *floruit* of a conservative scribe extending beyond his generation. However, in the case of a group of scripts belonging typologically to a certain generation, we can assume methodologically that the majority of the group were copied within the normal span of the generation.

While biblical manuscripts range in date from the late third century B.C. to the middle of the first century A.D., all extant copies of sectarian works fall in the Hasmonaean and Herodian periods. The earliest manuscripts of the *Rule of the Community* include two copies which are best dated in the first quarter of the first century B.C., and one papyrus copy in a proto-cursive script which, while more difficult to date, is earlier still.[17] Obviously none of these was copied before the founding of the community. And it is unlikely that even the oldest of them is the autograph copy.[18] Similarly, other sectarian manuscripts, including the Damascus Document,[19] appear first in copies which can be no later than the first half of the first century B.C.[20]

Certain conclusions must be drawn. The absence of sectarian manuscripts of the Archaic period suggests that the composition of the early sectarian works probably did not commence until the second half of the second century, B.C. To be sure, this is an argument from silence, but it is indicative.

The relative paucity of biblical manuscripts from the Archaic period points in the same direction. The first main

17. One of these is the well known 1QS; the other two are unpublished. The early Hasmonaean papyrus copy is tentatively designated 4QS[e].

18. In the case of 1QS, we can demonstrate its distance from the autograph. (1) Its text exhibits characteristic copyist's errors, as can be shown most easily by comparison with other texts; and (2) in col. V it presents an expanded text (cf. Milik, "Le travail d'édition . . ." p. 61.). Similarly, in another MS (4Q Testimonia) copied by the same scribe there is a quotation of an older sectarian work (4Q Psalms of Joshua, cf. Strugnell, *ibid.*, p. 65; Allegro, *JBL* 75 [1956], p. 186 f.).

19. In *CD* 16:3–4, an older Essene work, perhaps Jubilees, is referred to.

20. Certain works appear mostly in Herodian scripts (the commentaries), and some only in Herodian scripts (1QM). The latter fact tends to support the contention of Y. Yadin (see his thorough study, *mgylt mlḥmt bny 'wr bbny ḥwšk mmgylwt mdbr yhwdh*) and others who maintain that 1QM reflects a knowledge of Imperial Roman military practice.

period of the sect's life can hardly be pushed earlier than about 150 B.C.

The paleographical dates for the earliest extant copies of the *Rule* are much more instructive. They fix an ironclad *terminus ante quem* for the composition of early Essene works, and hence for the foundation of the sect. We cannot go later than the reign of Alexander Jannaeus for extant copies of this work, and the time of composition must almost certainly be pressed back before 100 B.C. to permit the textual development and parenetic expansions which characterize our earliest copies. Further we should postulate a certain interval between the decisive events which created the sect and sent it and the Righteous Teacher into exile in the desert, and the composition of the systematic discipline of the community. The Essene *Rule* is not a programmatic work written before the founding of the sect; it reflects the discipline of the first community in the wilderness of Qumrân at a time when its practices had been systematically worked out.[21] Similarly the Damascus Document was composed sometime after the death of the Righteous Teacher (which is referred to twice), yet before the Roman conquest of 63 B.C. as is shown both by paleographical evidence and internal evidence. In short, paleographical analysis of the texts now sets limits within which we must look for the events which gave rise to the sectarian movement: the upper limit, while not certain, is suitably drawn about 150 B.C.; the lower limit, which I should regard as definitively fixed, falls not far from 100 B.C.; in other terms from the priesthood of Jonathan (160–142 B.C.) to the reign of Alexander Jannaeus (103–76 B.C.).

We can also attempt to limit the historical range within which Essene origins fall by analysis of the archaeological

---

21. Certainly the Righteous Teacher is not responsible for the *Rule* in its extant form; he may be the author of an earlier work from which the two textual forms found at Qumrân were expanded.

22. See above, Chap. II, n. 46.

evidence for the foundation of the community center of Khirbet Qumrân. In the second chapter[23] we argued that on the basis of the coin series and related data we must fix the date of the earliest installations no earlier than the reign of Simon (142–134 B.C.), no later, probably, than the reign of John Hyrcanus I (134–104 B.C.).

It can be argued that the foundation of the community need not be coeval with work of the founder of the sect, or with the crucial events which led to its separation from the body of Judaism. However, such an argument can stand only with the greatest difficulty. All evidence points to the assumption that the Teacher led his flock into the desert, and certainly our earliest sectarian documents presume the existence of the settlement in the wilderness.

Methodologically, we should begin our study of the commentaries by seeking out the most explicit historical allusions, first of all, and relating them, if we can, to the history of the sect.

In a commentary on Nahum (4QpNah.) recently published,[24] there is an exposition of Nahum 2:12–13 in which names are named without the usual veil of a biblical sobriquet and events are brought together in such fashion that we can, I think, place them in a known historical context. The key readings are as follows: (l.2) "[This is to be interpreted as referring to Deme]trius, the Greek king who attempted to enter Jerusalem at the advice of 'Those who Seek Flattery'[25] . . ."; (l.3) ". . . the Greek kings from Antiochus until the

23. Chap. II, (pp. 42 ff.).

24. The document was published by J. M. Allegro in his article, "Further Light on the History of the Qumrân Sect," pp. 89–95.

25. The phrase *dwršy hḥlqwt* "seekers of flattery" is a designation taken from the "prediction" of Dan. 11:32 where it is said that "those who act wickedly against the covenant, he (Antiochus Epiphanes) will pervert with *flattery*." Presumably the term applies in the Qumrân texts to Jews with Hellenistic leanings, no doubt a broad category from the sectarian point of view.

accession[26] of the rulers of the Kittīyîm"; and (l.6–7) ". . . This is to be interpreted as referring to the 'Wrathful Lion' . . .[27] [ ]who hangs men alive . . ."

The exposition deals with a very small unit of Scripture, and in all probability deals with a single series of events. On this assumption we must look for a setting in the framework set by the text itself, in the era of the Greek kings between Antiochus and the establishment of Kittaean rulers in the East. The Antiochus in question is probably Antiochus IV, Epiphanes (175–163 B.C.), though a later important Seleucid such as Antiochus VII, Sidetes (138–129 B.C.), is not excluded. The Kittaean rulers seem clearly enough to be the Roman rulers who arrive on the scene beginning with Pompey, who conquered Jerusalem in 63 B.C. [28] In this framework

26. '*md* regularly has the technical sense, "to take office." Cf. the usage of *m'md*, "station, office."

27. The designation "Wrathful Lion" is most suitably applied to the Judaean opponent of Demetrius, and it seems clear enough, despite breaks in the text of ll. 5–8, that he is responsible for the crucifixions mentioned. Admittedly, however, this construction depends finally on one's interpretation of the whole.

28. Aemilius Scaurus, governor of the Syrian province in 62 B.C. which included Judaea, is mentioned by name ('*mylyws*) in an unpublished calendar from Cave IV, along with Sĕlāmṣïyôn (Alexandria 76–67 B.C.) and other known historical figures. J. T. Milik, who will publish the document, was kind enough to show the text to the writer in the summer of 1956.

The identification of the Kittīyîm (pronounced in this period *Kittï'im*) with the Romans, both in 4QpNah. and 1QpHab., and normally at least in IQM, appears to me to be established. The documents all date to the Roman period. And we have argued that they were *composed* in the Roman period on grounds quite independent of the Kittīyîm problem. In my opinion, the reading in 1QpHab. 9:4–5 ("This is to be interpreted as referring to the last priests of Jerusalem who gathered wealth and riches from the spoil of the peoples whose wealth and booty is to be given into the hand of the Kittaean army") must refer to Pompey's conquest. Cf. 1QpMic. 11–12:1; 4QpNah., 11. Any remaining doubts are dispelled by the Nahum *pēšer*.

Professor Rowley argues with erudition, however, against the identification (see most recently, "The Kittim and the Dead Sea Scrolls," pp. 92–109). Behind his argument is a strong inclination to

we must look for (1) an attempt by a Greek king named Demetrius to enter Jerusalem, preferably in an attack on a Judaean prince who (2) crucified men alive.

Of the Greek kings named Demetrius, Demetrius III (Eukairos), is the most suitable candidate.[29] His adversary was Alexander Jannaeus, the priest-king of Judaea from 103–76 B.C. Josephus records that an open civil war broke out in Jannaeus' reign, continuing for six years (93–88 B.C.) during which a reported fifty thousand Jews were killed. In 88 B.C. the desperate enemies of Jannaeus called upon Demetrius Eukairos for succor. Demetrius met Jannaeus at Shechem and decisively defeated him. However, Demetrius was not permitted to follow up his victory. The Jews who had asked his help and fought with him suddenly went over to the side of their archfoe, Jannaeus. This strange behavior can be

assume that identification of the Kittīyîm with the Romans disqualifies the view that Essene origins are pre-Roman. This is not the case, I think, any more than the mention of an Antiochus disqualifies a post-Maccabean date for the beginnings of the sect. The Righteous Teacher and the Wicked Priest are never directly associated with Antiochus, the Kittīyîm, or with the Wrathful Lion for that matter. Juxtaposition of the mention of events of sectarian beginnings and the mention of the Romans in 1QpHabakkuk in exposition of different sections of Habakkuk does not prejudice the question of the precise date of the Teacher's ministry; it only illustrates the fact discussed above that the commentaries contain traditions of exegesis developed over a considerable period of time, written down late.

29. Professor Rowley ("4QpNahum and the Teacher of Righteousness," pp. 188–93) has argued that Demetrius I (Soter) may be referred to in this context. Against his position it must be argued that Demetrius I is not described appropriately as having "attempted to enter into Jerusalem." It is true that two of his generals, Bacchides and the infamous Nicanor, were sent to Jerusalem (the king himself did not come), but both entered Jerusalem freely. Indeed both Bacchides and Nicanor used Jerusalem as headquarters for their actions against Judas in the hinterlands. When Nicanor was killed remnants of his army fled to Jerusalem for refuge; and Bacchides fortified the city against Jonathan (I Macc. 9:52 f.). It seems rather unlikely that one would speak of "an attempt to enter Jerusalem" unless the attempt was against opposition and was not carried out. And if it were a famous *general* who *entered* Jerusalem, why speak of the *king trying* to enter?

explained, I think, by assuming that Demetrius proposed (perhaps on the advice of Hellenists) to attack the capital and subjugate Judaea once more to the Seleucid crown. Only under such circumstances would there be sufficient incentive to induce Jewish rebels—and even in this case only the more orthodox—to desert to Jannaeus.[30] When Demetrius was forced to retire in the face of Jannaeus' new strength, the latter was successful in stamping out the rebels. In the process we are told that he crucified captives in wholesale lots.[31]

This construction, while theoretical in part, admirably fits our requirements. What does it tell us of the history of the Essenes? The Wrathful Lion and the events of his time discovered in the prophecy of Nahum by the sectarians certainly belong to "their history," i.e., to the "end of days." This is the pattern of exegesis in the commentaries. However, we have no way of knowing whether the terrible events in the reign of one of the illegitimate priests of Jerusalem (to speak from an Essene point of view) belong early or late in the history of the sect. There is no mention of the Righteous Teacher in connection with the events, and no reason to connect the Wrathful Lion with the figures of the era of Essene origins such as the wicked priest *par excellence* whose biblical sobriquet seems to be the False Oracle (*mattip hak-kāzāb*) or more simply the False One (*'iš hak-kāzāb*).[32] Just as we cannot date the foundation of the sect in the Roman era because of references to Pompey's conquest of Jerusalem in the Habakkuk Commentary or the mention of Aemilius Scaurus in the calendar from Cave IV, so we are not obliged to date the beginning of the movement in the time of Jannaeus. On the other hand we are quite near the minimal date fixed on archaeolog-

---

30. J. M. Allegro adopts this proposal for the specific occasion on which Demetrius "sought to enter Jerusalem" in his publication of 4QpNah., *op. cit.*, p. 92; cf. C. Rabin, "Alexander Jannaeus and the Pharisees," *JJS* 7 (1956), pp. 3–11.

31. Josephus, *Antiq.* XIII, 372–83; *War* I, 90–98.

31a. Cf. H. H. Rowley, "The Kittim and the Dead Sea Scrolls," p. 94.

32. See below, n. 88 and n. 89.

ical and paleographical grounds, and cannot absolutely exclude a date for the rise of the sect in the early reign of Jannaeus.[32a]

Our task is much simplified. We have learned something of the problems which are raised in the study of the expository writings of Qumrân and we have limited the scope of our search for the beginnings of the Qumrân sect to the second half of the second century B.C.

2. *The Righteous Teacher and the Wicked Priest*

The key to any sound reconstruction of the historical circumstances which gave rise to the Essene movement lies in an adequate explanation of the peculiarly priestly character of the early schismatic community.

In the extended introductory exposition of the Damascus Document are several crucial passages dealing with the origin of the sect. In one of these (*CD* 3:18–4:4)[33] the sectarian author discovers in I Samuel 2:35 and Ezekiel 44:15 prophecies of the origin of his sect. The passage reads as follows:

> And God in his wondrous secret counsels made atonement for their transgression and forgave their iniquity, and he built for them a "faithful (priestly) house"[34] the like of which has never arisen, formerly or lately. Those who hold fast to (this house) shall live forever, and all human glory is theirs, even as God promised them through Ezekiel the prophet, saying, "the priests and the Levites and[*sic!*] the sons of Zadok who kept the office of my Sanctuary when

32a. Josephus' testimony to the prophecy of Judas the Essene (*Antiq.* XIII, 311–13; *War* I, 78–80) in the reign of Aristobulus I (104–103 B.C.) argues strongly for a pre-Jannaeus date for Essene origins. Cf. Milik, *Découvertes*, p. 60.

33. See above, Chap. II, n. 122.

34. Cf. 1QS 8:9, where a parallel expression recalling I Sam. 2:35 is used of the sect.

the children of Israel went astray from me, they shall bring
me fat and blood." The "priests" are the repentant of Israel
who went out from the land of Judah . . . and the "sons of
Zadok" are the chosen of Israel, the "Elect of the Name"[35]
who shall arise in the end of days.[35a]

That the founder of the sect, the Righteous Teacher, was
himself a priest has long been taken for granted on the basis
of indirect evidence. His priestly origins are now certified in
a newly published text.[36] The "opposite number" of the Righteous Priest was the Wicked Priest, the archpersecutor of the
sect. The priests of Qumrân regarded the Jerusalem sanctuary as defiled, its priests false, its calendar unorthodox. In the
end of days the Essene priesthood would be re-established
in the New Jerusalem, the false priesthood overthrown for
ever. Meanwhile, the Essene community is organized as an
ideal priestly theocracy. Priests dominate its councils, take
precedence in its protocols; a priestly Messiah overshadows
the royal Messiah in visions of the New Age. The whole life
of the community is shaped in the interest of Priestly objec-
tives. In short the Essenes are a counter-Israel organized by a
counter-priesthood, " true" Israel led by the "legitimate"
priesthood.[37]

All this suggests that the origin of the Essene movement
must be sought for in the struggle of rival priestly houses, the
one hyperorthodox and presumably legitimate, the other less
orthodox but successful in gaining control of the high priesthood and Jerusalem cultus.[38] The founders of the sect would

35. A favorite biblical sobriquet of the sect taken from Num. 16:2;
cf. 1QSa II, 2, 11, 13. Probably the expression "the Name" is not to be
understood in its original sense in Num. 16:2, but as reference to the
divine name (cf. 1QS 6:27).

35a. Cf. 1QS 5:2, 9; 1QSa I, 2, 24; II, 3; 1QSb III, 22–23, etc.

36. See Chap. II, n. 114.

37. If the conclusions drawn at the close of Chap. II are correct, we
may add that the Essenes also instituted a counter sacrificial cultus.

38. This view, by no means new, is worked out most persuasively

thus be found among priests whose authority was lost, whose orthodox convictions were flouted, whose hopes for establishing a faithful theocracy in Israel had turned to despair, but who turned for comfort and new hope in an apocalyptic priestly community.

Within the chronological framework we have established, there is little difficulty in discovering the occasion for the birth of a dissident priestly sect. The history of the Maccabees is the story of the decay of the ancient line of Zadokite high priests, and the rise of a vigorous new house of reigning priests.

The last of the great high priests of the old Zadokite line was a priest of the Oniad family, Simon II, who died about 200 B.C.[39] Ben Sira sings the praises of Simon in Chapter 50 of Ecclesiasticus, ending with the pious hope that the "covenant of Phinehas", i.e., the high-priestly office,[40] will never pass from him or his descendants.[41] Ironically enough his line failed in his sons Onias III and Jason. The Oniad house was divided over the confused politico-religious issues of the day. Onias III, who had succeeded his father Simon, was pro-Egyptian by political persuasion and is pictured as defender of the ancient faith. In any case he opposed the strong policy of Hellenization imposed by Antiochus Epiphanes (175–163 B.C.). His brother Jason, whether out of personal ambition or because of genuine pro-Syrian sympathies we cannot be cer-

by Vermès and Milik. See most recently, G. Vermès, *Les manuscrits du Désert de Juda*, pp. 78–89; and J. T. Milik, *Découvertes*, Chap. III.

39. On the question of the identification of Simon with Simon the Just, see the discussion and literature cited by R. Marcus, *Josephus* (ed. Loeb) VII (Cambridge, 1943), Appendix B.

40. Cf. Num. 25:12–13; Eccles. 45:24; and 1 Macc. 2:54.

41. Presumably the Essenes approved of Ben Sira, since a copy of a Hebrew version appeared in Cave II, Qumrân. On the present passage, preserved in the quoted form only in the Hebrew text, and the significant passage in the hymn inserted in the Hebrew version at 51:12 ("Give thanks to Him who elects the sons of Zadok to be priests" [51:12:ix]), see J. Trinquet, "Les liens 'sadocites' de l'Ecrit de Damas, des manuscrits de la Mer Morte, et de l'Ecclésiastique," *VT* 1 (1951), pp. 287–92.

tain, allied himself with the Syrian party and was willing, even eager, to expedite the process of Hellenizing Jewry. In Jason's struggle for power he finally approached Antiochus, offering him a sum of money to recognize him as high priest in his brother's stead. Jason's move, however, set an ominous precedent. In the past the Greek kings had not interfered, normally, with the regular succession of the high priests. The Tobiad clan, long rivals of the high-priestly family for political sway in Judaea, had never dared to challenge directly the right of the Oniads to the supreme office in the land. But when the power to appoint high priests passed into the hands of Antiochus at the instigation of an Oniad, the Tobiads were quick to see an opportunity to break the power of the Oniad family. Their protégé was a certain Menelaus, the son of a Temple official, but not of Zadokite family.[42] Within four years of Jason's accession to office Menelaus succeeded in capturing Antiochus' appointment to the high priesthood. The strife between the rival houses led by Jason and Menelaus shortly became open civil war, and in the resulting chaos Antiochus found opportunity to carry out his fearful massacres, terminating in the desecration of the Temple in 167 B.C., and the complete Hellenization of the city. The stage was now set for the rise of the Maccabees, whose destiny it was to win independence for the Jews, and with it to establish a new high-priestly house.

In the early days of the Maccabean revolt, shortly before Mattathias' death in 166 B.C., we hear for the first time of a certain "congregation of the Ḥasîdîm (Assideans) . . . all of whom devote themselves to the Law" (I Macc. 2:42).[43]

42. On the ancestry of Menelaus, see 2 Macc. 4:23 (cf. 3:4); Josephus, *Antiq.* XII, 238; and the discussion of H. H. Rowley, *The Zadokite Fragments and the Dead Sea Scrolls*, p. 67, n. 7.

43. The latter phrase strikes a familiar chord; the Qumrân texts speak of "those who devote themselves" to the covenant, truth, community, or holiness. Cf. 1QS 5:1, 6, 8, 10, 21, 22; 6:13; 1Q14, X:7; and W. H. Brownlee, *The Dead Sea Manual of Discipline*, p. 7, n. 5, who already makes the combination with 1 Macc. 2:42.

Nothing is said explicitly in our sources of their origins or destiny. Presumably they included priestly and lay elements of strict faith who found themselves leaderless with the decay of the Zadokite priesthood in the reign of Antiochus. In the warfare between Jason and Menelaus they had no recourse but to stand aloof, since with the victory of either their cause was lost.

The Maccabean uprising gained their support, at least in its early stages. But they never rallied wholeheartedly to the Maccabean cause, it seems, and with the appointment of Alcimus, the successor of Menelaus, were quick to seek a reconciliation with the new high priest.[44] This circumstance is puzzling. Alcimus was the pro-Syrian appointee of the Seleucid throne.[45] We are told, on the one hand, that while the Maccabees actively opposed Alcimus, the Ḥasîdîm trusted him and sought to come to terms with him because he was "of the seed of Aaron." On the other hand, Josephus says flatly that he was not of the house of Onias III.[47] An explanation may be found for this set of circumstances if Alcimus were descended from a collateral branch of the Zadokite line,[48] and hence in some sense a legitimate high priest. At all events, Alcimus betrayed their trust, and they returned to the Maccabean camp.[49]

Probably in the congregation of the Ḥasîdîm, devoted to the ancient Law and no doubt to the Zadokite priesthood, un-

44. Cf. 1 Macc. 7:15 (vs. 2 Macc. 14:6).

45. Josephus, *Antiq.* XII, 387; 1 Macc. 7:5–9; 2 Macc. 14:3, 13; cf. *Antiq.* XX, 235. Alcimus was appointed about 162 B.C., probably by Antiochus Eupator, confirmed by Demetrius I (Soter). In any case, the conflicts in our sources are not serious ones.

46. 1 Macc. 7:14–16; Josephus, *Antiq.* XX, 235.

47. *Antiq.* XII, 387.

48. On Lysias' advice, Antiochus Eupator had Menelaus put to death. Yet the rightful successor, Onias IV, was by-passed. Presumably Lysias sought to conciliate the Jews and re-establish peace by siding neither with the Oniad nor Tobiad houses. *Antiq.* XII, 382–88.

49. 1 Macc. 7:13–17.

easy allies of the Maccabean warrior priests, we find ancestors of the Essene sectaries who appeared in the desert of Qumrân in the next generation.

Support for this view may be found in an introductory section of the Damascus Document:

> In the epoch of wrath, three hundred and ninety years[50] after he gave them into the power of Nebuchadnezzar, king of Babylon, he visited them and caused a root of planting[51] to sprout from Israel and from Aaron to possess His land[52] and to grow rich with the good things of His land. And they came to understand their iniquity and to know that they were guilty men; but they were like blind men or like those who grope for the way twenty years. And God recognized their works, that they sought Him with a whole heart and so raised up for them a Righteous Teacher to make them tread in the way of His heart and to instruct the last generations that which He would do in the last generation against the congregation of the false. (CD 1:5–12)

The scriptural number "390" (Ezek. 4:5) cannot be used for precise calculation.[53] It was a round number of prophecy put to Essene use. Perhaps the era to be spanned is from the Exile to the days of Antiochus Epiphanes.[54] The key figure, however, is the twenty years in which the priests and laity wandered like blind men before the commencement of the

50. On the construction of the phrase, see E. Wiesenberg's "Chronological Data in the Zadokite Fragments," VT 5 (1955), pp. 284–308. While his conclusions appear to me unacceptable, he has collected valuable data bearing on the problem.

51. A favorite appellation from prophecy (Is. 60:21; 61:3) applied by the sect to themselves. Cf. 1QS 8:5–8; I Cor. 3:9.

52. The expression (from Is. 60:21) is understood eschatologically as in 4QpPs. 37 (see Chap. II, n. 53).

53. Cf. the discussion and literature cited by Rowley, The Zadokite Fragments and the Dead Sea Scrolls, pp. 62–64.

54. Cf. 4QpNah., l. 3.

The cliffs of the wilderness of the Dead Sea viewed from the bed of the Wâdi Qumrân. In the background looms the great limestone cliff in which the first cave was found; below is the marl terrace which supports Khirbet Qumrân, the ruin of the Essene community center; the ruins form a silhouetted line in the center of the picture at the top of the cliff; to the left, high in the terrace may be seen an opening leading to Cave IV, the most productive of the Qumrân caves.

Advanced work in the eastern quarter of Khirbet Qumrân

The great common room of the Essene establishment
at Khirbet Qumrân. Photograph, J. Starcky.

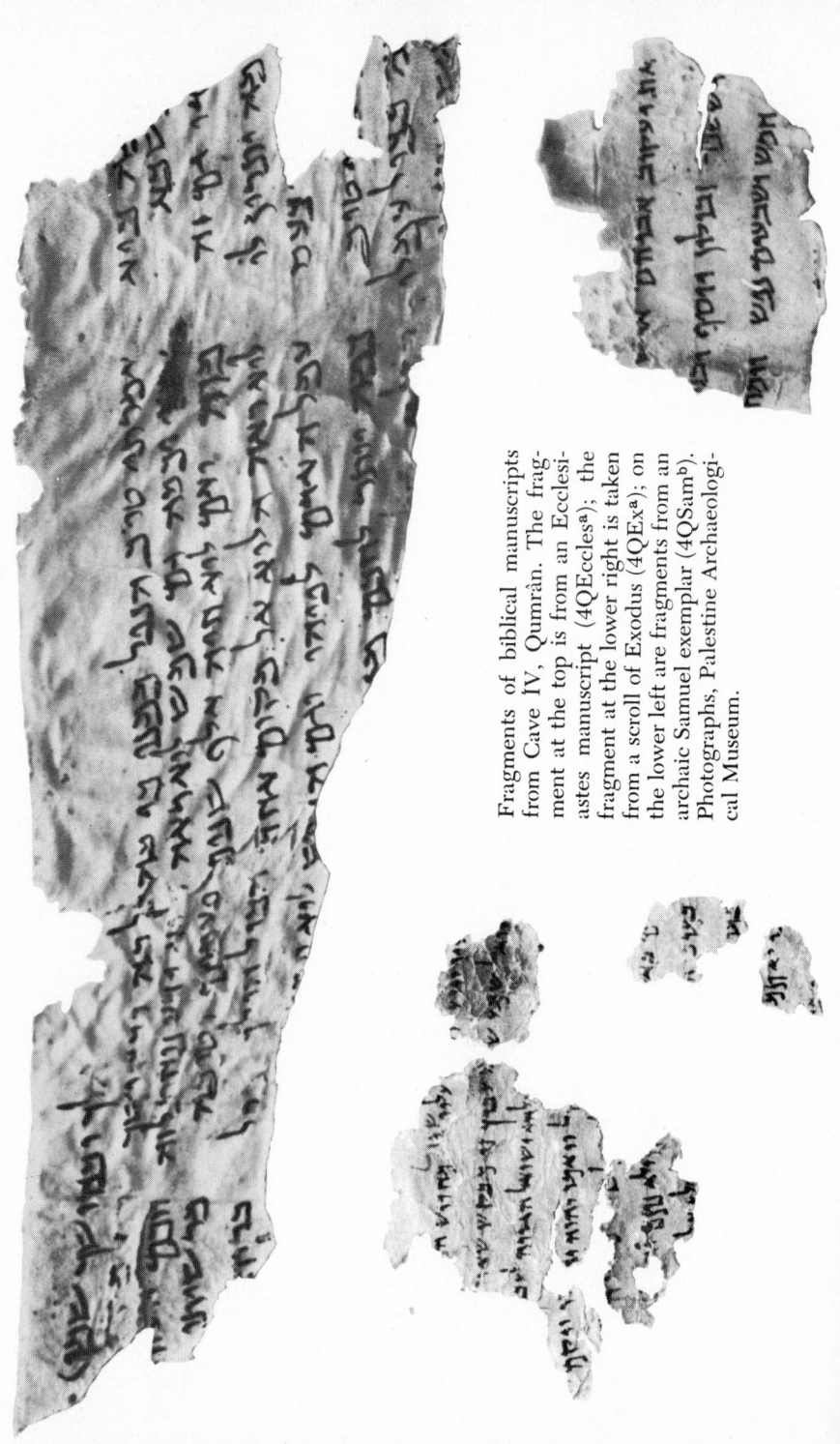

Fragments of biblical manuscripts from Cave IV, Qumrân. The fragment at the top is from an Ecclesiastes manuscript (4QEccles^a); the fragment at the lower right is taken from a scroll of Exodus (4QEx^a); on the lower left are fragments from an archaic Samuel exemplar (4QSam^b). Photographs, Palestine Archaeological Museum.

Righteous Teacher's ministry. The period of groping, that is, when the forerunners were "right-minded" but wrong in their discernment of their proper duty, best corresponds to the period in which the Ḥasîdîm were in active support of the Maccabees, roughly from the 160s to the 140s B.C.[55]

If these various assumptions are true, then the Righteous Teacher began his ministry late in the reign of Jonathan (160 –142 B.C.) or early in the reign of Simon (142–134 B.C.), and was a Zadokite priest of Hasidic sympathies. In any case, this construction of events points us precisely toward the period required by the external criteria of archaeolgical and paleographical analysis: the second half of the second century B.C.

The period of troubles for the Zadokite priesthood rose to a crisis after the death of Alcimus (159 B.C.).[56] No official high priest was appointed, apparently, for a period of some seven years.[56a] In this interval Jonathan together with his brother Simon gained control of the land outside Jerusalem, alternating between times of consolidation and periods in the field against the armies of Demetrius I; apparently a kind of rump government was established at Michmash with Jonathan at its head, while the Hellenistic party ruled in Jerusalem. In 152 B.C. Jonathan's fortunes shifted abruptly. Alexander Balas, the alleged son of Antiochus IV, appeared in Syria claiming Demetrius' throne. In the ensuing struggle Demetrius and Alexander began to bid for the support of Jonathan and his army, with the result that Jonathan first was enabled to seize Jerusalem and refortify the city and Temple (on the bid of Demetrius), and then by deftly shifting to the support of Alexander, to win appointment as high priest of the Jews.

55. Compare J. T. Milik's treatment, *Découvertes*, Appendice.

56. Cf. *Antiq.* XII, 413; 1 Macc. 9:54–57.

56a. Josephus, *Antiq.* XII, 414, 419, 434, states that Judas was made high priest by the people, and was high priest three years. In *Antiq.* XX, 237, however, there is a statement to the effect that there was a priestly interregnum of seven years. Finally 1 Macc. seems to place the death of Alcimus after that of Judas.

At the Feast of Tabernacles in 152 he formally was invested with the robes of his office.

This was the initial step in the usurpation of the high priesthood by the new Hasmonaean house. No doubt Jonathan's readiness to accept the Syrian king's appointment to the high priesthood confirmed the fears and crystallized the opposition of the Zadokite elements of the Ḥasîdîm, as well as some strict lay members belonging to this wing of Judaism. However, Jonathan's appointment to office followed the pattern initiated by Jason and Menelaus. He was charismatic leader of his people in the war for independence not yet won—a Syrian garrison still resided in Jerusalem—but *de facto* high priest, not by will of his people but by appointment of their suzerain.[56b] It was not yet wholly clear, from the point of view of the Zadokite priesthood, that a new high-priestly dynasty was being established once for all . . . though the handwriting on the wall can be read by the historian. The final and decisive step was to be taken by Simon, Jonathan's successor.

Meanwhile, Alexander and Demetrius passed from the Syrian scene, and two new rivals, Demetrius II and Tryphon, the latter as the ostensible protector of Alexander Balas' young son, Antiochus VI (145–142 B.C.), fought for supremacy over the Seleucid empire. Jonathan again advanced the interests of Jewish independence by playing one off against the other. However, Tryphon turned on Jonathan finally and by treachery captured him at Ptolemais. When word came from Ptolemais of his brother's captivity Simon at once took leadership and hastened to complete the walls of Jerusalem, fortifying the city in anticipation of Tryphon's attack.[57] After an attempt at negotiation of the release of Jonathan in which Tryphon proved false, Simon opposed the Syrian with the Jewish army. Tryphon chose prudently not to attack frontally

---

56b. Jonathan did not dare claim for his family the full right to the high-priestly office though he functioned as high priest. This suggests that Zadokite opposition to the Hasmonaeans had not yet been broken.

57. 1 Macc. 13:1–11.

but, circling, took his forces home to Syria through Trans-Jordan, murdering Jonathan en route (142 B.C.).

The lot had fallen upon Simon to bring to a completion the work of his warrior brothers. Simon is glorified as the "man of counsel" of the five Maccabean brothers in I Maccabees; and while Judas is appointed in the blessing of his father to be the captain in fighting the battle of the people, Simon is named "father" of the brethren, and indeed is mentioned first.[58] This reflects, of course, the major role of Simon in the eyes of this historian. Simon, the last of the brothers, was finally to achieve for the first time full independence for his people; he was to be established as the founder of a new high-priestly line.

Simon immediately upon Tryphon's withdrawal set to work fortifying his entire realm.[59] He offered recognition and support to Demetrius II, the rival of Tryphon, in exchange for full freedom from taxation, full recognition of Jewish control of all fortified sites in Judaea, forgiveness for all unpaid tribute and taxes, amnesty for all past disloyal acts against the Seleucid crown.[60] Demetrius, in his desperate need for support, had no alternative but to award all the privileges demanded by the Jews. Apparently Simon was recognized at this time by Demetrius as high priest.[61]

According to I Maccabees, a new era was established in Israel, dating from the first year of Simon (142 B.C.). Actually the full independence of Judaea is better reckoned from the following year when Simon succeeded at last in driving out the Syrian garrison from the citadel of Jerusalem, a quarter century after its establishment by Antiochus IV.[62] He further

58. 1 Macc. 2:65.

59. 1 Macc. 13:33; 14:33–34, 37–38.

60. 1 Macc. 13:34–40.

61. See 1 Macc. 13:36; 14:38.

Josephus (*Antiq.* XIII, 213) telescopes the first three years of Simon in such fashion that he is of no help in indicating the conditions under which Simon took up priestly duties.

62. 1 Macc. 13:49–53; cf. *Mĕgillat Ta'anît*, 5.

fortified the Temple hill alongside the citadel, as well as the citadel itself, and established himself there with his men.[63]

In the third year of Simon's reign, 140 B.C., a great assembly was held of "the priests and people and the heads of the nation and the elders of the country." The decree of the assembly was engraved in bronze and set up on stelae in Mount Zion. The decree, after the introductory formula, eulogizes "Simon, son of Mattathias . . . of the sons of Joarib and his brethren [who] exposed themselves to danger and stood firm against the enemies of their nation so that their sanctuary and their Law might be established and so have greatly glorified their nation."

And Jonathan assembled his people and became a high priest to them and was gathered to his people. And their enemies proposed to invade their country in order to devastate their country and stretch forth their hand against their sanctuary. Then rose Simon and fought for his nation and he spent much of his own wealth, armed the warriors of his people, and gave them pay. And he fortified the cities of Judaea . . .

And the people saw the faithfulness of Simon and the glory which he proposed to bring to his nation and they established him as their leader and highpriest because of all these things he had done, and for the justice and faith which he had shown to his people, and because he had striven in every way to exalt his people. And in his days, through his successful conducting of affairs, the (foreign) nations were removed from their country, as well as those (foreigners) who were in the City of David, i.e., those who were in Jerusalem, who had built a citadel for themselves from which they sallied forth to pollute the area about the sanctuary and greatly sully its purity. And he invested [this citadel] with Jews and fortified it for the security of the country and the city, and elevated the walls of Jerusalem.

63. 1 Macc. 13:53; 14:37.

King Demetrius confirmed the high priesthood to him in accord with these events, and made him one of his "Friends" and gave him great honor . . . (I Macc. 14:30–39.)

The most important part of the decree now follows in which it is officially affirmed that:[64]

The Jews and the priests were pleased that Simon should be their leader ($\dot{\eta}\gamma o\dot{\upsilon}\mu\epsilon\nu o\varsigma$), and high priest forever, until a faithful prophet should arise, and that he should be their general ($\sigma\tau\rho\alpha\tau\eta\gamma\dot{o}\varsigma$), and take charge of the holy things (of the sanctuary) . . . that he be obeyed by all and that all documents in the country be written in his name, and that he be dressed in purple and wear gold.

And none, neither one of the laity nor one of the priests should be allowed to set aside any part of these (decisions) or to countermand orders given by him or to gather an assembly in the country apart from him, or dress in purple and wear a gold ornament. Whoever should act contrary to these (decisions), or set aside any part of these should be liable to punishment.

All the people were pleased to grant Simon the right to act according to these words; and Simon accepted and was pleased to act as high priest and to be the general and governor of the Jews and of the priests and to be the chief of all. (I Macc. 14:41–47.)

Several points in the decree must be examined closely. The decree is more than a mere eulogy of Simon.[65] It officially proclaims that Simon and his sons are established as the progenitors of a perpetual high priesthood "until a faithful prophet arise" (in the last days). Moreover, the decree has

64. On the construction καὶ ὅτι at the beginning of 14:41, see F.–M. Abel, *Les livres des Maccabées* (Paris, 1949), p. 260, n. 41. However the syntactical (or textual) problem is to be solved, it is certain that the body of the (original) decree is to be found in vv. 41–47.

65. Cf. Abel, *loc. cit.* and the literature cited.

teeth; it warns against opposition to Simon, by layman or *priest*, including a prohibition of private assembly, threatening punishment to anyone who acts contrary to any of the stipulations of the decree. This decree reflects not merely a spontaneous welling-up of gratitude and praise for a hero. It is the decree of an assembly of priests and laity controlled by pro-Maccabean elements which officially recognizes the Hasmonaean dynasty and turns the *de facto* rights and privileges enjoyed by Jonathan into rights *de jure* for Simon's *house*.

Thus in the early years of Simon the high priesthood was irrevocably transferred from the Zadokites to the Hasmonaeans. We cannot expect our primary source, I Maccabees, with its overwhelmingly pro-Maccabean bias, to give attention to Zadokite opposition to Simon. No doubt, however, the priestly elements of Zadokite lineage furnished a continuing and steadily mounting opposition from the days of Jonathan's usurpation under the aegis of Alexander Balas until Simon's ultimate election by the priests and the people.

That there was opposition to such a shift from *de facto* to *de jure* status for a non-Zadokite high-priestly house is patent in the threat against those who give a show of disobedience. Probably also we must recognize a tacit acknowledgment that the legitimate priesthood is being set aside in the phrase ". . . high priest forever, until a faithful prophet arise." That is, the house of Simon is, in an ultimate sense, provisional, at least until pronounced legitimate over against the Zadokite house by the "faithful prophet" who will decide such matters in the last days. Simon's house is prepared to rule in the present age and abide by the decision of the eschatological spokesman of God.

With the decree condemning all opposition to Simon, we discern clearly the new high priest's determination to stamp out, indeed to persecute, those who refuse to recognize the full legitimacy of his office. This program, falling in the early years of Simon, seems to give the appropriate occasion for the crystallization of the Essene sect, its persecution and the persecution of its Righteous Teacher, and the exile in the wilderness of Judah. All was now lost from the point of view of pious Zadokite priests. Simon's power and popularity were overwhelming. His exaltation to the high-priestly office was by the election of the priesthood and elders of Israel, and not merely by the appointment of the Syrian suzerain. And Simon had gained hereditary rights to the high priesthood for his seed.[66]

The historical setting of Essene origins seems to be established by the convergence of our several lines of inquiry. The detailed task of seeking out concrete identifications of the main figures and events concealed in the veiled apocalyptic language of the Qumrân texts is more difficult and at best precarious. Nevertheless we propose to attempt tentative reconstructions of the careers of the Wicked Priest and the Righteous Teacher.

Our chief data for reconstructing the career of the Wicked Priest, the adversary of the Righteous Teacher, is found in the commentary on Habakkuk.[67]

Among the important passages for our purposes are the following. In 8:8–13 we read, "This is to be interpreted as referring to the Wicked Priest (quoting Hab. 2:6) who was called by a trustworthy name[67a] when he first took office, but

66. Probably at this time also the Hasidic party broke into two wings: the Pharisees and the Essenes. Presumably the Pharisees represent the "continuing" Hasidic movement, priests and especially a large portion of the laity who find a *modus vivendi* in the new circumstances, not in apocalypticism, but in going along for a season with the Hasmonaeans. On the other hand the Essene movement would be drawn especially from the Zadokite priesthood, together with some lay elements of strong apocalyptic bent led by the Righteous Teacher into separation from the main body of their Jewish brethren.

67. 1QpHab. 1:13; 8:8–13; 8:16–9:2; 9:9–12; 9:16–10:5; 11:12–15; 12:2–6; 12:7–10.

67a. The phrase appears in the Old Testament in contexts where one is called by another's name (cf. Gen. 48:6; Ezra 2:61; cf. 1 Chron. 23:14; Elliger, *SzHK*, p. 198). To be called by a "truthworthy name" may mean no more than that Simon had a good reputation. On the other hand it may be an allusion to the fact that Simon had the same name as

when he ruled over Israel became proud and forsook God and betrayed the statutes (of the Law) for the sake of wealth. He robbed and gathered the wealth of violent men who had rebelled against God, and seized the wealth of peoples, so further burdening himself with guilt. And he engaged in abominable practices, in every manner of impurity." The information provided is less specific than we should like. We learn that the Wicked Priest before or at the beginning of his rise to power had a good name. Either he was known as trustworthy or, perhaps, bore a name, Simon, which had good associations for the sectarians. The text is too vague to be certain. Further, the priest for the sake of wealth and ambition fattened himself with the loot of violence, most of it, no doubt, taken in wars against neighboring peoples. He appears to be rebuked for not "devoting" the spoil to God in accord with the laws of Holy War. Most of this data can be fitted with equal ease to any of the warrior high priests from Jonathan to Alexander Jannaeus. The first phrase, however, if it suggests a change in the status of the priest in the eyes of the sectarians, applies aptly only to Jonathan and Simon. Jonathan began as a military hero, only later accepting the high-priestly office. Simon was a man of counsel, self-effacing during his brothers' turns at leadership. On Jonathan's captivity he provided his substance as well as leadership in saving Jerusalem from Tryphon. Once established in power, however, he arrogated to himself and to his seed the high-priestly office, and affected a royal robe.

Several passages speak of the dreadful end of the Wicked Priest. IQpHabakkuk 9:9–12 is one of the more important of these.[68] "This is to be interpreted as referring to the Wicked

the beloved Simon II (the Just?) celebrated in Ben Sira, the last of the great Zadokite high priests.

68. 1QpHab. 8:16–9:2 also speaks of the horrors of the Wicked Priest's death, almost certainly. For a detailed discussion of some of the problems of the passage, see Elliger, *SzHK*, pp. 202–3. Cf. 9:16–10:5 (?). Regularly the author describes the death in hyperbolic images. The priest is struck down by a divine blow, suffers the pangs of the damned,

Priest whom, because of transgression against the Righteous Teacher and the men of his party, God gave into the hand of his enemies to bring him low with a mortal blow . . ." The passage immediately suggests Jonathan's end at the hand of Tryphon.[69] It may be applied also to the death of Simon at the hands of Ptolemy, son of Abubos (Ḥabūb) and his men.

In order to understand better the application of this passage to the peculiar conditions of Simon's demise, as well as to prepare a basis for additional passages shortly to be discussed, a review of the last days of Simon is desirable.

In 140 B.C., the year in which the decree confirming Simon in his high-priestly office was set up in Mount Zion, Demetrius was absent in Media fighting the Parthians. He was taken captive by the Parthians, and for a few years the Jews were untroubled by the contenders for the Seleucid throne, living in peace. "Simon's peace" is celebrated in the ode of I Maccabees 14:4–15; it was a period in which he consolidated his office and realm; however, the period of peace proved short-lived. In 138 Antiochus VII, Sidetes, brother of Demetrius, was successful in invading Syria, ousting Tryphon, and securing the realm. Almost immediately he took steps to reassert Syrian control of Judaea, demanding that the concessions granted by Demetrius (and by himself before he came to power) be given up. Simon, confident in his new strength, refused, and hostilities between the Seleucid power and the Jewish theocracy commenced anew.

Antiochus sent Kendebaios, one of his generals, to re-establish control of the Palestinian coastal plains preparatory to an attack on Judaea proper. Simon countered by sending his eldest two sons, Judas and John Hyrcanus, to oppose Kendebaios. Judas and John were successful in defeating the

etc. None of these figures can be made to walk on all fours. In effect all point to a violent death at the hand of enemies, and we can say little more.

On 1QpHab. 11:12–15, and 4QpPs. 37, Pl. 3b ll. 3–4, see below.

69. So Milik and Vermès.

Syrian general in the plain between Modin and Azotus. Antiochus was forced to seek other means to subdue the Jews under Simon.

I Maccabees turns abruptly from the defeat of Kendebaios to the tragic death of Simon and his sons. In February, 134 B.C., Simon, together with Judas (probably his eldest son[70]) and his youngest son, Mattathias, toured the cities of Judah, evidently reviewing the forts which he had built or which were under construction.[71] No doubt Simon was preparing against the attack of Antiochus Sidetes who struck later in the same year.[72]

In this connection, Simon and his sons descended to Jericho, administered by Ptolemy, son of Abubos. The latter appears to have been of Idumaean stock, more or less Judaized to judge from the fact that he had married into the high-priestly family. The district of Jericho was heavily Idumaean in population in this period, and normally formed a district separated from Judaea proper.[73] Unknown to Simon, Ptolemy had organized a plot of considerable proportions,[74] no doubt with

70. Cf. 1 Macc. 16:2, 14. In 16:2, Judas is named before John in speaking of the eldest two sons. On the other hand, John has already been appointed governor of Gezer (13:53) and may in fact be the eldest. Josephus, *Antiq.* XIII, 228, speaks of three sons, but in XIII, 247, speaks of another brother, probably in error.

71. 1 Macc. 16:14. ἐφοδεύειν is used here in its technical sense.

72. Josephus, *Antiq.* XIII, 236. Antiochus reduced Judaea in 134 B.C., beseiged Jersalem in 133–32, finally bringing the capitulation of John Hyrcanus and the destruction of the walls of Jerusalem. Cf. *Antiq.* XIII, 236–47; *War* I, 61 cf. 1 Macc. 16:23.

73. On Ptolemy's background, and the character of the Jericho "nome," see Abel, *Maccabées,* p. 280; *Histoire de la Palestine* I (Paris, 1952), p. 205.

74. 1 Macc. is laconic in reporting the character of Ptolemy's plot. We gather from the events that happened immediately following Simon's murder that Ptolemy's attempt to gain hegemony over Judaea was carefully ordered and had considerable support outside of Jerusalem. Men were dispatched to Gezer to kill the remaining heir, John Hyrcanus; others were dispatched to take possession of Jerusalem; letters were sent to the generals of the army of Simon to win their allegiance (1 Macc. 16:19–20).

the complicity of Antiochus VII,[75] to destroy Simon and his heirs, hoping to supplant Simon at Antiochus' appointment.

Ptolemy's opportunity came on the occasion of Simon's visit to the fortress of Doq, built on a high peak guarding Jericho.[76] I Maccabees (16:15) notes that the small fortress was built by Ptolemy. Presumably it was part of Simon's general program of fortifying Jericho carried out by Ptolemy as commanding officer, *strategós*, of Jericho. Ptolemy held a great banquet for Simon and his sons, having secreted certain of his men in the fortress. When Simon and his sons were drunk Ptolemy's men murdered Simon, and later his two sons.[77] Simon's remaining son, John Hyrcanus, was warned in time to protect himself against Ptolemy's assassins. His forces remained loyal so that he was able to overpower Ptolemy's partisans and assume the high priesthood before turning to face the armies of Antiochus Sidetes.

These events could well be described in Essene tradition in the words, "God delivered him into the hand of his enemies to bring him low with a mortal blow."[78]

75. The fact that Ptolemy immediately dispatched word of his *coup* to Antiochus Sidetes (1 Macc. 16:18), and asked for immediate assistance, suggests prior connivance on the part of Antiochus VII. Ptolemy could not hope to overthrow the popular and powerfully entrenched Maccabean party without backing from some quarter. No doubt he looked for support from dissident Hellenistic elements in Judaea, including the Idumaean faction. Ptolemy could not seek aid openly, however, and remain in Simon's confidence. It is thus even more likely that he acted with previous assurances of support from Antiochus.

76. For the location of Doq on the "Mount of Temptation," site of the later Byzantine monastery Δουκα, see Abel, *Géographie de la Palestine* II (Paris, 1938), 307; *Maccabées*, p. 281.

77. Cf. *Antiq.* XIII, 228–39; 1 Macc. 16:16.

78. In the late commentary to Ps. 37, in a fragment expounding Ps. 37:32–33 (*JBL* 75 [1956], Pl. 3b), the Wicked Priest is said to be given "into the hands of violent foreigners" (*'rysy gw'ym*), apparently, though the reading is not completely certain. The phrase can be applied specifically to Ptolemy and his men; more likely, however, in this instance it must be taken more generally, including the Seleucid role in the affair.

Three other passages, two in the Habakkuk roll, one in the so-called Testimonia of Cave IV, are most easily connected with the circumstances of Simon's death.

The Testimonia Document[79] lists biblical prophecies relating to the chief figures expected by the sect in the last days. The first quotation speaks of the "prophet like Moses."[80] The second quotation, from Numbers 24:15–17, concerns the Star of Jacob and the Scepter of Israel, the priestly and royal Messiahs respectively, expected by the sect.[81] The third quotation relates to the priesthood, quoting Deuteronomy 33:8–11, including the phrase "and taught thy judgments to Jacob, thy Torah to Israel." This may refer again to the priestly Messiah, but much more probably refers to the Righteous Teacher.[82] The fourth and final quotation is taken from the sectarian Psalms of Joshua, quoting the curse of Joshua upon Jericho in Joshua 6:26, "Cursed before the Lord be the man that rises up and rebuilds this city[ ]. At the cost of his first born shall he lay its foundation, and at the cost of his youngest son shall he set up its gates" (RSV). The exposition (from the Psalms of Joshua) continues: "and behold an accursed man, a son of Belial[83] shall come to power to be a trapper's

79. The list is published as Document IV in Allegro's article, "Further Messianic References in Qumran Literature," pp. 182–87 and Plate; cf. N. Wieder, "Notes on the New Documents from the Fourth Cave of Qumran," *JJS* 7 (1956), pp. 71–76.

80. The quotation is from the "Samaritan" recension of Exodus at Ex. 20:21 as first pointed out by Msgr. Patrick Skehan; cf. R. E. Brown, "The Messianism of Qumrân," *CBQ* 19 (1957), p. 82.

81. In the traditional exegesis of the sect, the Star and the Scepter are distinguished; cf. *CD* 7:19–20; Test. Levi 18:3. Milik's interpretation, that the citation applies only to the royal Messiah is therefore questionable (*DJD* I, pp. 121 f.).

82. The actual title of the Righteous Teacher is taken from Hos. 10:12 and Joel 2:23 (modified; cf. *CD* 6:11). However, Deut. 33:10 is most aptly applied to the Righteous Teacher (cf. Gaster, *op. cit.*, p. 5).

Allegro's reading *wy'yrw* should be corrected to *wy'wrw* (*ywrw* of *MT*); it is merely an orthographic aberrancy of familiar type.

83. The text reads *'rwr 'yš bly'l* corrected to read *'yš 'rwr 'yš bly'l*.

snare to his people and ruin to all his neighbors . . ." The
context is broken, and in the next line the two sons of the
accursed man are mentioned: "(so that) the two of them
shall become violent instruments, and they shall rebuild the
[city?]. . . and set up a wall and towers for it to make a
stronghold of wickedness [] . . . horrors in Ephraim and
Judah [] . . . [and they shall] commit sacrilege in the land
. . . [bl]ood like water[shall flow?] on the battlements of
the daughter of Zion and in the district of Jerusalem."

The passage assuredly applies to an archenemy of the sect,
and presumably therefore to the Wicked Priest. The application of the passage to Simon and his older and younger sons
Judas and Mattathias, and their deaths in Jericho is almost
too obvious to require comment. The slaughter in Jerusalem
and its environs described in the last lines reflects the attack
of Antiochus Sidetes upon Judaea in 134–132 B.C. immediately
following Simon's death.[84]

The original reading was probably *'yš 'rwr bn bly'l.*

84. One looks in vain for another historical setting for the passage.
J. T. Milik (*Découvertes, ad loc.*) has tried to make Jonathan and
Simon the "two sons," and apply the building of the city not to Jericho,
the original context, but to Jerusalem, alluded to in the last lines. The
difficulties here are obvious. The patriarch Mattathias had no part in the
building, and himself was scarcely the villain of the sect. Moreover, it
is awkward to apply a Jericho prophecy to Jerusalem, even given the
methods of exegesis used by the Essenes.

But if one grants that the curse is reapplied to Jerusalem, which is
certainly not impossible, we still must identify Simon with the accursed
one, his two sons with the "vessels of violence." Jonathan, Simon, and
John Hyrcanus all built the walls of Jerusalem and otherwise fortified
the city. Simon, however, is not only associated with the fortification of
the cities outside Jerusalem, but also with the rebuilding of the "City
of David," i.e., the citadel and its environs. On Simon's building operations, cf. 1 Macc. 13:10; 13:33; 13:52; 14:33; 14:37; Josephus' elaboration of 1 Macc. 13:52; 14:37 may not be historically sound (*Antiq.*
XIII, 215–17; *War* I, 50), but must also be taken into account. Moreover, Simon's adult sons who share rule with him defeat Kendebaios,
jointly administer his projects of fortification, and otherwise stand be-
side their ancient father. Finally the blood bath in Jerusalem in our
text appears to follow on the heels of the building projects, and hence
only can be the attack of Antiochus Sidetes following Simon's death.

Further support for the identification of the Wicked Priest with Simon is found in IQpHabakkuk 11:12–15: "This means the priest whose dishonor was greater than his honor. For he did not circumcize the foreskin of his heart but walked in ways of drunkenness in order to quench (his) thirst. But the cup of God's wrath will swallow him up . . . !" The drunken high priest not merely drinks in carousals, the cup of wrath swallows him. The comment admirably fits Simon's drunken demise.[85]

One more passage requires our attention, IQpHabakkuk 11:4–8: "This means the Wicked Priest who pursued after the Righteous Teacher to overwhelm him (or swallow him up) in the fierceness of his wrath at his house in exile.[85a] And in the season of the festival of rest, the Day of Atonement, he suddenly appeared before them to overwhelm them and to make them stumble on the fast day, their sabbath of rest." The attack of the Wicked Priest on the Righteous Teacher and his fellows[86] is made at the Teacher's establishment in exile. It falls on the *sectarian* fast day, not the orthodox one as is clear (1) from the fact that the religious calendar of the sect differs as we know from calendrical texts, and (2) from the fact that the priest is not presiding at his duties at the Temple.[87] If indeed the Wicked Priest attacked the sectarians in exile, it follows most naturally that he appeared *at Qumrân*. To be sure, it is quite conceivable that the sect hid elsewhere before constructing their permanent installations at Qumrân. But following the more obvious connection, we can apply our archaeological dating of the beginning of the community center to the question of the identity of the Wicked Priest.

85. So already G. Vermès, *op. cit.*, pp. 99–100.

85a. *'byt glwtw='l-byt glwtw* (Segal, Yeivin, *et al.*).

86. Cf. 1QpHab. 12:2–10 and 4QpPs. 37 (to vv. 32–33) for other allusions to the Wicked Priest's persecution of the Teacher and/or his party.

87. Cf. S. Talmon, "Yom Hakkippurim in the Habakkuk Scroll," *Biblica* 32 (1951), pp. 549–63; Milik, *Découvertes*, Chap. III.

The last years of Simon fall just within the upper limit for the foundation of the settlement of Qumrân.

A cycle of texts speak of the Wicked Priest (or possibly of another enemy roughly contemporary with the Wicked Priest) under the biblical appellation, the False Oracle,[88] or more simply the False One.[89] The title is taken from Micah 2:11, and is regularly combined in sectarian exposition with Ezekiel 13:8–12.[90] A typical example of this complex combination of texts is found in IQpHabakkuk 10:9–13, commenting on Habakkuk 2:12:"the interpretation of this [passage] relates to the False Oracle who caused the assembly[91] to go astray in building a city of vanity in blood and establishing a congregation in falsehood . . . their work will be in vain because those who reviled and reproached the Elect of God will enter into fiery judgments." How literally the commentator wishes the phrase "building a city" to be taken is hard to determine,[91a] but taken literally or figuratively, Jonathan and Simon both qualify, and perhaps John Hyrcanus as well. At all events, the main point is that the False Oracle leads the assembly to build a false congregation, a faithless Israel over against the Essene elect.

In other contexts we hear of those who, following the False One, deal treacherously against the New Covenant, and refuse to listen to the inspired words of the Righteous Teacher;[92] and of the house of Absalom which refuses to help the Righteous Teacher against the False One who "rejected the Law in the midst of their whole congre[gation]."[93] All of

88. 1QpHab. 10:9–13; *CD* 4:19–20; 8:2–13 (especially 12–13).

89. 1QpHab. 2:1–10; 5:9–12; *CD* 20:14–15; cf. the "Scoffer" or "Scoffers" (Is. 28:14), *CD* 1:13–21; 20:11 (14–15).

90. See *CD* 4:19–20; 8:2–13; and especially 1QpHab. 10:9–13.

91. The term is *rabbîm* which may mean "multitude" or more technically "democratic assembly" (frequent in the texts of Qumrân).

91a. Similarly the expression "builders of the wall" taken from Ezek. 13:10 may or may not be taken literally in *CD* 4:19; etc.

92. 1QpHab. 2:1–10; cf. *CD* 20:11, 14–15.

93. 1QpHab. 5:9–12. On the identity of "Absalom's house," cf. 1

these passages may reflect the public occasions upon which the Righteous Teacher opposed the "building" of a false high-priestly house, and its concomitant, a false congregation. And if this is the case, probably the Wicked Priest is identical with the False Oracle or False One. If not, the latter is to be identified with the Wicked Priest's successor or predecessor, that is with John Hyrcanus or Jonathan.[94]

In the course of our discussion we have spoken often of the Essene Master. A systematic reconstruction of his career is quite impossible. For all our labors, he remains a shadowy figure. We do not know even his name. There is no hint of his identity in our older sources. The Essene commentaries hide him under his scriptural title, the Righteous Teacher. They mention him fairly frequently,[95] but usually in very general contexts.

We have noted that the Righteous Teacher was a priest, a fervent supporter of the Zadokite high priesthood, and hence presumbably of Zadokite lineage himself. His ministry probably began sometime late in the reign of Jonathan. He suffered persecution and defeat at the hands of Simon, the Wicked Priest, and perhaps also under Jonathan, and/or John Hyrcanus. He was an inspired interpreter of the Scriptures, one "who spoke with authority." He won a following from the remnants of the Ḥasîdîm. He was a founder and in effect the

Macc. 13:11; 11:70; and D. N. Freedman, "The 'House of Absalom' in the Habakkuk Scroll," BASOR 114 (1949), pp. 11–12.

94. Abbé Milik has lately proposed to distinguish the two figures, identifying the False Oracle with John Hyrcanus. His chief evidence is that John had a reputation as a prophet (cf. Josephus, Antiq. XIII, 288–98, 300; etc.). The identification is quite attractive. Most likely the Righteous Teacher's ministry continued into Hyrcanus' reign, and, in any case, the two may have come into direct contact before John's accession to the high priesthood. Of course John, like Jonathan and Simon before him, engaged himself in refortifying Jerusalem (1 Macc. 16:23).

95. 1QpHab. 1:13; 2:2; 5:10; 7:4; 8:3; 9:9/10; 11:5; CD 1:11; 6:11; 20:1, 14, 28, 32; 1QpMic. 10:6; 4QPs. 37 II, 15 (Ps. 37:23b–24a); 4QpPs. 37:32–33 (?); 4QpPs. 37:14–15 (l.4).

author of the Essene faith. When Simon had established himself in the high priesthood "forever" and persecuted all who would gainsay him, the Righteous Teacher fled, leading his little congregation into exile in the wilderness of Qumrân. There he established his "eschatological" community, the community of the New Covenant. In exile he was still not secure from the wrath and persecution of the Wicked Priest, who on one occasion, at least, attacked the community on their private Day of Atonement.

We do not know the time or circumstance of the Righteous Teacher's death. It is unlikely that he survived the reign of John Hyrcanus. He may not have lived to hear of Simon's dreadful end in nearby Jericho. Many scholars have argued that he died violently under persecution at the hands of the Wicked Priest.[96] However, if this were the case, it is never stated explicitly. The passage discussed above (IQpHab. 11:4–8)in which it is said that the Wicked Priest pursued the Righteous Teacher to overwhelm him (or swallow him up) comes as close as any to implying that the Teacher was martyred. The Damascus Document speaks twice of the death of the Teacher but uses the passive expression "from the day the Teacher of the Community was gathered (to his fathers) . . ."[97] A newly published text bears on the question; unfortunately it is badly preserved. The passage being interpreted is Psalm 37:33: "The wicked watches the righteous and seeks to kill him; Yahweh will not abandon him in his hand . . ." The comment seems to read as follows: "This is to be interpreted as referring to the Wicked [Pries]t who [. . . the Righteous Teacher?] to kill him . . . but God will

96. A. Dupont-Sommer, the most articulate advocate of a martyr death, has defended his position systematically in "Le maître de justice fut-il mis à mort?" *VT* 1 (1951), pp. 200–15; and more recently in "Quelques remarques sur le Commentaire d'Habacuc, à propos d'un livre récent," *VT* 5 (1955), pp. 113–29, a review and answer to K. Elliger's *SzHK*.

97. *CD* 19:35–20:1; 20:14. The expression normally applies to peaceful death, but may apply to a violent death (e.g., 1 Macc. 14:30).

not ab[andon him in his hand . . .]" On the basis of the passage being commented upon, we with some confidence can reconstruct the exposition to apply to the Wicked Priest's attempt to kill the Righteous Teacher, and God's deliverance of the Teacher.[98] In light of this text I think we must say that while the Wicked Priest attempted to take his rival's life, the Righteous Teacher was spared, perhaps to be killed later by another adversary, perhaps to die of old age.[99]

98. 4QpPs. 37:32–33 (ll. 1–3). Allegro, "Further Light on the History of the Qumran Sect," pp. 94 f., attempts to avoid the plain meaning of the passage by referring the deliverance to eschatological times, having observed that the verb is future. Two things must be said: (1) the events of the Teacher's ministry are in a sense "eschatological," and (2) the tense of the verb is taken from the psalm quoted. The use of tenses in the commentaries is rarely helpful in interpretation, since *predictions* are being expounded, and the writer often shifts his point of view from that of scripture to that of his own time and vice versa.

99. Dupont-Sommer in his article, "Le Testament de Lévi (XVII–XVIII) et la secte juive de l'alliance," *Semitica* IV, pp. 33–53 (cf. *The Jewish Sect of Qumran and the Essenes* [London, 1954], pp. 38–57) attempts to use the Testament of Levi, especially Chap. 10: 14–15, 16, and 17–18 to support his view that the Righteous Teacher was martyred, and, indeed, was identified as the Messianic "savior of the world." The use of 10: 14–15, and 16 as witnesses to Essene history could hardly be defended on methodological grounds even at the time Dupont-Sommer wrote (before the extensive apocalyptic literature of Cave IV became known). The key elements in these passages including the conception of the Messiah as a transcendental "savior of the world," the slaying of the savior, the subsequent destruction of the Temple and dispersion of the Jews among the Gentiles, and the second coming of the Messiah, are suspect and have generally been assigned to the Christian stratum of the Testaments.

At all events we are now in a position to use Qumrân discoveries to lend weight to the view that the Testaments are indeed Judeo-Christian editions, in part reworked, of older Essene sources. See below, Chap. V, n. 6–7. Nor can the elements listed above be discovered in the extensive new apocalyptic materials from Qumrân. Cf. Chap. V, n. 7.

Similarly we must protest against the method of treatment of Chap. 17 by Dupont-Sommer. First of all he remarks that the term "jubilee" here by a "curious shift designates the time of a priesthood, of a pontificate, whatever its precise duration may have been" (p. 38), and proceeds to treat the priesthoods of the seven jubilees as a series of successive priests. It is possible that underlying the present form of the

The Essenes regarded their Master with a respect which approached adoration. Belief in his teachings was tantamount to salvation.[100] As Moses mediated the Old Covenant to Israel, so the Righteous Teacher instituted the Community of the Renewed Covenant, opened up the meaning of the ancient Scriptures, and established a new discipline in anticipation of the Messianic era. He was in the eyes of his later disciples an eschatological figure predicted in Scripture who was to aid in bringing the New Age to birth.[101]

document was a list of seven priests, and the formula "the Nth priest" (vv. [2], 4–7) was original, "in the Nth (jubilee)" (vv. 2, 3, 8) secondary. But we can scarcely deal so cavalierly with the meaning of the term "jubilee."

Dupont-Sommer then identifies the seven priests with seven of the Hasmonaean dynasty. Judas Maccabaeus is the first, called "annointed" who "shall rise to save the world." Presumably the Essene author was unaware that Judas never functioned as high priest. The last of the series is Aristobulus. Hyrcanus II is omitted in the interests of arriving at the number seven. Perhaps Professor Dupont-Sommer would now shift to Hyrcanus II as seventh, omitting Aristobulus.

Actually the chief offense of this construction of the list (ignoring for the moment the fashion in which the Righteous Teacher is related to the chapter) is in the sweeping approval given to Judas and Jonathan by an Essene, that is, a *Zadokite* author. In the writer's opinion such a view is little short of preposterous. Moreover, no adequate explanation is given to the distinction made between the two priests called "anointed" priests and praised, and the remainder, called merely "priests" and condemned. Why the sharp line drawn between Jonathan and Simon?

By such procedures the priests of Chap. 17 can be made to fit almost any chronology. As an example, taking up Dupont-Sommer's hypothesis that the list goes back to a series of seven priests terminating in the day of the Righteous Teacher, let us fit it to our own chronology. The two "anointed priests" will be the revered Simon (see above) and Onias III, both Zadokites. Trouble begins with the "priest" Jason, mounts with Menelaus. Alcimus is "possessed by darkness." So, too, Jonathan and Simon, the latter the worst of the lot. In this construction, the proper succession from Simon to Simon is followed, and an adequate explanation for the judgments upon each by the Essene priesthood is at hand. Such an analysis is at least as plausible as that of Dupont-Sommer.

100. 1QpHab. 8:1–3.

101. The question of the possible Messianic pretentions of the Righteous Teacher will be raised in Chap. V.

CHAPTER IV

The Old Testament
at Qumrâm

THE ESSENE MANUSCRIPTS, biblical and non-biblical, contribute new data to several areas of Old Testament study: the history of the Hebrew canon,[1] the development of Hebrew (and Aramaic) dialects, scripts, orthographies, and scribal procedures, and—the fields which will be selected arbitrarily for treatment here—the historical criticism of the Old Testament, and the history of the Old Testament text.

1.   The Scrolls and Historical Criticism

While the most fruitful fields of study lie elsewhere, the new manuscripts are not without interest for the historian of Old Testament literature. Almost certainly we must cease to date any biblical work belonging to the Former or Latter Prophets (not to mention the Torah), or any extensive pericope within these books, later than the early second century

1. The subject of canon is briefly touched upon by the writer in "Qumrân Cave I," pp. 122 f., and by H. L. Ginsberg in his excellent article, "The Dead Sea Manuscript Finds: New Light on *Eretz Yisrael* in the Greco-Roman Period," from *Israel: Its Role in Civilization*, ed. Moshe Davis (New York, 1956), pp. 45–49.

B.C. To be sure, this *terminus ad quem* is exceedingly late and merely confirms recent trends in the analysis of the latest materials in prophetic literature. It is none the less a gain to have manuscripts, albeit fragmentary and incomplete, of the books of the Pentateuch, the Prophets, especially the Twelve, dating from the second century B.C.,[2] which rule out categorically speculations about extremely late additions to prophetic works.[3]

Indeed it is probable that no canonical work postdates the Maccabean age. An exception, at least theoretically, may be made in the case of the Book of Esther, missing at Qumrân. More likely, however, Esther was rejected by the sectaries, as suggested by H. L. Ginsberg,[4] or is missing purely by chance. Ecclesiastes, sometimes dated in the second, or even in the first century B.C., by older scholars, appears in one exemplar from Cave IV (4QQoh[a]) which dates ca. 175–150 B.C.[5] Since the text of the manuscript reveals textual develop-

2. The oldest MSS from Qumrân IV include the following (all of which antedate the oldest of the Cave I MSS, 1QIsa[a]): 4QEx[f] and 4QSam[b] from the third century B.C.; 4QEx[e]; 4QDeut[a]; 4QIsa[a]; 4QJer[a]; 4QXII[a] 4QXII[c]; 4QJob[a]; 4QPsa[a]; 4Qq[0]h[a] from the second century B.C. A fairly large group of biblical MSS belongs to the late second century or early first century B.C., none of which are listed here. For illustrations of the script of certain of the unpublished MSS listed above, and a discussion of the typological sequence of the Qumrân texts, see the writer, "The Oldest Manuscripts from Qumrân," pp. 147–65.

3. For example, Dupont-Sommer, as late as 1950, speculated about the possibility of bringing such materials as the Servant Passages of Isa., Dan. 9, Zech. 12, etc., down into the first century B.C. (*The Dead Sea Scrolls*, p. 96), on the grounds that the Essene Righteous Teacher might be reflected in them. Such speculations were not to be taken seriously by Old Testament specialists for several reasons. But the appearance of second-century copies of each of the above-mentioned passages provides the *coup de grâce* to any such aberrant theories. Here, as elsewhere, the further study of Essene materials themselves disproves earlier hypotheses based on undisciplined examination of Essene literature.

4. "The Dead Sea Manuscript Finds . . ." pp. 39–57, especially p.52.

5. Cf. J. Muilenburg, "A Qoheleth Scroll from Qumrân," *BASOR*

ment, it is demonstrably not the autograph, and hence the date of composition must be pushed back into the third century. A second-century B.C. copy of the canonical Psalter (4QPsa), though fragmentary, indicates that the collection of canonical psalms was fixed by Maccabean times, bearing out the current tendency to date the latest canonical psalms in the Persian period.[6]

Psalm studies will be strongly affected also by the appearance in Essene circles of collections of hymns of Maccabean and Hasmonaean date. They include many categories of material of which the Thanksgiving Hymns (1Q and 4QH) are but a single type.[7] Analysis of the literary types, the prosody, and the language and theological motifs of these documents will greatly expand our knowledge of the development of late Old Testament psalmody on the one hand, and will illuminate on the other hand difficult problems in the study of the literary types and prosodic canons of New Testament psalms (especially in the prologue of Luke) and poetry. Preliminary study already indicates that the psalms of the Maccabean period are much developed beyond the latest of Old Testament psalms; their language is neoclassical, not classical; sapiential forms and language have profoundly influenced hymnic style. Older patterns of symmetry (meter) and many classical forms of thought rhyme (*parallelismus membrorum*) have largely broken down or been lost.[8] The hymns are archaistic. They imitate biblical psalms to such an

135 (October 1954), pp. 20–28; cf. Cross, "The Oldest Manuscripts from Qumrân," pp. 153, 162.

6. Other grounds for a Persian dating of the Psalter are given below. Cf. the writer's earlier discussion in *BA* 17 (1954), p. 3; and P. Hyatt, "The Dead Sea Discoveries: Retrospect and Challenge," *JBL* 76 (1957), p. 5.

7. Provisionally, see J. Strugnell, "Travail . . ." p.65.

8. These tendencies are already at work, of course, in late Old Testament poetry. The failure of New Testament scholars to recognize this development has hindered advances in the analysis of poetic materials embedded in the New Testament, notably in the Gospels.

extent that most Essene hymns are patchworks of phrases from the Psalter, and, notably from the Prophets; yet the mood and theological structure differ strikingly from canonical psalms. For suitable parallels one must look to the hymns, especially the apocalyptic hymns, of the Apocrypha and New Testament.

In one rather striking instance, a Qumrân document promises to throw light on oral, or possibly literary, sources lying behind the fixed edition of an Old Testament book. In 1956 J. T. Milik identified and published a few fragments of a Cave IV document, designated the "Prayer of Nabonidus," after its first line: "The words of the prayer which Nabonidus, king of Assyria and Babylon, the great king, prayed . . ."[9] The prayer relates how Nabonidus came down with a "dread disease by the decree of the Most High God," was "set apart from men" for a seven-year period in the Arabian oasis of Teima. A Jewish diviner, presumably Daniel—the broken text does not reveal his name—intervenes, speaks of the king's worship of "gods of gold, bronze, iron, wood, stone, silver . . ." (Cf. Dan. 5:4.)

The document is closely related in language, style and genre to the cycle of tales collected and edited in Daniel 1–6 (so-called Daniel A). It is strongly reminiscent of Daniel 4, the story of Nebuchadnezzar's being driven from men for seven years, during which he learns that the "Most High rules the kingdom of men . . ." ending with the snatch of poetry in which the king "blesses the Most High and praises and honors Him who lives forever." In fact there is every reason to believe that the new document preserves a more primitive form of the tale. It is well known that Nabonidus gave over the regency of his realm to his son Belshazzar in order to spend long periods of time in Teima; while Nebuchadnezzar, to judge from extrabiblical data, did not give up his throne.

9. " 'Prière de Nabonide' et autres écrits d'un cycle de Daniel," *RB* 63 (1956), pp. 407–15; cf. David Noel Freedman, "The Prayer of Nabonidus," *BASOR* 145 (February 1957), pp. 31 f.

Moreover, in the following legend of Belshazzar's feast, the
substitution of Nebuchadnezzar for Nabonidus as the father
of Belshazzar (Dan. 5:2) is most suggestive. Evidently in an
older stage of tradition, the cycle included stories of Nebuchadnezzar (cf. Dan. 1–3), Nabonidus (Dan. 4), and Belshazzar (Dan. 5).[10] The change of names, as well as the
development of the elaborate details of Nebuchadnezzar's
theriomania, is best attributed to the refracting tendencies of
oral transmission, in this case the shift of a legend from a lesser
to a greater name. It is not necessary to think of the Prayer of
Nabonidus as a literary source of the canonical Daniel, or
even to give the prayer priority in terms of its written composition. The prayer may simply derive from a parallel, but
more conservative line of orally transmitted material.[11]

2. The Archaic Text of the Old Testament

The most direct and obvious contribution of the Qumrân
scrolls is in the field of Old Testament textual studies.[12] At
the outset we may remark that the new scrolls give evidence
of the antiquity of the type of textual tradition which has

10. This suggests that in the riddle of Dan. 5:25–28, the kings
referred to originally as a mina, shekel, and half shekel, were Nebuchadnezzar, *Nabonidus*, and Belshazzar respectively, as pointed out by
Freedman, *ibid.* Cf. H. L. Ginsberg's discussion, *Studies in Daniel*
(New York, 1948), pp. 24–26.

11. With the publication of the Habakkuk Commentary, scholars
duly noted that the work treated only the first two chapters of
Habakkuk. Since it is generally accepted that the psalm of Chap. 3
was not composed by the prophet, a number of scholars jumped to the
conclusion that prophecy and psalm had not yet been wedded when
the commentary was composed. This position cannot hold. The Qumrân
commentaries often treat short pericopes, a psalm, a section of chapters,
and only rarely the whole of a short prophetic book.

12. This discussion of the text of the Old Testament at Qumrân is
a revised and expanded form of material published in the writer's
article, "The Dead Sea Scrolls," in Vol. XII of *The Interpreter's Bible*
(New York-Nashville, 1957), copyrighted by the Abingdon Press in
1957. Copyrighted material is used here by permission.

survived in the form of the traditional Hebrew Bible.[12a] Again the scrolls preserve many new readings some of which are superior to received readings, some of which are inferior. Nevertheless, the textual scholar finds the chief interest of the scrolls neither in their testimony to the age of our received text (which has never been seriously doubted), nor merely in individual readings as such. The real importance of the biblical scrolls lies in the data they yield for the reconstruction of the textual history of the Old Testament.

To make this point clear, perhaps it will be useful to glance backward at the state of textual studies before the coming of the Qumrân and Murabba'ât scrolls.

The eighteenth and nineteenth centuries witnessed the assiduous collection and study of extant Hebrew manuscripts, together with the ancient versions into which the Hebrew had been translated. These studies led to the first systematic reconstructions of the history of the Old Testament text. The culmination of this stage of study is found in the works of Paul de Lagarde, who stated categorically that all medieval Hebrew manuscripts were descended from a common ancestor, a single master scroll. This official text, according to Lagarde, could be dated no earlier than the first century of the Christian era. That is, these studies seemed to establish that about A.D. 100, in the days of Aqiba, the rabbis had fixed an authoritative Hebrew text, chosen arbitrarily from the more or less fluid textual traditions alive in the pre-Christian period, and that this official text in effect destroyed all variant lines of tradition in normative Judaism.[13] Old Testament textual criticism found itself at an impasse.

12a. That is to say, a proto-Masoretic recension for certain books is present at Qumrân. As we shall see, this tradition was chosen by the rabbis, who, after further recensional activity, established the base of the *textus receptus*, the traditional consonantal text. See below.

13. See Lagarde, *Anmerkungen zur griechischen Übersetzung der Proverbien* (Leipzig, 1863). Cf. Reider, *Prolegomena to a Greek-Hebrew and Hebrew-Greek Index to Aquila* (Philadelphia, 1916), pp. 81 ff.; H. M. Orlinsky, *On the Present State of Proto-Septuagint Studies*

(*AOS Offprint Series 13*) (New Haven, 1941), pp. 81–91; especially p. 84 and references; R. H. Pfeiffer, *Introduction to the Old Testament* (New York, 1941), pp. 78, 79; B. J. Roberts, *The Old Testament Text and Versions* (Cardiff, 1951), pp. 23–29.

Attacks on Lagarde's position show at most that he overstates his case. All medieval manuscripts stem from a single, narrow, recensional base. This is evidenced not only by the early, pre-Tiberian manuscripts from the Cairo Genizah, but decisively now by the appearance of the Murabba'ât fragments, especially the great Minor Prophets scroll (not to be confused with the Greek recension of the Minor Prophets). Medieval variants, whether in biblical manuscripts, or in rabbinic texts (see Aptowitzer, *Das Schriftwort in der rabbinischen Literatur* [*Sitzungsberichte der kais. Akad. der Wiss. in Wien*. Phil.-Hist. Klasse Bd. 153:6, 1906; 160:7, 1908], and H. L. Strack, *Prolegomena critica in Vetus Testamentum hebraicum*, Leipzig, 1873) are for the most part merely orthographic, or secondary, a witness to subsequent development of variant readings which for a number of reasons may coincide with older witnesses, the Septuagint, etc. In the Targums, Aquila, and Jerome, some genuine survivals of readings which predate the official recension of ca. A.D. 100 are expected, since in each case older materials were used alongside the new standard text.

Part of the difficulty arises from differing presuppositions as to the state of the Hebrew text in the pre-Christian period. For those who presume an extremely conservative development of the Hebrew textual tradition, the variants of the post-Aqiba period loom large. For those who suppose that the pre-Christian period was marked by a Hebrew text which exhibited widely different recensional traditions, the medieval variants appear to be negligible. As we shall see, the pre-Christian Hebrew text exhibits *recensional* variation which differs *toto caelo* from the variation exhibited after the promulgation of the official Hebrew (consonantal) text.

The general reaction against Lagardian positions, therefore, represented today especially by the Kahle-Sperber school (cf. Kahle, "Untersuchungen zur Geschichte des Pentateuchtextes," *TSK* 88 [1915], pp. 432–39), has gone much too far. The text established about A.D. 100 appears to be the culmination of rabbinic recensional activity which began perhaps a century or more earlier, to judge from the Qumrân texts (cf. Cross, "A New Qumrân Biblical Fragment Related to the Original Hebrew Underlying the Septuagint," *BASOR* 132 [December 1953], p. 24, n. 36). Barthélemy's Greek recension of the Septuagint is evidence of this early trend. There is no doubt that our copy dates at the latest from the first century A.D., and preferably about the turn of the Christian era, and represents an early attempt *to revise the LXX* into conformity with the proto-Masoretic text. (On the dating see Barthélemy, *op. cit.*, p. 19; and C. H. Roberts quoted by P. Kahle, ". . . Die im August 1952 entdeckte Lederrolle . . ." *TLZ* 79 [1954], col. 81). It may be noted that in his article devoted precisely to this

There were only a few hints of the state of the text in the era sealed off by the promulgation of a standard text. The Pentateuch of the Samaritans, having been transmitted along different channels, preserved an alternate form of the text for the Torah.[14] Actually, however, the Samaritan provided little help toward reconstructing the early history of the Hebrew text. This was due not only to its restricted scope, but to certain confusions which attended its early study. Generally it was presumed to be an extremely early branch of tradition separating from the main Jewish line at the time of the early Samaritan rift (fifth century B.C.). In fact its text is a relatively late branch, going back at earliest to Hasmonaean times. [15] That this was the case has long been likely on historical grounds. It is now clear both on paleographical grounds—the Samaritan script is a derivative of the Paleo-Hebrew script

new recension, Kahle fails to deal with this point, that the scroll is a Jewish revision, *not* translation, which takes the pre-Christian Septuagint as its base. The failure is most curious, since this is easily the most significant characteristic of the text, as well as most damaging evidence against Kahle's theories of Septuagint origins.

The Murabba'ât texts certify that the consonantal base of the *textus receptus* had been fixed finally by the days of the Second Revolt, and that Lagarde was, after all, right in principle. Indeed the evidence from Murabba'ât indicates that even the principles of orthographic practice (use of vowel letters, *matres lectionis*) became fixed at this time. While minor orthographic variations appear, as well as a few variants of other types, they are no more significant than variants in Tiberian Masoretic manuscripts; the relatively fluid orthographic practice of the Hasmonaean and Herodian periods known from Qumrân has vanished, once for all.

14. A non-Masoretic text type also appears in some of the Apocryphal and Pseudepigraphical works, which being rejected by rabbinical Judaism, did not undergo revision. Cf. Kahle, "Untersuchungen . . ." pp. 399–410; *The Cairo Genizah* [The Schweich Lectures 1941] (London, 1947), pp. 147–8.

15. Cf. the writer's remarks in "A Report on the Biblical Fragments of Cave Four . . ." p. 12, n. 5a. Contrast Kahle, "Untersuchungen . . ."; Roberts, *The Old Testament Text and Versions*, pp. 188–96; and M. Greenberg, "The Stabilization of the Text of the Hebrew Bible, Reviewed in the Light of the Biblical Materials from the Judean Desert," *JAOS* 76 (1956), 161–63.

which was revived or became resurgent in the Maccabean era of nationalistic archaism—and on orthographic grounds.[16] The text type found in the Samaritan is difficult to categorize. On the one hand it stands very close to the proto-Masoretic text. Yet it has a large number of readings in agreement with the Septuagint. Again, it is replete with inferior readings: expansion, transposition, insertion of parallels from other passages or books, readings of a type which must have been introduced at a fairly early date when the text was relatively fluid. They are not the result of specifically Samaritan recensional activity in all probability.[17] In any case the Samaritan Pentateuch has been only of limited use in the task of recovering a more primitive form of the Hebrew text of the Old Testament.

The best hope for a break-through into the unknown era before the promulgation of the official textual recension of the rabbis lay in the Septuagint, the standard Greek Old Testament of the early Church, which according to tradition traced its lineage to an Alexandrian translation of the third-second centuries B.C. Perhaps by reconstructing the Hebrew underlying this antique version, the textual critic might gain detailed knowledge of the development of the early text, enabling him thereby to reconstruct a more nearly original form of the Hebrew Bible.

This was not an easy path to the pre-rabbinic Bible. Two difficult and complex problems required resolution before the Septuagint could be used confidently to reconstruct an old Hebrew text type. In the first place, Septuagint scholars had to establish the original form of the Old Greek translation (the proto-Septuagint) out of a maze of manuscripts be-

16. That is, Samaritan orthography reflects neither the restricted use of *matres lectionis* characteristic of the third century and earlier, nor the revised spelling principles of the rabbinic text. Rather it exhibits the characteristic full orthography of the Maccabean and especially Hasmonaean eras. Cf. Cross, "The Oldest Manuscripts from Qumrân," p. 165.

17. Cf. Kahle, "Untersuchungen . . ." pp. 399–410. (See below.)

longing to Christian recensions of the Old Greek, and its daughter versions. This required the grouping of the manuscripts, the versions, and citations in ancient authors into families and then the establishment of the text types belonging to the recensions of the Septuagint known, especially, from Jerome: the Hesychian (Egyptian), Lucianic (Syrian), and Hexaplaric (Palestinian), as well as unknown recensions to be detected by inductive critical procedures. The task was further involved by the presence of contamination of the transmission of the Septuagint by later Jewish Greek texts which had been successively revised back into conformity with the developing Hebrew text. Such recensions include the Greek text of the Minor Prophets partially published by Barthélemy,[18] probably identical with the Quinta of the Hexapla, which revises the Septuagint by a late pre-Christian Hebrew text (closely allied with the proto-Masoretic tradition), and especially Theodotion and Aquila, both of which appear to be based on the earlier Jewish recension, revising it to conform to the authoritative Hebrew text which emerged about A.D. 100.[19]

18. Bibliography on the Barthélemy recension is listed in notes 33 and 35 of Chap. I.

19. The above description is, of course, oversimple. The number of Jewish revisions of the Septuagint may be larger than the present evidence suggests, and the detailed relationships between such and the "Three," Theodotion, Aquila, and Symmachus, may be more complex than is suggested by first study. The problems of proto-Lucian, proto-Theodotion, Rahlfs' and Katz's "R" recension, etc., will require complete re-examination in light of the new texts of the *LXX* from Qumrân, and the new Greek data from the "undesignated provenience," as well as the Hebrew texts from these finds and from Murabba'ât. (On these texts, see Chap. I, especially n. 21, 23, and 33–35.)

All the new evidence seems to suggest that these problems will be solved in the general framework of the proto-Septuagint hypothesis formulated by Lagarde and developed by Rahlfs, Montgomery, Margolis, and in the present generation by Orlinsky, Katz, and especially Ziegler. That is to say, the remnants of Greek texts at variance with the standard Septuagint and which appear to be pre-Hexaplaric in date, are now most easily explained as surviving from Jewish revision(s) of the Septuagint. Not only do we now possess such a recension, but we

The task of supplying the materials from which the proto-Septuagint text can be recovered is by no means completed. Progress has been made in the seventy-five years since Lagarde initiated his program, despite pauses to solve unexpected complexities, and occasional loss of faith by some in the very existence of a proto-Septuagint which consisted of more than a congeries of distinct and competing Greek translations. The still incomplete edition of the Larger Cambridge Septuagint, the continuing publication of the great Göttingen edition of the Septuagint, recently at an increased tempo, and the publication of individual studies of which Margolis' *The Book of Joshua in Greek* is the outstanding example, are major advances. Nevertheless the determination of the text of the Septuagint in a given Old Testament passage is one of the most exacting tasks of the biblical scholar, and in some portions of the Old Testament, fortunately decreasing steadily in extent, remains a precarious task at best.

If we can presume that we know what the text of the Septuagint is, a second formidable difficulty appears when the Septuagint comes to be used as a witness to the archaic Hebrew text. Does the Septuagint in a given passage witness to an ancient Hebrew text at variance with the *textus receptus,* or are its divergent readings to be explained away as due to translation procedures? Does the Septuagint reflect in distorted form the *Hebraica veritas* as assumed by Origen and Jerome as well as ancient Jewish scholars, or does it often

possess the various Hebrew text types reflected by it, by the "Three" and, indeed, by the proto-Septuagint itself.

For recent discussions of the proto-Septuagint question, see Orlinsky, *On the Present State of Proto-Septuagint Studies* (cf. "The Septuagint–Its Use in Textual Criticism," *BA* 9 [1946], pp. 21–34); "Current Progress and Problems in Septuagint Research," in *The Study of the Bible Today and Tomorrow,* ed., H. R. Willoughby (Chicago, 1947); P. Katz, "Septuagintal Studies in the Mid-Century . . ."; "Das Problem des Urtextes der Septuaginta, *ThZ* 5 (1949), pp. 1–24; J. W. Wevers, "Septuaginta Forschungen . . ."; P. Kahle, *The Cairo Genizah,* Chap. II:2; Roberts, *Old Testament Text . . .* pp. 104–19.

testify in faithful fashion to a different Hebrew text from
the one we have always known?

These questions gave rise to sharp debate in the nineteenth century. The issue was joined between supporters of the
antiquity and fidelity of the Masoretic tradition who would
explain away the apparently divergent readings of the Septuagint, and those who insisted on laying their Septuagint side
by side with the traditional Hebrew Bible—as if the two were
variant manuscripts which by comparison could be forced to
yield a text superior to both. On the side of the medieval
Hebrew text stood such figures as Fränkel and Löhr; in support of the importance of the Old Greek for textual criticism
stood Thenius, Lagarde, and the master, Julius Wellhausen.
The debate persists into the twentieth century. Indeed the
polemic against the trustworthiness of the Septuagint translators and the usefulness of their version as a witness to the
pre-Masoretic text had come close to winning the day. How
can the critic be sure, said this school of thought, that when
the Greek translator departs radically from the received text,
the Hebrew manuscript from which he translated also de-
viates? Could not these deviations be caused by bad translation techniques? Was the Greek a literal and faithful translation of its *Vorlage*? Or was it full of error, paraphrasing, and
arbitrary changes? Increasingly scholars have looked upon the
Septuagint with a jaundiced eye, and, following the lead
especially of H. S. Nyberg, a new conservative respect for the
medieval Hebrew text has gained sway.[20]

Then with the discovery of the Qumrân scrolls we were
suddenly catapulted over the alleged barrier into the for-

20. Cf. H. S. Nyberg, "Das textkritische Problem des Alten Testaments am Hoseabuche demonstriert," ZAW 52 (NF 11), 1934, pp.
241–54; *Studien zum Hoseabuche* (Uppsala, 1935); P. A. H. De Boer,
Research into the Text of I Samuel I-XVI (Amsterdam, 1938), and
sequent studies in *Oudtestamentische Studien I* (1942) and VI (1949).
Cf. the literature, especially that of the Gehman school discussed by
Wevers, "Septuaginta-Forschungen, II. Die Septuaginta als Übiset-
zungsurkunde," *ThR* 22 (1954), pp. 171–90.

bidden land. The great Isaiah scroll of Cave I was published first. It proved rather an anticlimax. While it conserved thousands of variant readings, few of its readings were significant, and even fewer superior to the traditional readings. It seemed that the defenders of the traditional Hebrew Bible were vindicated, and that the work of the rabbis in preparing the official text current in the second century A.D. had had negligible effect on the history of textual transmission. Certainly it was true that the text of Isaiah preserved in the Masora was based on an extremely early textual type, already at home in Palestine in the late second century B.C.[21]

There was one ambiguity in this construction of the evidence. Isaiah in the Septuagint is not one of those books where traditional renderings and those of the Greek translation clash. Isaiah in Greek appears to have been translated from a manuscript quite close to the proto-Masoretic tradition. However, it was difficult to be certain, since the translation of Isaiah is among the poorest in the Greek Bible.[22] What was needed was a group of manuscripts from other biblical books where the

21. The literature on the Isaiah scroll (1QIsa[a]) is quite extensive. A general discussion may be found in M. Burrows, *The Dead Sea Scrolls*, pp. 301–15, and full bibliographic notes for textual studies of the early finds may be found in his bibliography, pp. 420–35; of the older studies, noteworthy are the contributions of Baumgartner, Beegle, Hempel, Kahle, Loewinger, Milik, and Orlinsky. The most recent discussions dealing with the text of Isaiah at Qumrân are those of W. F. Albright, "New Light on Early Recensions of the Hebrew Bible," *BASOR* 140 (1955), pp. 27–33; P. W. Skehan, "The Text of Isaias at Qumrân," *CBQ* 8 (1955), pp. 38–43; and a paper published in *Actes du 2e Congrès international pour l'étude de l'Ancien Testament*, Strasbourg, 1956 (seen by the writer in preparation); M. Greenberg, "The Stabilization of the Text of the Hebrew Bible . . ." pp. 163 f.; and H. M. Orlinsky, "Notes on the Present State of the Textual Criticism of the Judean Biblical Cave Scrolls," in *A Stubborn Faith* (Papers on Old Testament and Related Subjects Presented to Honor William Andrew Irwin), ed. E. C. Hobbs (Dallas, 1956), pp. 117–31.

22. See J. Ziegler, *Untersuchungen zur Septuaginta des Buches Isaias* (Münster i. W., 1934).

Septuagint translation was good, where it was extremely literal when it agreed with Masoretic readings, but where in places it branched radically from this later standard text. This was the case, for example, in the historical books, especially in Joshua and Samuel. It is also true of Jeremiah, where the Septuagint omits or changes the order of large sections of material. Ideally, of course, the scholar needs samplings from the whole Old Testament in order to reconstruct a valid history of its transmission.

The recovery of nearly a hundred biblical scrolls from Cave IV came, therefore, as incredibly good fortune. Here at last was the material for sampling the textual types extant in virtually every book of the Old Testament. Here was a substantial basis for the establishment of the archaic, pre-Masoretic history of the Hebrew Bible. Moreover, thanks to the Murabba'ât texts which extend the series from Qumrân down into the second century A.D., we have direct evidence for the first time as to just what happened to the text in the crucial era before, during, and after the time when the official text was fixed.

Initial study was directed to the historical books, especially to Samuel.[23] The text of Samuel contained in the three scrolls from Cave IV is widely at variance with that of the traditional Masoretic Bible; it follows systematically the rendering of the Septuagint of Samuel.[24] For example, in the few published fragments of the archaic Samuel text (4QSam[b]), there are some thirteen readings in which the Qumrân text agrees with the Greek against the readings of the received text, four readings in which the Qumrân text agrees with the traditional text against the Septuagint. The ratio of readings in agreement

23. Cross, "A New Qumrân Biblical Fragment . . ." pp. 15–26; "The Oldest Manuscripts from Qumrân," pp. 165–72.

24. The older Samuel MS (4QSam[b]) often preserves a text superior to both the Septuagint and Hebrew *textus receptus*. The non-specialist can find a translation of one such passage in my article, "The Oldest Manuscripts from Qumrân," p. 171.

with the Septuagint against the Masoretic text is even higher in the large Samuel manuscript (4QSam^a).[25]

Other historical books (Joshua, Samuel, Kings) follow suit, in so far as they are preserved, in presenting the tradition of the Septuagint. It now becomes clear, at least in these books, that the Septuagint's divergent text was due less to "translation idiosyncrasies" than to the type of text which it translated. These manuscripts establish once for all that in the historical books the Septuagint translators faithfully and with extreme literalness reproduced their Hebrew *Vorlage*.[26] And this means that the Septuagint of the historical books must be resurrected as a primary tool of the Old Testament critic. This is a repudiation of much of the textual theory and method developed and applied to the Hebrew text of Samuel during the last generation.[27]

All this does not mean that the Septuagint in the historical books presents a text which is *necessarily* superior to the Masoretic text. The question of which witness is superior is another problem, to be decided in individual readings. It does mean that the Septuagint reflects accurately a Hebrew textual tradition at home in Egypt in the third–second cen-

25. Cf. Cross, "A New Qumrân Biblical Fragment . . ."; *passim;* E.Vogt, "Textus praemasoreticus ex Qumran," *Biblica* 35 (1954), pp. 263–66; and J. Hempel, "Ein textgeschichtlich bedeutsamer Fund," *ZAW* 65 (1953), pp. 296–98.

26. The literalness of the Septuagint of Samuel is not, of course, the mechanical and tortured literalness of Aquila. However, the translator reflects systematically in his translation, shifts of tense, the presence or absence of the article, and so on, so far as Greek idiom permits. Study of the method of the translator over against the Qumrân text soon teaches one his technique, so that from his translation his *Vorlage* can be predicted with high accuracy. Save for a very few poetic passages (e.g., the Song of Hannah) where the Greek text probably had a prehistory, paraphrasing is virtually absent from the Septuagint of Samuel, and no evidence is to be found of conscious changes made by the translator on theological or otherwise tendentious grounds.

27. Among the studies of the text of Samuel, for example, that which needs least revision in light of the new evidence is Wellhausen's *Der Text der Bücher Samuelis* published in 1871.

turies B.C., and that thanks to the Qumrân manuscripts we have the means to control its evidence.[28]

The state of the text in other books of the Old Testament is a more complicated one. Among no less than thirty Pentateuchal manuscripts from Cave IV, Qumrân, at least three sharply defined textual traditions persist.[29] The majority of the texts are allied closely with the proto-Masoretic tradition. However, the text type underlying the Septuagint is well represented. For example, there is the Deuteronomy manuscript of which fragments of Deuteronomy 32 were published by Monsignor Patrick Skehan. It preserves a text derivative from the Hebrew recension underlying the Septuagint in a passage where the *textus receptus* is defective, so that by comparison of the three texts, a text superior to any one of the witnesses may be reconstructed.[30]

28. In fact comparative studies of the text of Samuel are tending to indicate that the Masoretic text here is based on an extremely narrow and often inferior textual recension. Its text is often defective as the result of systematic revision (see below, n. 57). Textual scholars are accustomed to the fact that a *textus receptus* is normally a conflate text; the reverse is true of Samuel; it is a text characterized by frequent and extensive haplography. On the other hand the Hebrew underlying the Septuagint is a full text, sometimes conflate, frequently original. That the two texts stand at opposite poles in their textual development is a most fortunate circumstance for the critic who wishes to reconstruct their common ancestor and thereby press back to an extremely early form of the Hebrew text.

29. Cf. Cross, "A Report on the Biblical Fragments of Cave Four . . ." p. 12; *"Le travail d'édition . . ."* p. 56.

30. Skehan, "A Fragment of the 'Song of Moses' (Deut. 32) from Qumrân," *BASOR* 136 (December, 1954), pp. 12–15; cf. Albright, "New Light on Early Recensions of the Hebrew Bible," p. 32, n. 27.

The textual history of Deut. 32:43 in 4Q, *LXX*, and *MT* can be diagrammed as follows:

Original Text

hrnynw šmym 'mw   whbw 'wz (?) lw bny 'lhym
ky dm bnyw yqwm   wkpr 'dmt 'mw
            Shout for joy, O heavens, before him;
            And ascribe might to him, O sons of God;

For he avenges the blood of his children,
And purges the people's land.

Proto-Masoretic Text

hrnynw [šmym 'mw
whbw 'wz (?) lw bny 'lhym
hrnynw] gwym 'mw
ky dm <'bdyw> yqwm
Etc.

Shout for joy, [O Heavens, before him,
And ascribe might to him, O sons of God;
Shout for joy,] O nations <for his people>;
For he avenges the blood of his <servants>,
Etc.

Proto-4Q Deuteronomy

hrnynw šmym 'mw
[whbw 'wz (?) lw bny 'lhym
hrnynw gwym 'mw]
whšthww lw kl 'lhym
ky dm bnyw yqwm

Shout for joy, O heavens, *before him*,
[And ascribe might to him, O sons of God;
Shout for joy, O nations, *before him*,]
And bow down to him, all ye divine ones;
For he avenges the blood of his children,
Etc.

The following points may be observed in v. 43a. The corruption of the *MT* is best explained on the basis of a text in which one doublet, *hrnynw šmym 'mw* and *hrnynw gwym 'mw*, but only this doublet, appears. As pointed out to me by John Strugnell, LXX μετὰ τοῦ λαοῦ αὐτοῦ is merely a double rendering of *'mw* (a familiar phenomenon in the *LXX*). The shifts to *gwym* here, and to *'bdyw* in the next bicolon are secondary though perhaps early variants which modernize the primitive diction of the passage. In both cases, therefore, *LXX* and 4Q are superior to *MT*.

The text of 4Q presumes a double conflation. Not only is there the doublet underlying the *haplography* of *MT*, but a second doublet appears. *whšthww lw kl 'lhym*, taken from Ps. 97:7 (or its source), no doubt because of its strong resemblance to the original *whbw 'wz lw bny 'lhym* (cf. Ps. 29). On the Greek rendering ἄγγελοι θεοῦ for *bny 'lhym*, cf. Deut. 32:8 LXX, and the text referred to by Skehan, p. 12.

The doubly conflate text presumed by the reconstruction above actually appears, though in a slightly different order, in the *LXX*.

In v. 43b the loss of *wlmśn'yw yšlm* is best explained as haplography

One Exodus manuscript (4QExᵃ) belongs systematically to the Egyptian textual tradition reflected in the Septuagint; though at points it appears to offer a more consistent form of that tradition than the Septuagint itself. For example, in the first five verses of this manuscript, partially preserved on a single fragment, no fewer than six certain variants are to be found, four on the preserved leather, two fixed by reconstruction of the fragment.[31] Four readings are in agreement

in a (hemi-)stichometric manuscript. However, the entire bicolon *wnqm yšyb lṣryw wlmśn'yw yšlm* is intrusive from Deut. 32:41, two verses earlier, where it is surely original. Here it constitutes not poetic parallelism, but mere tautology. Its introduction may have been occasioned by the combination *yqwm-wnqm*, as suggested by John Strugnell.

31. The first fragment of 4QExᵃ reads as follows (Ex. 1:1–5):

    1.]'t y'qwb 'byhm 'yš[(v.1)
    2.]yśśkr zbwlwn ywsp wbný[(v.3)
    3.]ḥmš wšb'ym npš wymt[(vv.5–6)

    1.]with Jacob their father, each[
    2.]Issachar, Zebulun, Joseph and Benj[amin
    3.]seventy-five persons. And (Joseph) died[

The following variants are significant. In l.1, 4Q adds *'byhm*, "their father," with *LXX* (τῷ πατρὶ αὐτῶν). In l.2, 4Q adds *ywsp*, "Joseph" in his proper position as a son of Rachel (see Gen. 46:19); the reading is found neither in the Greek nor received Hebrew text. However, the phrase *wywsp hyh bmṣrym* ("and Joseph was in Egypt") is omitted in l.3 (between *npš* and *wymt*). In the *LXX* tradition the phrase is not found at the end of v.5, but is placed following Ἀσηρ. (v.4.). A reconstruction of the text of 4Q indicates that the phrase is lacking also following *'šr*, i.e., where it is inserted in the *LXX*.

Perhaps the easiest explanation of textual history of these readings is to suppose that the reading *ywsp* in v.3 together with the omission of the phrase *wywsp hyh bmṣrym* belongs to one textual tradition, the omission of *ywsp* in v.3 together with the insertion of *wywsp hyh bmṣrym* to another, surviving in the proto-Masoretic tradition. It is probable that Joseph once appeared in the list in v.3. Later the discrepancy was noticed, *ywsp* suppressed, and the phrase *wywsp hyh bmṣrym* inserted. If the phrase is taken to be secondary, then the uncertain position of the phrase, inserted at one point in *LXX*, at another in *MT*, is readily explained.

In v.5 , *MT* reads *wyhy kl npš yṣ'y yrk y'qb*, *LXX* ἦσαν δὲ πᾶσαι ψυχαὶ

with the Septuagint; one is unique, but probably points to an Egyptian text form superior to that used by the translators of the Septuagint; one probably agrees with the Masoretic text against the Septuagint.[32]

There are also manuscripts from Cave IV which ally themselves with that line of tradition of which the Samaritan is a collateral witness. One of these is a Paleo-Hebrew Exodus recently published by Skehan.[33] Another unpublished example is a Numbers manuscript in Jewish ("square") script (4QNum[b]).[34] This latter manuscript, however, is by no means a simple or consistent witness to the Samaritan recension, or

ἐξ Ιακωβ. In reconstructing 4Q, it becomes clear that there is insufficient room for the full reading of MT. 4Q like the LXX appears to be shorter. As for the original reading, we cannot speak with any certainty; the reading of MT may be influenced by Gen. 46:26, that of the LXX by Gen. 46:26 or 27.

In l.3 v.5, 4Q reads ḥmš šb'ym, "seventy-five," with LXX (πέντε καὶ ἑβδομήκοντα), against MT šb'ym, "seventy." The number is based on the LXX tradition which appears in Gen. 46, where (46:20, 27) five additional descendants of Joseph are listed; cf. Deut. 10:10 (LXX), and Acts 7:14. In short, 4Q here represents a recensional reading characteristic of the Vorlage of the Septuagint in Genesis and Deuteronomy as well as Exodus.

The LXX of Ex. 1:1–5 may be at variance with MT in three other readings: v.1 ταῦτα for MT w'lh; v.2 Ιουδας for wyhwdh; v.5 omission of ψυχαί in virtually all witnesses, MT npš. It is impossible to be certain of 4Q readings in all but the last of these instances; in v.5, 4Q reads npš with MT, possibly against the tradition of the LXX.

The fragment may be reconstructed as follows:

1. [<>'lh šmwt bny yśr'l hb'ym mṣrymh] 't y'qwb 'byhm 'yš [wbytw]

2. [b'w r'wbn šm'wn lwy <w>yhwdh] yśśkr zbwlwn ywsp wbny[myn dn]

3. [wnptly gd w'šr wyhy kwl npš <ly'qwb?>] ḥmš šb'ym npš wymt [ywsp]

32. The statistics on 4Q Ex[a] 1:1–5 listed in my Interpreter's Bible article, p. 655, are incorrect, owing to an unfortunate lapse in which the wrong figures were transferred from my workbook.

33. "Exodus in the Samaritan Recension from Qumrân," JBL 74 (1955), pp. 182–87.

34. "Le travail d'édition . . ." p. 56.

even to the proto-Samaritan recension. While it contains expansions characteristic of this recension[35] and regularly follows less striking Samaritan variants, its contacts with the Septuagint tradition are even more striking. To be sure, the standard Samaritan text frequently agrees with the text underlying the Greek; however, in this manuscript the agreement is far more extensive, and often its text sides with the Septuagint over against both the *textus receptus* and the Samaritan.[36]

The text of Jeremiah is of particular interest. In the recension underlying the Septuagint text it is one eighth shorter than in the Hebrew Bible. Scholars have suggested that the translators simply abbreviated their text for their own reasons. Other scholars have maintained that two ancient recensions are responsible for the differences.[37] From Qumrân comes a fragmentary Hebrew manuscript, which, where preserved, follows the short text of Jeremiah found hitherto only in Greek. In Chapter 10, for example, the Septuagint omits no fewer than four verses, and shifts the order of a fifth. The Qumrân Jeremiah (4QJer^b) omits the four verses and shifts the order in identical fashion.[38] The longer recension is also present at Qumrân.

35. For example, Deut. 3:21 is inserted after Num. 27:23, a reading otherwise attested only in the Samaritan and Samareitikon. And after Num. 20:13, Deut. 3:23–24 is inserted; the Samaritan is likewise expanded here by the addition of Deut. 3:24.

36. The following are chosen at random: in Num. 35:21, 4Q and LXX add *mwt ymwt hrwsh* after *hw'* (LXX θανάτῳ θανατούσθω ὁ φονεύων); Num. 26:33 in 4Q and LXX reads *w'lh šmwt bnwt* (καὶ ταῦτα τὰ ὀνόματα τῶν θυγατέρων) versus MT and Samaritan *wšm bnwt*.

37. Cf. Orlinsky, *On the Present State of Proto-Septuagint Studies,* p. 85; W. F. Albright, "New Light on Early Recensions . . ." p. 28 and references.

38. The fragment of 4QJer^b cited contains the left portion of a column of text. Ends of lines are preserved with the text of Jer. 9:22–10:18. Lines 5–7 give the reading in question.

l. 5 wbz]hb yyphw bmqbwt	[=MT v. 4]
l. 6]tklt w'rgmn	[=MT v. 9]
l. 7]y'bdw mn 'r"	[=MT v. 11]

As for the remaining books of the Old Testament, a number of books are preserved in texts which belong to the proto-Masoretic family: Isaiah as we have seen, Ezekiel, and the Book of the Twelve (Minor Prophets). It is still premature to discuss the text of the Hagiographa at Qumrân. Study has not proceeded far enough and some manuscripts appear to present complicated textual problems.[39]

3. Early Recensions of the Old Testament

Sufficient materials are available now to permit first attempts to reconstruct in outline the early Hebrew recensions (or local texts) of the Pentateuch, the Historical Books, and perhaps Isaiah and Jeremiah. An excellent beginning has been made by W. F. Albright in his programmatic study, "New Light on Early Recensions of the Hebrew Bible."[40] However, the ground is not yet sure, and many missteps will be taken before sure results can be hoped for. The following suggestions, therefore, are provisional; they attempt to comprehend the evidence as presented above.

First of all we may inquire into the history of the Hebrew recension which underlies the Septuagint of Samuel. As in the case of the Pentateuch, so no doubt in that of Samuel, the text type was present in Egypt in the early Ptolemaic period when the Septuagint began to be translated. Albright has argued that behind the translators' Hebrew text stands a recension edited sometime in the fifth—fourth centuries B.C. in Egypt.

There is, however, other strong evidence which ties this

Reconstruction demonstrates what can be seen even with a casual comparison of the text with *MT* and *LXX*, that with *LXX*, 4QJer[b] transposes v. 5 after v.9, and omits vv. 6–8 and 10. It will be noted also that 4Q transposes *MT* *bmsmrwt* *wbmqbwt* to read *bmqbwt* [*w<b>msmrwt*] with *LXX*, ἐν σφύραις καί ἥλοις.

39. For brief comments on the Daniel manuscripts, see the writer, "Le travail d'édition . . ." p. 58.

40. Cf. n. 21.

old recension to Palestine. For example, examination of the passages of the large Samuel manuscript (4QSam^a) which are paralleled in Chronicles gives direct evidence that the Chronicler often utilized an edition of Samuel closer to the tradition of the Cave IV scroll than to that which survived in the Masoretic recension.[40a] This suggests that the text type underlying the Septuagint, which is closely allied to that used by the Chronicler not long after 400 B.C. in Palestine, is derived from an Old Palestinian recension.[41] Again, the archaic Samuel

40a. An example of the interesting affinities between 4QSam^a and Chron. on the one hand and LXX to Sam. on the other hand is found in a fragmentary column at the end of 4QSam^a.

II Sam 24:16b wml'k yhwh hyh 'm grn h'wrnh hybsy <   >
I Chron. 21:15b   wml'k yhwh 'md 'm grn 'rnn hybsy wyś' . . .
4QSam^a [wml'k y]hwh 'wmd '[m grn 'rw]n' hybsy wyś" [

[II Sam 24:16b+   ]
I Chron. 21:16a . . . h'rṣ wbyn hšmym wḥrbw šlwph bydw . . .
4QSam^a]h'rṣ wbyṅ [hšmy]m wḥr[b]w šlwph bydw[

II Sam 24:17a-MT: . . . w'nky <   > h'wyty w'lh hṣ'n mh 'św
II Sam 24:17a-LXX^{OL} . . . w'nky hr'h hr'wty w'lh hṣ'n mh 'św
I Chron. 21:17a . . . <   > whr' hr'wty w'lh hṣ'n mh 'św
4QSam^a [w']ṅky hr'h hr'ty w'lh h[ṣ'n

Several points are to be noted. 4QSam^a and I Chron. 21:16 preserve a verse which has dropped out of MT by haplography (wyś' dwyd . . .wy'mr dwyd) as well as agree against Samuel in reading 'md/'wmd for hyh in 24:16b=21:15b. In II Sam 17a, 4QSam^a and LXX to Sam agree against MT. Chron. (21:17a) stands closer to 4QSam^a than to MT Sam. That hr'ty is the superior reading is evident. Resh and waw are virtually identical in the Jewish book hand of the third century B.C. The matres lectionis waw and yodh, probably introduced after the third century, were most easily confused in the late first century B.C.

41. By "Old Palestinian" we mean the text type current in Palestine at the end of the fifth century B.C. (i.e., according to our chronology, the time of Ezra). No doubt this text was developed from materials which had passed through the hands of the Exilic, i.e., early Babylonian community. By the "Babylonian" text, however, we mean the text of the "continuing" or late Babylonian community which persisted after the Restoration, and after the return of Ezra. This "Babylonian" text diverges from the "Old Palestinian" text after the introduction of the latter into Palestine. It is questionable whether we can

manuscript (4QSam[b]) obviously reflects at many points a text which antedates both the proto-Masoretic recension and that underlying the Septuagint,[42] though its affinities are clearly with the latter. Since the manuscript itself dates from the end of the third century, and there is no strong reason to suppose that several texts imported from Egypt came to Qumrân,[43] we must conclude that it is a witness to a collateral line of tradition that persists in Palestine from a time antedating the divergence of the Chronicler's Palestinian text of Samuel and the Hebrew textual tradition surviving in Egypt. Perhaps it is easiest to suppose that this Old Palestinian text type derives from the fifth-century Jewish community in Palestine, and that the ancestral Egyptian textual tradition diverged from this Old Palestinian text no earlier than the fourth century, no later than the early third century B.C.[44]

We are left with the problem of the origin of the proto-Masoretic recension of Samuel. No exemplars of its text are found at Qumrân, but there is no reason to suppose that it did not exist in the pre-Christian period. The analogy of other books, Isaiah, Jeremiah, the Pentateuch, warn us that the proto-Masoretic tradition is sometimes old, and not merely the creation of the recensional activities of the rabbis, and that the appearance of one recension at Qumrân does not

detect any readings derived from sources surviving in Palestine from pre-Exilic times, though such may explain some of the radical divergences of later local texts.

42. Cf. Albright, ". . . Early Recensions . . ." p. 33; and Cross, "The Earliest Manuscripts from Qumrân," p. 172.

43. It is not impossible, of course, that a number of the Qumrân texts came from Egypt. There are a number of lines of potential connection between the Essenes and Alexandrian Jewry. The presence of Greek Septuagint manuscripts at Qumrân as well as the manuscripts under consideration could be explained by such contacts.

44. Albright's evidence for Egyptian influence on the Hebrew tradition used by the Greek translators is most convincing in the Pentateuch. The question as to whether or not the Historical Books underwent recensional work in Egypt, and if so when, perhaps should be left open.

exclude the presence of another. Moreover, the proto-Masoretic text of Samuel is clearly the result of systematic revision.[45] Can we suppose it to be a late Palestinian recension which ousted the Old Palestinian surviving both in Egypt and at Qumrân? The radical divergence of its text as well as its frequently inferior readings speak against such a conclusion. A recension in Palestine should have produced both a better text and a text closer to the Egypto-Palestinian family. We can hardly suppose the proto-Masoretic recension to be a "standard" text, while a text superior in many ways, and certainly standard in the day of the Chronicler, is reckoned a vulgar text. If, then, Egypt and Palestine are eliminated as possible localities for the development of the proto-Masoretic text, we may look to Babylon. It is not impossible that the ancestral proto-Masoretic tradition developed independently in Babylon (after the return of the Exiles) and was reintroduced into Palestine in the Hellenistic period or later.[46]

The evidence for reconstructing the history of the local recensions of the Pentateuch is rapidly accumulating; however, the problems are more complicated, and the recensional distinctions less clear cut than in the case of Samuel.

The Paleo-Hebrew text of Exodus, and especially the Num-

---

45. Monsignor Skehan has called an excellent example to my attention. In II Sam. 4:1,2 the *MT* reads *wyšm' bn š'wl* . . . *hyw bn š'wl* . . . The latter phrase makes no sense whatever; the former is not happy. In both the *LXX* and 4QSam[a] the reading is *wyšm' mpybšt bn š'wl*, which grammatically makes perfect sense. However, Mephibosheth is an obvious blunder. Ishbosheth is meant in both instances. The reviser of the text did not replace the erroneous reading with the correct one; rather he excised the mistake and left the text standing. In the case of *hyw lmpybšt bn š'wl*, he cut out not only *mpybšt* but also *l* and forgot to replace it before *bn šwl*, leaving nonsense. Precisely the same phenomena, the excising of a mistake and thereby the creation of a defective (and senseless) text appears in II Sam. 3:7. Here again *LXX* and (in part) 4Q preserve the full but corrupt text to which *MT* is secondary.

46. Albright has proposed such an origin for the great Isaiah scroll (IQIsa[a]) on the basis of correct vocalizations of Babylonian names in its text.

bers scroll described above, furnish materials for reconstructing the prehistory of the Samaritan recension. As we have seen, the Samaritan recension proper branches off in the early Hasmonaean period.[47] It differs from the "proto-Samaritan" text at Qumrân only slightly; these differences would include, no doubt, the specifically sectarian readings—by chance the passages in question are not extant at Qumrân—and closer affinities to the proto-Masoretic tradition.[48] There is not the slightest reason to suppose that the "proto-Samaritan" is in any sense a sectarian recension. In its textual characteristics it stands between the proto-Masoretic recension and the Egyptian recension preserved in the Septuagint as well as at Qumrân. Contrary to both the Egyptian and the proto-Masoretic traditions, however, it is characterized by free expansion, "modernizing" revisions, insertion of parallel passages, and the like, most of its changes being transparently secondary. Such a process must have taken some time; these peculiarities are the product of traditional growth, not recensional endeavor.

Similarly, if Albright is correct, the Egyptian influences reflected in the Hebrew underlying the Septuagint suggest that the Old Egyptian recension was made no later than the fourth century.[49] Probably the Egyptian textual tradition and the proto-Masoretic tradition separated as early as the fifth century, and the "proto-Samaritan" cannot have diverged much later.

There can be no doubt that the proto-Samaritan text is Palestinian. If for no other reason, this can be argued from the fact that the Paleo-Hebrew script survives thanks to its transmission in texts of this type. The origin of the proto-Masoretic tradition is less than clear. Possibly it was a text in use in official circles from the fifth century onward in Palestine, being transmitted independently, though side by side with the

47. See above, n. 15,16.
48. See n. 34.
49. Albright, *op. cit.*, p. 30.

developing vulgar text represented in the proto-Samaritan. On the other hand it may be that it is a type which developed outside Palestine in the fourth and third centuries (presumably in Babylon) later being reintroduced—though in no case later than the Maccabean period. This would explain the repudiation of the traditional Paleo-Hebrew script in the rabbinic period (an unexpected development), as well as the influence of the proto-Masoretic text on the Samaritan (*sensu stricto*) recension.

These details are enough to indicate that the biblical scrolls from Qumrân begin a new period in the study of the text of the Old Testament. Perhaps it is not too much to hope that in proper time, Old Testament scholars will be able to establish a genuinely critical or eclectic text of the Old Testament which would reconstruct a pre-Christian state of the Old Testament. At all events, the new finds will chart new courses by which progress will be made toward a more accurate, more intelligible Old Testament.

CHAPTER V

The Essenes and the Primitive Church

STUDENTS OF CHRISTIAN origins have regularly traced the historical continuities which intimately connect Christianity and Pharisaic Judaism. Thanks particularly to the rich traditional materials preserved by the later rabbis, we have been able to reconstruct much of Pharisaic faith and practice in the pre-Christian period, although it has never been entirely clear how much tradition has shaped the picture of earlier Jewish practice in the image of the normative Judaism which was crystallized out of the Pharisaism which alone of the Jewish movements of pre-Christian times survived the catastrophic Jewish wars against Rome. Since Pharisaism is the best-known, and certainly the dominant branch of early Judaism, there has been a natural tendency to equate it with the Judaism of the first centuries before and after the initiation of the Christian era, and Christianity has often been seen as its simple derivative. Jesus himself has been called a renegade Pharisee and, the New Testament polemic against the Pharisees notwithstanding, with some justification. Certainly Pharisaism formed a major part of the Jewish matrix in which Christianity was conceived, and from which it drew its life and understanding. There can be no doubt that Pharisaism was an important line along which the heritage of Old Israel was transmitted to the Jewish-Christian community which claimed to be the New Israel.

The early Church, however, was not the child of a single parent. Its lineage must also be traced historically to those sectarian Jewish communities whose life and cult provided the "setting in life" for apocalypticism. The language of the early Christian community, including that of the sayings attributed to Jesus, is shot through with the terminology of the Jewish apocalyptic; and the early Church conceived itself to be precisely an eschatological community. We do well, therefore, if we are to understand these motives in her structure and thought, to discover the faith and forms of the apocalyptic communities which preceded Christianity.

The Essenes prove to be the bearers, and in no small part the producers, of the apocalyptic tradition of Judaism. As we have seen, an extraordinarily rich and extensive apocalyptic literature appears in the Essene library of Qumrân. Cycles of Enoch literature, Testaments literature, Daniel literature, pseudo-Jeremianic literature, and pseudo-Mosaic literature, as well as a score of apocalyptic types hitherto unknown, have proved to be at home among the Essenes of Qumrân, and hence, presumably, among the Essene cells of Palestine generally. No doubt Essene editions of certain apocalyptic works are based on sources composed in the Hasidic "congregations"[1] or like communities of the Maccabean or late pre-Maccabean era. Such an explanation evidently obtains in the case of the rich Daniel literature at Qumrân,[2] only a portion of which

1. The Ḥasîdîm in I Macc. 2:42 receive the significant designation, συναγωγὴ Ἀσιδαίων , "congregation of the Ḥasîdîm." Our best source, as we have seen, distinguishes this "congregation" from both the Hellenist and Maccabean parties. To what degree they were an organized group in their "dedication to the Law," we cannot say with certainty. It seems highly probable, however, that in their movement they anticipated the separatist traits of the Pharisees and Essenes, and formed structured congregations or at least loose associations.

2. Cf. Milik, " 'Prière de Nabonide' et autres écrits d'un cycle de Daniel," p. 415.

escaped later condemnation by Pharisaic Judaism. In the case of other apocalypses it is difficult to determine whether they are properly designated "Essene" or "proto-Essene." The concrete contacts in theology, terminology, calendrical peculiarities, and priestly interests, between the editions of Enoch, Jubilees, and the Testaments of Levi and Naphtali found at Qumrân[3] on the one hand, and the demonstrably sectarian works of Qumrân on the other, are so systematic and detailed that we must place the composition of these works within a single line of tradition. There can be no question here of isolated apocalyptists composing spontaneous works reflecting merely private or individual idiosyncrasies of doctrine or calendar. These works are molded by a common tradition, forged within the life of a continuing community with more or less separatist tendencies.[4] That is to say, much of the apocalyptic literature found at Qumrân originates in Essene or proto-Essene (presumably Hasidic) communities and expresses not only their common speculative interests, but their common "eschatological existence" as a community.[5]

In some sense the primitive Church is the continuation of this communal and apocalyptic tradition. It is not merely by chance that so much of the surviving literature of apocalyptic affinities was suppressed in normative Jewish circles and survived almost solely in a Christian milieu. And it is most significant that the literary genres featured in the "Qumrân" apocalyptic remained living literary forms in the Jewish-

3. The qualification, found at Qumrân, is to be noted. The later editions of Enoch and the Testaments introduce apocalyptic traditions belonging to a different stratum and will be discussed below.

4. See most recently on the Essene origin of Enoch, the Testaments, Jubilees, etc., R. Marcus, "The Qumrân Scrolls and Early Judaism," pp. 9–17. Cf. H. H. Rowley, Jewish Apocalyptic and the Dead Sea Scrolls [Wood Lecture, 1957] (London, 1957), passim; and H. L. Ginsberg, "The Dead Sea Manuscript Finds . . ." pp. 45–49.

5. It is worthy of note that the Qumrân library has not produced works composed in Jewish circles hostile to the sectarians. For example, there is no trace of the strongly pro-Maccabean histories of the Maccabees. See further below, n.7.

Christian community at the same time they were dying in Judaism at large. The direct use of Essene or proto-Essene materials in Christian compositions, and, indeed, the publication of Christian compilations of Essene or proto-Essene sources can now be documented impressively.[6]

6. For example, the early Enoch literature is directly quoted in the New Testament, and had strong influence on several books, notably Revelation (cf. Charles, *Apocrypha and Pseudepigrapha* II, pp. 180 ff). Again, it seems increasingly clear, from provisional examination of the documents of Cave IV, that those views are correct which insist that the received editions of 1 Enoch and the Testaments of the Twelve Patriarchs came from Jewish-Christian hands which supplemented and reworked (rather than merely interpolated) Essene editions. On the (Judeo-) Christian origin of the Testaments, see M. DeJonge, *The Testaments of the Twelve Partriarchs: A Study of Their Text, Composition, and Origin* (Manchester, 1954); Milik's review of DeJonge (in light of Cave IV materials), *RB* 62 (1955), pp. 297–98; and "Le Testament de Lévi en araméen," *ibid.*, pp. 398–406, especially pp. 405–6. Cf. Braun's discussion and citation of older literature, "L'arrière-fond judaïque du quartrième évangile et la Communauté de l'Alliance," *RB* 62 (1955), p. 5, n. 4. Milik has recently identified a second source of the Christian edition of the Testaments at Qumrân, fragments of a Testament of Naphtali, which adds weight to his analysis.

On the Qumrân Enoch literature, see Milik's remarks in "Le travail d'édition. . ." p. 60.

Another illustration is the doctrine of the "Two Ways" found in the Rule of the Community (1QS). The theme is implicit in the Gospel of John (cf. Braum, *op. cit.*, p. 18), and this and like Essene formulations are found in the Didache, the Epistle of Barnabas, and elsewhere. Cf. J.-P. Audet, "Affinités littéraires et doctrinales du 'Manuel de Discipline,'" *RB* 59 (1952), pp. 219–38; 60 (1953), pp. 41–82.

On Essene features in the Jewish-Christian Ebionite movement, see the judicious discussions of O. Cullmann, "Die neuentdeckten Qumran Texte und das Judenchristentum der Pseudoklementinen," in *Neutestamentliche Studien für Rudolf Bultmann* (Berlin, 1951), pp. 35–51; J. A. Fitzmeyer, "The Qumran Scrolls, the Ebionites and their Literature," *Theological Studies* 16 (1955), pp. 335–72.

K. G. Kuhn, in "Les rouleaux de cuivre . . ." p. 203, n.1, has made the plausible suggestion that II Cor. 6:14–7:1 is cited (freely) by Paul from an Essene source.

It is extraordinary that the Essenes are not named in the New Testament. I know of no fully adequate explanation of this circumstance. Certainly it is not to be attributed to ignorance. We may find a partial explanation in the lack of antipathy of the early Church toward the

The full import of the continuities which bind together the earlier apocalyptic communities of Palestine with the primitive Christian community cannot be indicated, however,by reference to the survivals of Essene literary materials in Christian circles or the borrowings of Essene or Hasidic themes in Christian literary composition. We have known some of the Jewish apocalyptic writings from ancient times, of course, and these, together with more recently discovered works belonging to the same tradition, have played an increasingly important part in scientific New Testament studies. It is a commonplace of New Testament research today that the Jewish apocalyptic exerted a profound and direct influence on earliest Christianity. The new finds will extend our knowledge of this literature greatly, to be sure, and give us fresh means to analyze and describe its development[7] as well as its relationship to the Christian apocalyptic.

Essenes. We hear of the other major parties of Judaism largely in polemical passages. On the other hand, there *are* polemical passages in the New Testament which are most easily explained as directed against the Essenes. The best example is Col. 2:16–23, where reference is made to matters of calendar, priestly laws of purity, worship of angels, etc.

7. The later apocalyptic materials, II Baruch, the Similitudes of Enoch (=I Enoch, 37–71), II Enoch, II Esdras (IV Ezra), The Assumption of Moses, the Testaments of the Twelve Patriarchs, *et al.* are not to be found at Qumrân, although in some cases sources of the above-named works or materials of a similar genre are extant. We have noted above that Testaments of Levi and Naphtali, earlier than, but related to the Testaments of the Patriarchs, have been found. The failure of the Similitudes of Enoch to put in an appearance among the multiple fragmentary copies of Enoch from Qumrân is especially noteworthy. As suggested by Milik, the silence of Qumrân in this instance is most impressive, and seems a good indication that this part at least of the Enoch cycle is post-Essene in date, and Christian in its received form. On the pseudo-Jeremianic literature, see J. Strugnell, "Le travail d'édition . . ." p. 65.

Students of the apocalyptic will immediately note that the Qumrân apocalyptic systematically fails to present materials containing allusions to the figure of the "Son of Man" or to a Messianism strongly influenced by elements associated with the "Heavenly Man" (the most recent discussion of these problems together with references to an extensive liter-

Nevertheless, a new factor has entered. We have known little or nothing heretofore of the *Sitz im Leben* of the Jewish apocalyptic, the communities out of whose special faith and life the apocalyptic sprang as a characteristic expression. The background of the institutions and patterns typical of the communal life of the earliest Church in an earlier apocalyptic milieu can now be investigated seriously for the first time. The Essene literature enables us to discover the concrete Jewish setting in which an apocalyptic understanding of history was living and integral to communal existence. Like the primitive Church, the Essene community was distinguished from Pharisaic associations and other movements within Judaism precisely in its consciousness "of being already the called and chosen Congregation of the end of days."[8] Contrary to the tendency of New Testament theologians to assume that the "eschatological existence" of the early Church, that is, its community life lived in anticipation of the Kingdom of God, together with the forms shaped by this life, was a uniquely Christian phenomenon, we must now affirm that in the Essene communities we discover antecedents of Christian forms and concepts.[9]

ature may be found in S. Mowinckel, *He That Cometh* [New York, 1956], pp. 261–450). We must assume that a developed "transcendental" Messianism belonged either to (1) a post-Essene stage of the development of the apocalyptic or, less plausibly, to (2) another, parallel apocalyptic tradition.

8. The phrase is taken from Bultmann (*Theology of the New Testament*, trans., K. Grobel [New York, 1951] Vol. I, p. 42). The full context of Bultmann's phrase is noteworthy: ". . . when regarded from the history-of-religions point of view, the earliest church presents itself as an eschatological sect within Judaism, distinguished from other sects and trends, not only by the fact that it awaits the crucified Jesus of Nazareth as Son of Man, but especially by the fact that it is conscious of being already the called and chosen Congregation of the end of days."

9. The relation of the movement of John the Baptist to the Essenes on the one hand, and to the earliest Christian community on the other, may explain some of these continuities between the early apocalyptic traditions and the eschatological structure of early Christian thought

In the pages to follow we shall investigate the theological
language common to the Essene and Christian sects, the common eschatological doctrines, and the related organizational
and liturgical institutions belonging to the two "apocalyptic
communities." There will be no serious attempt to deal ex-
haustively with the parallels between the Qumrân documents
and the New Testament, even in the areas we have chosen for
discussion.[10] One grows somewhat weary of the listing of

and practice. (Cf. Cullmann, "The Significance of the Qumran Texts
. . ." *JBL* 74 [1955], pp. 218 f.). John himself seems to have derived
from priestly forebears. The little we know of his message fits very
well into the context of the priestly apocalypticism of the Essenes.
Moreover, it is quite likely that the members of his sect formed congregations, and, like the Essenes and early Christians, constituted
themselves a community of the elect, baptized in repentance and in
anticipation of the imminent New Age. On the other hand we cannot
reconstruct either the life or teachings of the Baptist movement in
any detail from the laconic, and sometimes tendentious notices in the
New Testament, so that it is impossible to say, I believe, whether John
and his disciples constituted an Essene splinter group or a parallel
apocalyptic movement. It seems methodologically dubious to argue on
the basis of John's desert life that he was at one time associated with
the desert community of Qumrân. At best we can affirm that there are
contacts between the preaching of John and the teaching of the
Essenes of Palestine (and Qumrân).

Perhaps the strongest argument that the Baptist movement mediated
between the Essene and Christian communities is to be found precisely
in the ambivalence of the New Testament writers' attitude toward
John. On John the Baptist's relationship to the Essenes, see further
Braun, "L'arrière-fond judaïque du quatrième évangile et la Communauté de l'Alliance," pp. 41 f.; Metzinger, "Die Handschriftenfunde
am Toten Meer und das Neue Testament," *Biblica* 36 (1955), pp.
457–81; Brownlee, "John the Baptist in the New Light of Ancient
Scrolls," *Interpretation* 9 (1955), pp. 71–90. (Cf. "A Comparison of
the Covenanters of the Dead Sea Scrolls with Pre-Christian Jewish
Sects," *BA* 13 [1950], pp. 49–72.) Older literature may be found in
Carl H. Kraeling, *John the Baptist* (New York, 1951).

10. Among the many general studies of the Qumrân manuscripts
and the New Testament, we may select the following for special reference: K. G. Kuhn, "Die in Palästina gefundenen hebräischen Texte
und das Neue Testament," *ZTK* 47 (1950), pp. 192–211; W. Gros-
souw, "The Dead Sea Scrolls and the New Testament: A Preliminary
Survey," *Studia Catholica* 26 (1951), pp. 289–99; 27 (1952), pp.

parallels, for parallels as such may be casual or meaningful in determining relationships, depending on the integrity of each side of the parallel in its theological, dogmatic, or cultic context. Rather we propose to investigate certain parallels in theological language, cultic procedures, and ethos which appear to belong to a related apocalyptic framework, and which therefore may illuminate one of the historical lines along which the prophetic faith of "Old Israel" passed, transmitted and transmuted by Essene Judaism, to the "New Israel," the primitive Church.

1. Common Theological Language: The Gospel of John[11]

Linguistic and conceptual contacts between the scrolls and the New Testament are nowhere more in evidence than in the Gospel of John.[12] Such phrases as "the spirit of truth and

1–8; K. G. Kuhn, "πειρασμός-ἁμαρτία-σάρξ im Neuen Testament und die damit zusammenhängenden Vorstellungen," ZTK 49 (1952), pp. 200–22; J. Coppens, "Les documents du Désert de Juda et les origins du Christianisme," Anal. Lovan. II:41 (1953); F.-M. Braun, "L'arrière-fond judaïque du quatrième évangile et la Communauté de L'Alliance," pp. 5–44 (broader than its title indicates); O. Cullmann, "The Significance of the Qumrân Texts for Research into the Beginnings of Christianity," JBL 74 (1955), pp. 213–26; A. Metzinger, "Die Handschriftenfunde am Toten Meer und das Neue Testament," pp. 457–81; Burrows, The Dead Sea Scrolls, Chap. XV, pp. 326–45; Frank M. Cross, "The Dead Sea Scrolls," IB XII, pp. 657–67 (cf. "The Essenes and the New Testament," The Christian Century, August 24, 1955, pp. 968–71; and "The Scrolls from the Judean Desert," Archaeology 9:1 [Spring, 1956], pp. 48–53); R. E. Murphy, "The Dead Sea Scrolls and New Testament Comparisons," CBQ 18 (1956), pp. 263–72; and The Dead Sea Scrolls and the Bible (Westminster, Maryland, 1956), pp. 55–108; W. D. Davies, "The Dead Sea Scrolls and Christian Origins," Religion in Life 26 (1957), pp. 246–63.

11. This section, and parts of sections 2 and 3 of this chapter are a revised and expanded form of material published in the writer's article, "The Dead Sea Scrolls," in Vol. XII of the Interpreter's Bible, copyrighted by the Abingdon Press in 1957. Copyrighted material is used here by permission.

12. Already there is an extensive literature in this field. In

deceit" (I Jn. 4:6),[13] "the light of life" (Jn. 8:12),[14] "to do the
truth" (Jn. 3:21),[15] sons of light (Jn. 12:36),[16] "life eternal"
(Jn. 3:15,16; and *passim*),[17] familiar elements in the Johannine
vocabulary, are also characteristic of the diction of the sectarian writings. More important are the repeatedly contrasted
themes which sound a kind of counterpoint in both Johannine and Essene literature: light and darkness, truth and error
or lying, spirit and flesh, love and hate, death and life. As in
the scrolls, religious "knowing" has a special flavor and wide
usage in John; however, "knowledge" as a revealed, especially
eschatological knowledge, which belongs properly to the community of the saved, its most striking usage in the Essene
literature, has its best parallels in Paul and Matthew.[18] In both

addition to the discussions to be found in the general articles cited
in n. 10, the following articles which deal primarily with Johannine
parallels may be noted: L. Mowry, "The Dead Sea Scrolls and the Background for the Gospel of John," *BA* 17 (1954), pp. 78–97; R. E. Brown,
"The Qumrân Scrolls and the Johannine Gospel and Epistles," *CBQ* 17
(1955), pp. 403–19; 559–74; A. Dupont-Sommer, "La mère du Messie
et la mère de l'Aspic dans un hymne de Qoumran," *RHR* 147 (1955),
pp. 174–88 (parallels to Rev. 12); J. V. Chamberlain, "Another Qumran
Thanksgiving Psalm," *JNES* XIV (1955), pp. 32–41; "Further Elucidation of a Messianic Thanksgiving Psalm from Qumrân," *ibid.*, pp.
181 f.; L. Silberman, "Language and Structure in the *Hodayot*
(1QH3)," *JBL* 75 (1956), pp. 96–106; S. Mowinckel, "Some Remarks on *Hodayot* 39.5–20," *JBL* 75 (1956), p. 276; and W. F. Albright, "Recent Discoveries in Palestine and the Gospel of St.
John," in the *Background of the New Testament and Its Eschatology*,
pp. 153–71.

13. *rwhy 'mt w'wl* (1QS 4:23). *rwḥ 'mt* and *rwḥ 'wl* also appear
standing alone often in Qumrân literature.

14. *b'wr hḥyym* (1QS 3:7).

15. *l'śwt 'mt* (1QS 1:5, etc.).

16. *bny 'wr* (1QS 1:9; and especially 1QM *passim*).

17. *ḥyy nṣh* (1QS 4:7, etc.).

18. Typical of Johannine usage is Jn. 17:3, "And this is life eternal
that they know you, the one true God and him whom you sent, Jesus
Christ" (cf. I Jn. 4:7 f.). Compare 1QS 2:2–3: "May he bless you
with every good thing and keep you from all evil, and illuminate your
heart with the wisdom of life, and favor you with eternal knowledge."

John and the scrolls juridical language is common, and in both may be found a tendency to treat the inner teaching or sacraments of the community as esoteric.[19] The gift of salvation is not known by "flesh," but through the "spirit." "Unless a man be born again of water and the spirit, he cannot enter into the Kingdom of God" (Jn. 3:5); "Then God in his faithfulness (or by his truth) will purify all the works of man, and cleanse for himself the body of man, in order to consume every wicked spirit from the midst of his flesh, and to make him pure with (a) holy spirit from every wicked deed; and he will sprinkle on him (a) spirit of truth like water for impurity . . . so as to give the righteous understanding in the knowledge of the Most High. . ." (1QS 4:20–22.)[20]

In both the Essene literature and in the Johannine writings there is the strongest emphasis on unity and community. The Essenes call themselves the Community,[21] literally the Unity.

On the Johannine use, see R. Bultmann, "γινώσκω, κτλ." *TWzNT*, ed. G. Kittel, Band I, pp. 711–13.

On the usage of "knowledge" in the scrolls and elsewhere in the New Testament, and the relationships to Gnostic usage, see especially K. G. Kuhn, "Die Sektenschrift und die iranische Religion," *ZTK* 49 (1952), pp. 296–316; W. D. Davies, " 'Knowledge' in the Dead Sea Scrolls and Mt. 11:25–30," *HTR* 46 (1953), pp. 113–29; and F. Nötscher, *Zur theologischen Terminologie der Qumran-Texte* (Bonn, 1956), pp. 15–79.

19. On the juridical language of John, see Théo Preiss, *Life in Christ* (London, 1954) (from *La Vie en Christ* [Neuchâtel, 1951]), pp. 4–31. Preiss remarks of the Johannine literature, "In a style of grandiose monotony, it develops a few unchanging themes . . ." (p. 10). No better description could be given of the theological sections of the sectarian document. There can be little doubt that the origins of the Johannine style must be sought after in Essene circles.

On the esoteric elements in John, especially in connection with the Eucharist, see J. Jeremias, *Die Abendmahlsworte Jesu,* 2nd ed. (Göttingen, 1949), pp. 58–62.

20. Cf. Y. Yadin, "A Note on DSD IV:20," *JBL* 74 (1955), pp. 40–43.

21. *hyḥd,* "unity" "togetherness." The translation "community" is poor in English, since it permits secular connotations or the wide English usage to blur its narrow meaning. Moreover, the term in our texts has specific theological overtones; it applies to the "eschatological"

This oneness is a sign of the kingdom which is dawning and to which they belong, and is a gift of the spirit. The Johannine phrases, "that they may be one," "become perfectly one" (Jn. 17:11,21,23) use typical Essene diction.[22] The quality of life in the true community is to be marked by love of brother; this is a basic theme of Essene discipline, and, of course, the repeated motive of the Johannine writings, especially I John. The Essene Rule also requires that one "hate all the children of darkness," even as he must "love all children of light."[23] The note of hate is not characteristic of the New Testament ethic of disinterested love; however, as often has been remarked, the Johannine emphasis, unlike that of the New Testament in general, is almost exclusively on love within the "little flock"; and a note of hostility toward the "world" occasionally appears,[24] which, while milder than the Essene exhortation "to hate," is nevertheless reminiscent of it.

According to Essene doctrine, the world is in the grip of two warring spirits, created by God from the beginning: the Spirit of Truth and the Spirit of Wickedness or Perversity.[25]

community or *Heilsgemeinschaft*, or to its activities "in common" *byhd*, etc.). A good number of the passages in published texts are collected by Habermann, *'dh w'dwt* (Jerusalem, 1952), pp. 136,7. Note such phrases as *byhd 'l, byhd 'mt(w), lbryt yhd 'wlmym, bryt hyhd, lyhd qwdš, byhd'stw, lyhd b'mtw, lyhd bryt 'wlm*, where the normal theological connotations are made explicit.

22. Note the Semitic and presumably "Essene" form of the following: ἵνα ὦσιν τετελειωμένοι εἰς ἕν (Jn. 17:23); *lhywt lyhd* (1QS 5:2); συναγάγῃ εἰς ἕν (Jn. 11:52); *bh'spm lyhd* (1QS 5:7). Cf. Eph. 4:3–5.

23. 1QS 1:9–10; cf. Mt. 5:43,44, which seems to be a reaction against such an emphasis.

24. E. g., I Jn. 2:15; 3:13. See the discussion of Braun, pp. 19,20; and especially Brown, pp. 561–64.

25. On the doctrine of the Spirit at Qumrân, see E. Schweizer, "Gegenwart des Geistes und eschatologische Hoffnung bei Zarathustra, spätjüdischen Gruppen, Gnostikern und den Zeugen des Neuen Testamentes," *The Background of the New Testament and Its Eschatology*, pp. 482–508; and W. D. Davies, "Paul and the Dead Sea Scrolls: Flesh and Spirit," in *The Scrolls and the New Testament*, pp. 157–82.

The Spirit of Wickedness is none other than Belial, the "Prince of Darkness," Satan. The Spirit of Truth is otherwise called the holy spirit (not identical with the Holy Spirit, though often hard to distinguish), the "Prince of Lights," the "Angel of Truth." All men have their "lot" in one of these spirits, and thus are children of light or darkness.[26] These two powers are locked in a titanic warfare, a struggle which mounts to a climax in the last times (compare Revelation and the War scroll). The war is waged, not only between the opposing arrays of spirits and their human hosts, but also within the heart of each "son of light."[27] For the people of the scrolls the end of the war is in sight. God is about to destroy forever the rule of the Spirit of Perversion, and bring an end to all darkness and wickedness. In the Johannine literature, however, although the struggle persists, and a final Armaggedon is to be fought[27a], yet the crisis of the battle is past, Jesus the Christ has "overcome the world" (i.e., the domain of the Prince of Darkness).[28]

Our remarks may be illustrated by the following passage from the Rule of the Community (1QS 3:17–23):

> [God] created man to rule the world and He established two spirits by which (man) would walk until the time appointed for His Visitation (i.e., Last Judgment): these are the spirits of Truth and Deceit (or Wickedness). In a

26. Cf. Jn. 8:42–47; I Jn. 5:19 (as well as II Cor. 6:14–7:11), etc.; and especially 1QS 3:13–4:26.

27. 1QS 4:23–26. It is in this framework that the New Testament concepts of temptation, predestination, and justification must be understood (as well as corresponding ideas in the scrolls). See K. G. Kuhn's admirable analysis, "$\pi\epsilon\iota\rho\alpha\sigma\mu\acute{o}\varsigma$-$\dot{\alpha}\mu\alpha\rho\tau\acute{\iota}\alpha$-$\sigma\acute{\alpha}\rho\xi$ im Neuen Testament . . ." and Nötscher, *Zur theologischen Terminologie der Qumran-Texte*, pp. 173–82. On the scrolls and "justification" see above, Chap. III, n. 85.

27a. *Pace* Bultmann.

28. See Father Brown's discussion, pp. 410–12. On the *Kampf-situation* in the thought of Jesus, see Kuhn, pp. 219 ff., who draws attention to the following pertinent passages: Mt. 10:34; Mt. 12:28 f. and parallels.

source of light are the origins of (the Spirit of) Truth and from a well of darkness the origins of (the Spirit of) Error. The rule of the children of righteousness is in the hand of the Prince of Light (so that) they walk in ways of light; the rule of [all] children of error is in the hand of the Angel of Darkness (so that) they walk in ways of darkness; and when any of the children of righteousness err, it is through the Angel of Darkness . . . and all the spirits allotted to him (attempt to) make the children of light stumble, but the God of Israel and His Angel of Truth are a help to all sons of light.

The passage may be compared with the following citations from I John:

Children let no one lead you astray. He who does righteousness is righteous, as he is righteous; he who commits sin is of the devil, for the devil has sinned from the beginning. To this end the Son of God was made manifest, that he might destroy the works of the devil. None that is born of God commits sin, for His seed abides in him (so that) he is not able to sin, because he is born of God. By this the children of God are made known, and the children of the devil. Everyone who does not do righteousness is not of God . . . (I Jn. 3:7–10.)

Beloved, do not trust every spirit, but test the spirits, whether they are from God . . . By this you know the spirit of God: every spirit which confesses that Jesus Christ has come in flesh is from God, and every spirit which does not confess Jesus is not from God; and this is the (spirit) of the antichrist . . . Children, you are of God, and have conquered them, for he who is in you is greater than he who is in the world. They are of the world; for this reason what they say is of the world and the world listens (obediently) to them. We are of God; he who knows God listens to us; he who is not of God does not listen to us. By this we know the Spirit of Truth and the Spirit of Deceit. (I Jn. 4:1–6)

In both the Rule and I John we recognize a similar "spirit-spirit" dualism, a powerful doctrine of predestination which allots some to God or the Spirit of Truth, others to the devil or the Spirit of Deceit. In both, the diabolical spirit struggles against the children of God (or of light). In both, the children of light have knowledge which permits them to distinguish between the spirits of truth and deceit. Because of the aid of God or the Spirit of Truth, the children of light do righteousness, but those under the dominion of the devil walk in ways of darkness. We have noted above that the work of Jesus gives a new note of victory. We may note also that the Johannine dualism is differently expressed. In the Johannine literature the Spirit is normally God's own spirit or Christ's own spirit (cf. I John 4:13). In the Qumrân Rule the Spirit of Truth has a "greater distance" from God; the hypostatized Spirit *of* God has become largely identified with an angelic creature, the spirit *from* God, and their functions combined.[28a]

The "Prince of Light" or "Spirit of Truth" is appointed, according to the Essenes, as a *helper* to all children of light.[29] The figure of the *Paraclete* or Advocate of John (Jn. 14:17; 15:26; 16:13; I Jn. 5:6–8[30]) is derived from this complex of ideas. His function, described as "to witness," to "intercede," "to speak," yet "*not on his own authority*" (Jn. 16:13), has always been puzzling, for it does not fit the expected description of

28a. Cf. the remarks of W. D. Davies on the differences between the doctrine of the Spirit of God in the New Testament and the doctrine of the two spirits in the Qumrân literature in his article, "Paul and the Dead Sea Scrolls: Flesh and Spirit," *the Scrolls and the New Testament*, pp. 157–82.

29. Cf. 1QM 13:10 *šr m'wr m'z pqdth l'wzrnw;* 1QS 3:24, 25 *w'l yšr'l wml'k 'mtw 'zr lkwl bny 'wr;* and 1QM 17:6–8.

30. Often in the Johannine material the functions of the Spirit of Truth as (1) bearer of light, (2) leader of the armies of God, and (3) Advocate or witness are shifted to the Christ. Cf. (1) Jn. 9:5; 12:46; (2) Rev. 12:7–12 parallel to 19:11–21; and (3) I Jn. 2:1.

the Holy Spirit. And the origin and meaning of the term *Paraclete* as an appellation of the Spirit of Truth has been much in dispute.[31] In the light of the new Essene parallels, we now understand the title and vocation of the Advocate/ Spirit of Truth for the first time with some clarity.

The origin of the concept is found in the heavenly court of Yahweh in the Old Testament where in scenes of judgment Satan as prosecuting attorney stands over against the Angel of the Lord as advocate or witness.[32] In the elaborate angelology and dualism of the Essenes, partly under Iranian influence, the Old Testament origins are blurred and transmuted so that the two angels become the two opposing principles or spirits of truth and error, light and darkness. In the cosmic struggle the heavenly accuser becomes the diabolical tempter of the

31. As early as 1933, S. Mowinckel, on the basis chiefly of Essene material in the Testaments of the Twelve Patriarchs, was able to reconstruct much of the Old Testament and Jewish background of the *Paraclete* figure. See his studies, "Die Vorstellungen der Spätjudentums von heiligen Geist als Fürsprecher und der johanneische Paraklet," *ZNW* 32 (1933), pp. 97–130; and "Hiobs gō'ēl und Zeuge im Himmel," in *Vom Alten Testament* (Marti Festschrift), ed. K. Budde (Geissen, 1925), pp. 207–12; Cf. N. Johannson, *Parakletoi* (Lund, 1940), pp. 3–178; and especially Théo Preiss, *Life in Christ*, pp. 19–25.

However, Mowinckel's work has been widely ignored, especially by members of the Bultmann school in Germany; this is unfortunate since the new texts (e.g., those quoted in n. 29) directly support Mowinckel. The opinion of Bultmann himself has been expressed most recently in his *Theology of the New Testament* I (New York, 1955), p. 88n. For the present state (pre-Qumrân!) of the discussion, see W. Michaelis, "Zur Herkunft des johanneische Paraklet-Titels," in *Coniectanea Neotestamentica* XI (Lund 1947), pp. 147–62; G. Bornkamm, "Der Paraklet in Johannesevangelium," in *Festschrift Rudolf Bultmann* (Stuttgart, 1949), pp. 12–35.

32. See especially I Kings 22:19–24; Zech. 3; and Job, especially in 16:19 and 19:25 where the "Heavenly Witness" is to be identified with the "Angel of the Lord," as first pointed out by Mowinckel (see above n. 31; called to my attention by Professor G. Ernest Wright). The function of the angel, or divine messenger as witness in heavenly court scenes is found already in ancient Canaanite mythology (as I have been reminded by G. E. Mendenhall).

sons of light, the Prince of Darkness who is at war with the Prince of Light. The heavenly advocate becomes the Spirit of Truth, a holy spirit which testifies to truth in the heart of those in the "inheritance" of truth, as well as the accuser of the children of darkness.[33] In John the Essene dualism is partly resolved, but reflections of the Essene structure of thought still survive. This is especially clear in the Johannine advocate, but also to a lesser degree in the special function of the Spirit in Acts and in Paul.

These Essene parallels to John and the Johannine Epistles will come as a surprise only to those students of John who have attempted to read John as a work under strong Greek influence. It now turns out—as a small coterie of scholars have long maintained—that John has its strongest affinities, not with the Greek world, or Philonic Judaism, but with Palestinian Judaism. Its concepts of truth, knowledge, spirit, and even the Word[34] must be seen, not as rooted in Greek or Gnostic thought, but as concepts emerging precisely out of sectarian Judaism. So that rather than being the most Hellenistic of the Gospels, John now proves to be in some ways the most Jewish.

Ultimately these conclusions will bear on critical theories in regard to the origin of John.[35] We must look for a *Sitz im Leben* for the development of Johannine tradition where Jewish Christianity was dominant, and where Essene influences persisted. Some have suggested that John may be

33. Cf. Test. of Judah 20. Preiss (*Life in Christ,* p. 20) comments on this passage, "Similarly in Jn. 16:7 ff. the Spirit of Truth will convict the world of sin . . . It plays the part of accuser before the world . . . But as soon as man has received the truth in faith the roles are reversed; the Satanic Spirit of Error will seek to accuse him . . . while the Spirit of Truth as Paraclete will witness to him of the certainty of the love of God."

34. Actually, no equivalent of $\dot{o}$ $\lambda\acute{o}\gamma o\varsigma$ in the Johannine sense can be documented in the scrolls. However, intimate parallels to the Prologue of John, in style, content, and vocabulary appear in the new documents. Cf. Braun, pp. 15–16; 1QS 11:11; 1QS 3:15–17.

35. See especially, W. F. Albright, "Recent Discoveries in Palestine . . ."

regarded no longer as the latest and most evolved of the Gospels, but the most primitive, and that the formative locus of its tradition was Jerusalem before its destruction. This is not to suggest that the present form of the book has not had an elaborate literary history; the point is that John preserves authentic historical material which first took form in an Aramaic or Hebrew milieu where Essene currents still ran strong.

2. *Some Common Eschatological Motifs*

Both the Essenes and the primitive Church believed that the last age was imminent; indeed they were living in the last times; they were the last generation. In some sense the new age had dawned; at least its signs were discernible in the events of their day. History had reached its crisis. The powers of darkness and light were poised for the final, decisive struggle. The Church was exhorted to "put on the full armor of God . . . to stand against the wiles of the devil . . . to be able to withstand the evil day, and having done so to stand" (Ephes. 6:10–17); the Essenes divided their little community into battle divisions and drew up a liturgy of Armageddon.

In the prophecies of the Old Testament the Essenes saw predicted the events of their own day.[36] Where the prophets spoke of the last days and their signs (and even where they did not), the sectarian commentators discovered fulfillment in the history of their own times or in the inner life of their sect. Those with "knowledge" should now recognize that the final war had begun. They must "decide," understanding by faith and the spirit the fulfillment of prophecy, expectant of the consummation of history.

Of themselves the Essenes wrote, quoting Isaiah: "When these things come to pass in Israel to the Community . . . they will separate themselves from the midst of the abode of

36. See Chap. III, *ad loc.*

perverse men to go into the desert to prepare there the way of the Lord according as it is written, 'In the desert prepare ye the Way (of the Lord), make straight in the wilderness a highway for our God' " (1QS 8:12–14).

Thus this people understood themselves to be in the situation of John the Baptist, of whom the New Testament quotes the identical passage of Isaiah. Jesus' early teachings are in much the same eschatological framework.[37] The man in the early Church lives in a "later" moment. He believes that the Messiah has come and that his resurrection signals the beginning of the New Creation. Yet he lives in a like tension. The Kingdom delays, the "world" remains. He must partake proleptically of life in the Kingdom to come, anticipating the coming day when ambiguity will end, the world be transformed, an end be brought to all wicked flesh, and the Kingdom of God fulfilled.

The Essenes therefore search the Scriptures and interpret their prophecies eschatologically. As several scholars have pointed out, Essene exegesis has no real parallel either in Rabbinic Judaism, or in Philonic Judaism.[38] Their interpretation is neither legalistic nor allegorical. But it falls precisely into the pattern of the New Testament's use of the Old Testament. In both, exegesis is "historical" (i.e., eschatological), and pneumatic.[39]

37. Cf. James M. Robinson, "Jesus' Understanding of History," *JBR* 1955, pp. 17–24.

38. Cf. L. Mowry, "The Dead Sea Scrolls and the Gospel of John," pp. 93 f. G. Vermès in his article "À propos des Commentaires biblique découverts à Qumrân," *RHPR* 35, pp. 95–102, after distinguishing the Qumrân *pĕšārîm* from both the *midrash* and Philonic exegesis, attempts to find parallels in the Targumim, but without notable success. Cf. C. Rabin, "Notes on the Habakkuk Scroll and the Zadokite Documents," *VT* V (1955), pp. 148–62.

39. Krister Stendahl in his volume, *The School of St. Matthew* (Uppsala, 1954), pp. 181–202, has stressed the affinity between presuppositions and style in quoting the Old Testament in Essene and New Testament composition. He notes the "apocalyptic" character of Old Testament interpretation common to both, but also attempts more pre-

The Essenes believed themselves to be the people of the New Covenant. They yearly celebrated the renewing of this New or "Eternal" Covenant,[40] no doubt recalling Jeremiah's prediction of a new covenant (Jer. 31:31). They understood this "New Covenant" to be at once the "renewed (old) covenant" and the "eternal covenant" to be established at the end of days; i.e., precisely in the New Testament sense.

The Essenes had a most developed Messianism. They expected an eschatological prophet recalling Deuteronomy 18:15–18.[41] This figure has a counterpart in the New Testament in John the Baptist. However, it is interesting that in John's Gospel, the Baptist denies that he is Elijah, and also that he is the expected prophet, implying that Jesus is the prophet to come.[42] And in Acts 3:22 Jesus is identified in Peter's sermon precisely with the prophet of Deuteronomy

cise definition of what he calls the *péšer* mode of citation and interpretation, common to Qumrân commentaries and certain of the quotations of the Old Testament in the New, especially "the formula quotations" of Matthew. Here he finds a freedom of citation based partly on a thorough knowledge of Hebrew text types and translations, partly on techniques which permit the learned expositor to manipulate an Old Testament passage to fit sectarian interests. Stendahl wrote before the character of the Old Testament text at Qumrân had become fully known, so that his work presumes a view of the Old Testament text which virtually identifies the text of the early Christian era with the single Masoretic tradition. In view of the relatively fluid state of the Old Testament in the earliest Christian period, his results must be qualified at a number of points.

The question of testimonia lists allegedly used in composition of New Testament works must also be re-examined in light of our new knowledge of the complex character of the Hebrew text in the early Christian period, and, as well, in light of the testimonia literature from Qumrân.

40. J. T. Milik in an oral communication indicates that on the basis of new data, including a reading in an unpublished text, he can establish that the festival of the New Covenant among the sectarians fell on Pentecost (i.e., at the traditional time when the law was given at Sinai). This suggests intriguing possibilities for interpreting the setting of the event of Pentecost in the New Testament.

41. Cf. 1QS 9:11; and 4Q Testimonia.

42. Jn. 1:21, 25; 6:14; 7:40.

18:15–18.[43] Moreover, the category of "Messianic prophet" has left many traces in the earliest Church's interpretation of the work of Jesus.

A second eschatological figure is the Anointed Priest. He is the faithful priest of prophecy, the Star of Jacob, the Messiah of Aaron.[44] He is the primary figure of the New Age in the priestly apocalypticism of the Essenes. Jesus is never specifically designated the Messiah of Aaron, though there are reminiscences of this and like categories in the New Testament.[45] In the Testament of Joseph[46] the Messianic priest is called the Lamb, who takes precedence over the Lion of Judah, the royal Messiah; no doubt we must combine this figure with that of the *militant* Lamb in Revelation. Most obvious is the interpretation of Jesus as the heavenly high

43. On the Ebionite identification of Jesus with the "true prophet," see Fitzmyer, "The Qumrân Scrolls, the Ebionites and Their Literature," pp. 356–58.

44. In addition to Milik's study in *DJD I*, pp. 121 f., see K. G. Kuhn, "Die beiden Messias Aarons und Israel," *NTS* I (1954/55), pp. 168–79; G. Friedrich, "Beobachtungen zur messianischen Hohepriesterwartung in den Synoptikern," *ZTK* 53 (1956), pp. 265–311, especially the introductory survey; W. H. Brownlee, "Messianic Motifs of Qumrân and the New Testament," *NTS* 3 (1956/57), pp. 12–30; and the excellent study of R. E. Brown, "The Messianism of Qumrân," *CBQ* 19 (1957), pp. 53–82. Literature predating the publication of 1QSa and 1QSb, especially, and to some degree that predating the partial publication of 4Q Testimonia, "Patriarchal Blessings," and "Florilegium," is now antiquated. One may be singled out for its perception, M. Burrows, "The Messiahs of Aaron and Israel," *ATR* 1952, pp. 203–6.

45. G. Friedrich (*op. cit.*, pp. 275–305) has attempted to demonstrate that strong traces of a priestly Messianism are to be found in the Synoptics, and proposes that alongside the Christologies of the Davidic Messiah, the Suffering Servant, and the "Son of Man," we must now make room for a high-priestly Christology. In detail, however, his analysis is rarely convincing.

46. Chap. 19. To be sure there is a Christian hand visible in the chapter, and any attempt to analyze the elements into older and later strands is bound to be partly subjective; nevertheless, it appears that the figures of the Lamb and Lion stand behind the present form of the text.

priest in the Epistle to the Hebrews.[47] Here Jesus is the combined priestly and royal Anointed in the type of Melchizedek, the priest-king of Salem in the days of Abraham. One suspects a conscious attempt of the early Church to adjust its Christology to the Messianic expectations of the Essenes, or rather to see in its single Messianic figure the fulfillment of all the Messianic longings of the past.[48]

The Essenes also expected the coming of the Davidic or royal Messiah. He would be lay head of the New Israel, commander of the troops in the Final War, and universal king.[49] Various proof texts of the Old Testament are quoted by the Essenes predicting the scion of David, some of which are used of Jesus in the New Testament. Of course the identification of Jesus as the Davidic Christ or Messiah of Israel dominates New Testament confessions.

The Messianic doctrine of the Essenes, including certain of its peculiar features, is closely related to that of the early Church. In both, the Messiah(s) appear in the end of days to receive an eternal kingdom; in each the royal Messiah appears bearing a sword, and defeats the earthly and cosmic powers of wickedness; in both there are priestly, royal, and prophetic elements in their Messianic expectations. There are also noteworthy distinctions. Nowhere at Qumrân, at least so far, is there a hint of "highest" New Testament Christology: the pre-existence of the Messiah, the Second Adam, the Son of Man. In the (later edition of the) Testament of Levi, Chapter 18, in a hymn to the Messianic high priest, we find passages reminiscent of these doctrines. The Messiah here leads the return to Paradise and feeds the saints upon the tree of life. However, the material is suspect and cannot be used to

47. Rev. 17:14 (cf. T. Jos. 19:8!). Cf. Charles, *The Revelation of St. John* [ICC] I, pp. cxiii f.; especially n. 2.

48. Cf. G. Friedrich, *op. cit.*, p. 303.

49. Cf. 4QpIsa. D: 1–5; 1QSb V: 20–29; 1QM 5:1; 12:10–15 (?); 1QSa II:11–22; 4Q Patr. Blessings; 4Q Florilegium; etc.

Note in 1QSb:V:29, the prince is compared with a lion. Cf. Rev. 5:5, the "Lion of Judah"; Test. Jos. 19:8; etc.

establish Essene doctrine. In short, both in Essene circles and in the early Church we find a developed apocalyptic Messianism.[50] In the Qumrân literature, however, the Messiah has not yet become a heavenly savior. Nor is there any evidence in the Essene documents that the Messianic figures were confused or combined as they were in the early Church's Christology.[51][52]

The question may be raised as to the role of the Righteous Teacher in the eschatology of the Essenes. He was an "eschatological" figure predicted in Scripture who was to aid in bringing the New Age to birth.[53] Is he one of the three, prophet, priest, or king?

The vocation of the Righteous Teacher during his lifetime must be described as that of forerunner of the Messianic figures. I think there can be no question of his disciples attributing Messianic rank to a Teacher who died before the full dawning of the Messianic age and remained dead during the subsequent life of the sect![54] This need not prejudice neces-

50. Cf. above Chap. III, n. 63, and Brown, pp. 59–63, 79.

51. Dupont-Sommer has argued (cf. "Le Testament de Lévi [XVII-XVIII] et la secte juive de l'alliance," pp. 47–53) that the three offices were combined and applied to the Righteous Teacher. His crucial evidence is drawn from the Testaments of the Twelve Patriarchs, evidence which appears to us to be inadmissible.

52. W. H. Brownlee, "Messianic Motifs of Qumrân . . ." pp. 17–30, has suggested that the motif of the Suffering Servant is applied to the Messiah and to the eschatological Prophet in the Qumrân literature adumbrating the identification of Jesus with the Servant of II Isaiah. He builds his case essentially on two crucial passages: 1QS 4:20–23 and 1QH 3:6–18. The interpretation of both is disputed. On the former, the interpretation of Y. Yadin, "A Note on DSD IV, 20," *JBL* 74 (1955), pp. 40–43, seems clearly superior to that of Brownlee. As to the latter, I am inclined to a non-Messianic interpretation (Mowinckel, Silberman, *et al.* cf. n. 12); but even if the Messianic interpretation is assumed, it would seem to have no necessary connection with the theme of the *suffering* Messiah.

53. See Chap. III, esp. n. 82.

54. There are no references to a resurrection of the Righteous Teacher in the Qumrân literature; on pHab. 11:4–8, see Elliger *SzHK* 213–18; R. de Vaux, *RB* 58 (1951), pp. 437 ff.

sarily the question of a possible second coming of the Teacher in the Age-to-Come.[54a] Among the least ambiguous passsages relating to the Messianic figures are the following:

> All the men who entered into the New Covenant in the "Land of Damascus," but have again acted faithlessly and turned aside from the well of living water, shall not be reckoned in the council of the people, nor inscribed in their book, from the day the Teacher of the Community died until the Messiah(s) of Aaron and of Israel arise.[55] [*CD* 19:34 (=8:21)–20:1]
>
> . . . and they shall not deviate from the whole counsel of the Torah to walk in any stubbornness of their (own) heart but shall be judged by the first decisions (laws) by which the men of the Community commenced to be disciplined, until a Prophet comes and the Messiahs of Aaron and Israel. (1QS 9:9–11.)

The former passage cleanly separates the Messianic advents from the lifetime of the Teacher. The latter asserts that the rules of the Community, presumably enacted in the early days by the Teacher and his flock, are binding until the coming of an eschatological prophet and the appearance of the priestly and royal Messiahs. This appears to distinguish between the work of the Teacher in establishing the community and the work of the Prophet who appears alongside the Messiahs.[56]

While in Judaism the forerunners of the Messianic age include Elijah and the "prophet like Moses,"[57] I do not believe

54a. Cf. K. Stendahl, "The Scrolls and the New Testament, an Introduction and a Perspective."

55. . . . *mywm h'sp* [] *mwrh hyh<>d 'd 'md mšyh<y>* (with Kuhn, Milik, *et al.*) *m'hrn wmyśr'l.* If the form *mšyh* is not emended, the same sense is gained by reading "the Messiah from Aaron and (the one) from Israel." Cf. 1QS 9:9–11.

56. Cf. Brown, pp. 73 f.

57. On the concept of "forerunner" in Jewish eschatology, see most

that the Teacher is to be thought of as a prophetic forerunner. He is, of course, a Zadokite priest. This need not disqualify him from a prophetic office. And certain of his gifts and works suggest prophetic powers. He understands all the words of the prophets by divine inspiration. He opens the books of the Law. However, the high priest properly performed an oracular function,[58] and the late high priests claimed gifts of prophecy.[59] Moreover, teaching is first of all a priestly function.[60] If our interpretation of the Testimonia is correct, the passage quoting Deuteronomy 33:8–11 relating to the oracular and teaching duties of the priesthood is applied by the sect to the Righteous Teacher,[61] following (1) the passage relating to the prophet like Moses, and (2) the Star and the Scepter, the priestly and royal Messiahs respectively. Moreover, the revealed title of the Essene Master is precisely "Righteous Teacher." While he may be referred to in other ways, the title par excellence chosen by the sect from ancient prophecy[62] is neither a prophetic nor Messianic designation. It is a priestly designation, chosen, we suspect, because other traditional titles were for one reason or another less appropriate. A parallel may be found in the Johannine designation of John the Baptist. Here John is portrayed as rejecting the titles of Christ, Elijah, and "the prophet." He is a forerunner, to be sure, but who? The solution is to name him "the Voice crying in the Wilderness." So a new title for the forerunner is sought out to fit John's circumstances. Similarly, to the question,

recently, Mowinckel, *He That Cometh*, pp. 298–302. Mowinckel also takes the Righteous Teacher to be a forerunner.

58. Cf. the "ephod of prophecy" given to Levi in T. Levi, 8:2; the title "False Oracle" taken from prophetic contexts in sectarian exposition (see above Chap. III, esp. nn. 88, 89.) presumes the "prophetic" office of high priest, Cf. K. Elliger *SzHK*, p. 209.

59. Cf. Josephus, *Antiq*. XIII, 288–98; 300; etc.; Jn. 11:51.

60. In *CD* 5:5 Zadok is portrayed as an inspired teacher of Torah. Cf. also the discussion of the expression *dôrēš hat-tôrāh*, n. 71.

61. See above, Chap. III, esp. nn. 80–82.

62. Cf. Chap. III, n. 82.

"Is the Essene master the prophet, the Messiah of Aaron or Israel?" I think we must answer: "No, he is the Righteous Teacher of Scripture."

We have been speaking of the Righteous Teacher's role as forerunner during his ministry. There is, however, a further question. Is the Righteous Teacher to return after death, and if so, will he appear as prophet, priest, king—or as righteous teacher?

There is one passage which can be utilized plausibly to suggest the reappearance of the Righteous Teacher in the Messianic age. This is a well-known and long-debated passage from the Damascus Document, an exposition of Numbers 21:18.[63] The expositor is describing events during the epoch of the "ruin of the land" or the epoch of "wickedness."

But God remembered the covenant of the forefathers, and raised up from Aaron men of understanding, and from Israel wise men, and he made them listen (obediently), so that they dug the well, *the well which the princes dug, which the nobles of the people delved with the staff* (meḥôqēq). *The well* is the Torah, and *those who dig it* are the penitents of Israel who went out from the land of Judah and sojourned in the Land of Damascus . . .

And the *Staff* (mᵉḥôqēq) is the expositor of the Law (dôrēš hat-tôrāh) . . . and *the nobles of the people* are those that come to dig the well with precepts (mᵉḥôqᵉqôt) which the Staff laid down, that they might walk in them during the whole epoch of wickedness. Except for them they cannot grasp (the Law)[64] until the Righteous Teacher[65] arises in the end of days (6:2–11).

The last phrase, "until the Righteous Teacher arises in the

---

63. Direct quotations from Numbers are in italics.

64. See Rabin, *The Zadokite Fragments*, pp. 22,23.

65. Usually the biblical title is distorted to môrēh haṣ-ṣédeq; here it is yôrēh haṣ-ṣédeq.

end of days" is in itself ambiguous; it may apply to the contemporary life of the sect seen from the perspective of the "whole era of wickedness" or it may refer to the Messianic era after the death of the Righteous Teacher. Context must determine which is the correct understanding. The era of the "devastation of the land,"[66] otherwise called the "era of wrath,"[67] applies to the interval between the demise of the Davidic kingdom[68] before the power of Babylon,[69] and the rise of the sect. The exposition of Numbers 21:18 here as elsewhere is applied to the sect itself, not to the ancient Jewish community.[70]

The crux of the passage is the identification of the Staff, the expositor of the Law. He holds a priestly office.[71] He is a figure of the past, possibly of the remote past,[72] more likely of the time of the beginnings of the sect. In the latter case he is most easily identified with the Righteous Teacher or with an early Hasidic leader, a precursor of the Teacher at the earliest beginnings of the sect, twenty years before the in-

66. *CD* 5:20–21.

67. *CD* 1:5–6.

68. *CD* 3:9–10.

69. *CD* 1:5–6.

70. Cf. *CD* 8:35 (19:21); Chap. II, n. 46.

71. The term "Staff" in 4Q Patr. Blessings applies to the historical, royal covenant of David. The term *dôrēš hat-tôrāh*, however, applies to the priestly office of teaching or studying the Law. In *CD* 7:18–19 it is applied to the *Star*, the priestly Messiah, the counterpart of the Scepter, the royal Messiah: "the *Star* is the expositor of the Law who comes to Damascus" (*hb' dmśq*, i.e., who will come to the Essene community). In 4QFlor. the expositor of the Law is associated with the Davidic Messiah and hence we most easily take the expression to apply to the priestly office, in this instance again the priestly Messiah: "He is the Scion of David who arises (*h'wmd*, i.e., who will arise; the participial construction is the same as in the preceeding quotation) with the expositor of the Law."

72. See the writer's remarks in his *Interpreter's Bible* article, p. 664, n. 117; an identification in the remote past, with Aaron or Zadok, now appears less likely to me.

itiation of the Teacher's ministry.[73] In some respects, identification with a Hasidic founder seems the better solution of the two. It would explain the fact that the Staff is not specifically called the Righteous Teacher, and the expression "until the Righteous Teacher arises in the end of days" need apply only to the ministry of the Righteous Teacher as forerunner.

If indeed we identify the Staff with the Righteous Teacher, then it follows that the Teacher is expected to return in the Messianic era. Under this hypothesis, we can then proceed to the conclusion that he will return as the priestly Messiah. His priestly lineage disqualifies him as a candidate for the Davidic Messiahship; and it is unlikely that the Righteous Teacher would properly function as an inspired interpreter of prophecy alongside the priestly Messiah.

There are obvious difficulties in this whole line of argument. The Teacher of Righteousness is nowhere explicitly identified with the coming priestly Messiah.[74] He is not specifically

73. Cf. CD 1:5–11. S. Mowinckel ("The Hebrew Equivalent of Taxo in Ass. Mos. ix," *Supplement to VT* I [Leiden, 1953], pp. 88–96; cf. *He That Cometh*, pp. 300 f.) has identified the man called Taxo in the Assumption of Moses with the Staff of the Damascus Document arguing that τάξων is the Greek equivalent of *meḥôqēq*. The combination is the best suggested to date, though not wholly certain. Taxo was of the tribe of Levi, according to the Assumption, and in a time of a second dreadful visitation (that is, after the Babylonian captivity), exhorted his sons to fast three days, and then on the fourth enter a cave and die in order that God's Kingdom come. There is nothing historically impossible in identifying Taxo either with the Righteous Teacher or with a Hasidic predecessor of the Teacher.

74. John Allegro, in his article, "Further Messianic References in Qumrân Literature," assumes that the appearance of the epithet, "expositor of the Law," in a context where it is clearly applied to the priestly Messiah (4Q Flor.) proves that the Teacher must be identified with the priestly Messiah. Actually the importance of the new passage is that it tends to confirm the view that the Star associated with the Scepter in *CD* 7:18–19 is the *priestly* Messiah. The expression "expositor of the Law" is not a "revealed" title of an eschatological figure named in Scripture. More probably it designates a priestly function appropriate to the Staff of history, to the priest of the New Age, or to the Righteous Teacher. As it happens, however, the expression is never associated directly with the title "Righteous Teacher."

identified with the Staff. It is noteworthy that the one passage which makes plausible this series of deductions is in the Damascus Document, and that all the literature from Qumrân has not yielded sufficient data to resolve the question. If the Essenes did expect their Teacher to return as the priestly Messiah, they have been exceedingly indirect in expressing their hope. The New Testament preoccupation with the death and Messiahship of Jesus is in significant contrast.[74a] Perhaps the whole question is best left unsettled until new data are forthcoming from the caves of Qumrân.

3. The Order and Liturgical Institutions of the "Apocalyptic Communities"

The scroll material is especially rich in materials which illuminate the origins of the organizational structure of the early Church, especially the Church in Acts.[75] Throughout

In connection with the expression *dôrēš hat-tôrāh*, it may be noted that in 1QS 6:5 the rule is laid down that in each Essene community there must be one who functions as the expositor of the Law, *'yš dwrš btwrh*. Cf. 5:11, 8:15, Jubilees 23:26, etc.

Allegro argues in effect that the Righteous Teacher=the Staff; the Staff=the expositor of the Law; the expositor of the Law=the priestly Messiah. Therefore the Righteous Teacher=the priestly Messiah. That is, a=b; b=c; c=d; *ergo*, a=d. This logic would be excellent if Mr. Allegro were not dealing with apocalyptists, who unfortunately do not lay out their materials mathematically. One could add another step: the Staff=the Davidic covenant; *ergo*, the Righteous Teacher is the Davidic covenant (a=b; b=e; e=a). Furthermore, his first equation is not clearly established; and if our understanding of *dôrēš hat-tôrāh* as an (ideal) priestly function is correct, then Allegro can prove at best that each of these figures . . . expounds the Torah.

74a. Cf. the writer's remarks in the *New Republic*, April 9, 1956, p. 19.

75. See especially, S. E. Johnson, "The Dead Sea Manual of Discipline and the Jerusalem Church of Acts," *ZAW* 66 (1954), pp. 106–20; B. Reicke, "Die Verfassung der Urgemeinde im Lichte jüdischer Dokumente," *ThZ* 10 (1954), pp. 95–112; Cross, "The Scrolls and the New Testament," the *Christian Century*, August 24, 1955, pp. 968–71; J.

the history of Christianity there have been debates concerning
the nature of Church government in Apostolic times. Some
have contended that the order was democratic, government
without stated offices, others that it was presbyterian, following the practice of the synagogue, still others that its form of
government was monarchic, governed by bishops. Actually
elements of each of these types of organization appear in the
New Testament. Scholars have increasingly attempted to fit
them into an evolution moving from the free and congre-
gational order to a more rigid monarchic structure.

The Essenes were a priestly and lay community, governed
by hereditary priests in cultic affairs, by laymen in their common religious and "secular" life. There is, of course, no precise
counterpart in Christianity to the dominance of the Aaronic
office. The organization of the Essenes is most instructive,
however, once this qualification is made.

The ruling assembly of the Essenes, made up of all the
mature members of the covenanted community is called the
Rabbîm, literally, the "Many." It is a technical term in Hebrew
which appears in literal translation in the New Testament
with similar technical meaning.[76] The Jerusalem council is so
designated in Acts 15:12; the assembly which chooses the
Seven and places them before the Apostles is so named in
Acts 6:2,5; Silas and Judas together with Paul and Barnabas
assemble the "Many" of the Church at Antioch to hear the
report of the "Many"in Jerusalem (15:30).

Within the "Many" was a higher judicatory consisting of
twelve laymen and three priests. These were the types of the
twelve princes of the tribal assembly in the Mosaic era, together with three priests representing the princes of the three

Daniélou, "La communauté de Qumrân et l'organization de l'Eglise
ancienne," *RHPR* 35 (1955), pp. 104–15.

76. The same term may be applied in non-sectarian Judaism with
reference to members of a synagogue or *ḥªbûrāh;* in this case it does
not, apparently, carry the technical meaning of a body with democratic
powers.

clans of Levi,[77] as seems clear from the role and number of the princes in the War scroll. The circle of the Twelve in the early Church in part parallels the Essene Twelve. For example, the Essene inner circle, according to the Rule of the Community, when it is established in Israel (in the last days) will be ". . . an eternal planting (Is. 60:21; 61:3), a holy temple for Israel . . . faithful witnesses in judgment, the Elect of (God's) favor to atone for the earth, and to mete out punishment to the wicked. It (the inner circle) is the tried (foundation) wall (misquoting Is. 28:16), the precious corner whose foundations shall not be shaken . . ."[78] Revelation 21:14 (cf. Eph. 2:20; Heb. 11:10) alludes to the same passage (Is. 28:16; cf. Ezek. 48:31), recording that the wall of the New Jerusalem "had twelve foundations and on them the names of the twelve Apostles of the Lamb." In Luke 22:30 Jesus addresses the Twelve: "You are those who have continued with me in my trials; as my father appointed a kingdom for me, so do I appoint for you that you may eat and drink at my table in my kingdom, and sit on thrones *judging the twelve tribes* of Israel." Here again is the theme of the twelve "judges" of the *eschaton* after the pattern of the old princes of the tribal assembly of Israel.[79]

Finally, to mount another stage, the highest office of the Essene community, aside from that of the presiding priest, was that of the inspector, *mᵉbaqqēr*.[80] He was president of the sessions of the "Many," fiscal agent of the community, director of labors, religious and secular, in charge of training

77. This was first called to my attention by J. T. Milik.

78. 1QS 8:5–8.

79. Compare also the more general application of Is. 28:16 to the Church in I Pet. 2:4-5. The two figures, the "planting" and the "building" used in the Essene text are also combined in application to the Church in I Cor. 3:9. Of course the description of the Church in the figure of a holy temple is a familiar motif in Pauline writings (I Cor. 3:16; II Cor. 6:16).

80. *mᵉbaqqēr* probably has as its Greek equivalent ἐπιμελητής, used by Josephus of the Essene overseers.

and examining those who applied for membership in the community. He was to act as shepherd (*CD* 13:7–9). Scholars have long recognized here a parallel to the Christian shepherd, the bishop or ἐπίσκοπος, a term applied to Jesus in I Peter 2:25 (together with the designation "shepherd"), but usually to leaders in the early Church. Yet the parallel left something to be desired, since the normal Hebrew equivalent of ἐπίσκοπος is *pāqîd*. However, even this difficulty is resolved in Qumrân material. In one passage (1QS 6:12–14) the *mᵉbaqqêr* is called the *pāqîd* "at the head of the Many," that is, the "bishop of the Many."[81]

Thus a democratic assembly, a council of twelve, and an episcopal overseer all belong to the pattern of community or-

---

81. Cf. the writer's remarks, "Qumrân Cave I," p. 124.

Recently J. T. Milik (*Découvertes, ad loc.*), has observed that the presiding priest of the community (who must be distinguished from the *mᵉbaqqêr;* cf. 14:8–9) is described as follows in *CD* 14:7, *hkwhn 'šr ypqd ⟨br⟩'š hrbym,* "the priest appointed overseer at the head of the Many"; and in an unpublished text, *hkwhn hmpqd 'l hrbym,* "the priest appointed overseer over the Many." On the basis of this data he suggests the official title of the lay official is *mᵉbaqqêr,* of the priestly official, *pāqîd.*

The situation is not so simple. The *pāqîd* of 1QS 6:14 is not the presiding priest, but the *mᵉbaqqêr.* This is evident not merely because of its parallelism with 6:12, but because the *pāqîd* here mentioned is functioning as *mᵉbaqqêr.* The text reads, "and everyone who volunteers from Israel to be added to the Communal Council (the Essene membership), the one who is overseer (*pāqîd*) at the head of the Many shall try him as to his intelligence and his works . . . he shall make him to understand all the rulings of the Community" (6: 13–15). In *CD* 13:11–13 we read: "and everyone who is added to his congregation, he [the *mᵉbaqqêr;* cf. 13:6, 13] shall examine him (*ypdhw*) as to his works and his intelligence . . . and he shall inscribe him in his place according to his situation in the party [lit. lot] of the truth. Let no one of all the members of the Camp assume authority to bring someone into the congregation contrary to the will of the *mᵉbaqqêr* of the Camp." The identity of function of the *pāqîd* of 1QS and the *mᵉbaqqêr* of *CD* is obvious not only in the general sense of the passages, but in the frequent verbal contacts between the passages. We have here two forms of a single rule of organization.

Perhaps the term *pāqîd* could have been used of either official, at least in the early period.

ganization among the Essenes. It would appear that the early Church appropriated and modified offices and institutions belonging to older apocalyptic communities in developing its own organizational structure.

The central "sacraments" of the Essene community appear to be its baptism(s) and its communal meal. The baptism of the Essenes, like that of John, was on repentance of sins into the eschatological community of God.[82] Contrary to early Christian usage, the Essenes seem to have practiced daily priestly lustrations as well as baptism on entrance into the New Covenant of the Community.[83] It is also possible that they repeated the initiatory rite of baptism at the yearly ceremony of covenant renewal.[84]

In the discussion of the communal meal of the Essenes in Chapter II[85] we argued that the meal must be understood as a liturgical anticipation of the Messianic banquet. The anticipation of the banquet of the Kingdom is a strong element also in the New Testament accounts of the Lord's Supper and in the later Eucharistic practice of the Palestinian Church. In the Markan account we read, "Truly I say to you, I shall not drink again of the fruit of the vine until that day when I drink it new in the kingdom of God" (14:25); in the Lukan version it is even stronger, especially if one follows the shorter text (22:14–19a); and it appears as well in the Pauline and later formulae; "For as often as you eat this bread and drink the cup, you proclaim the Lord's death *until he comes*" (I Cor. 12:26); "marana-tha, Come our Lord," and "the holy vine

82. 1QS 5:8–23; especially 5:13–14 (the passage is discussed in detail above, Chap. II, n. 96a). Cf. 2:25–3:12, especially 3:4–7 where baptism is connected not only with repentance and covenant, but also with the gift of the spirit; 4:20–22; etc.

83. The practice of a baptism of initiation in combination with practice of daily ritual washings persists among the Ebionites. Cf. the discussion of Fitzmyer, "The Qumrân Scrolls, the Ebionites and their Literature," pp. 365 ff.

84. Cf. Chap. II, n. 96a.

85. Pp. 62–7.

of David thy servant which was made known to us through
Jesus . . ." (*Didache* 9:2; 10:6.)[86]

The Church of Acts (Acts 2:46, etc.) ate common meals
regularly, "partaking of the food in joy." Indeed these ban-
quets of joyous anticipation led to the excesses referred to
in Jude 12 and I Corinthians 11, and to the later reforms
which in turn led to the separation of the Eucharist proper
from the regular common meals of the faithful.

What is the background of the institution of common meals
of the entire community, eaten in anticipation of the
Messianic banquet? The Passover, the other element in the
background of the Lord's Supper, can give no suitable context.[87] It is a yearly feast of memorial, eaten in private in
families, and is not, properly, an eschatological festival. The
Essene meal gives the first suitable answer.

This is not to suggest that the Church merely took over an
Essene meal. Within the Lord's Supper are notable original

86. Many other allusions to the Messianic banquet appear which
occur in Eucharistic contexts, or which seem to be shaped by liturgical
usage in the early Church; e.g., Rev. 19:9, "Blessed are those who
are invited to the marriage supper of the Lamb." In Lk. 22:30, we
read ". . . that you may eat and drink at my table in my kingdom . . ."; this saying is placed in the context of a dispute over rank
at the Lord's Supper. The account of the miracle at Cana has frequently been held to have Eucharistic overtones. In any case Jesus'
reply to his mother when told that the wine had failed is obscure; "O
woman, what have you to do with me? My hour has not yet come."
Normally, "the hour" refers elsewhere in John to his Passion and death.
Why does Jesus refuse (at least at first) to provide the wine at the
feast because his "hour" has not come? Perhaps Jesus is portrayed
here as alluding to the day when he properly will provide wine as host
at the Messianic feast.

87. For recent attempts to equate the Lord's Supper with the Passover, see J. Jeremias, *Die Abendsmahlsworte Jesu;* and A. J. B. Hig-
gins, *The Lord's Supper in the New Testament* (London, 1952).

A. Jaubert in a recent article (see Chap. I, n. 71) has argued with
no little weight that the Gospel accounts are best understood if Jesus
celebrated his Last Supper on the date of Passover in the Essene (and
old religious) calendar, while the Crucifixion took place on the eve of
the official Jewish Passover.

elements: the formulas which transform the old Passover into the feast of the New Covenant memorialize the sacrifice of the body and blood of the victim, the pledge of the covenant.[88] And there is no reason, I think, to suppose that the combination of the two elements, the memorial of the sacrifice and the anticipation of the Messianic banquet does not exist already in the most primitive traditions of the Jerusalem community.

The extreme emphasis on rank at the Essene banquet is noteworthy. It seems hardly by chance that in the Gospels of Luke (22:24–30) and John (13:12–16), teaching which repudiates the desire for rank among the disciples is placed in discourses at the Last Supper. Elsewhere we also hear Jesus condemning those who seek places of rank in his kingdom. Moreover, in the parable of the banquet in Luke 14:15–24 (cf. Mt. 22:1–14), which in its present context is told in reply to one who says, "Blessed is he who shall eat bread in the kingdom of God," we find the remarkable expression, "For I tell you, none of those men who were invited shall taste my banquet"; while the feast of the Essenes is for "the Men of the Name Who are Invited to the Festival."[89]

We have noted that the life of the sect is understood as life in anticipation of the Kingdom of God. This eschatological community is made concrete not only in the common meal of the Messiah but also in the sharing of goods. Entry into the Essene community meant giving up all private property. In the New Testament Church, especially in Palestine, a similar practice obtains: "Now the congregation of believers were of

88. The rite of the renewal of the covenant among the Essenes is not, so far as we can tell, directly related to their communion meals, the former being an annual affair.

89. J. T. Milik and D. Barthélemy (*DJD I*, p. 117) have called attention to this parable of the banquet in connection with the list of rules which prohibited men who were maimed, unclean, blind, etc., from entering into the inner councils and cultus of the Essene community. Jesus, in absolute contrast, asserts that "the poor and maimed and blind and lame" will be brought in to the banquet (Lk. 14:21)! It is difficult to suppose that the parable is not told in conscious reaction to sectarian doctrine.

one heart and soul, and no one said that any of the things he possessed were his own, but they had everything in common (Acts 4:32; cf. 4:32–5:11); "And all who believed were together and had all things in common . . . And day by day attending the temple together and breaking bread together (in common meals) in their homes, they partook of food with glad and generous hearts" (Acts 2:44–46).

Again, as we have seen, many (though not all) Essenes eschewed marriage.[90] They were soldiers already mustered and prepared for the Holy War of the End Time. Being engaged in the war of God, they took up the ancient ritual prescriptions of the Old Testament for Holy War, keeping the "purity of their camps." They refrained from sexual intercourse and marriage, which disqualified one for war, kept the stringent sanitary regulations of Holy War, and all the rest. Theirs was not a genuine asceticism, but an eschatological asceticism. They did not, it seems, reject marriage as such, but marriage in the present circumstances.

Compare this structure of thought with the following passage in Paul's letter to the Corinthians: "I mean, brethren, the appointed time has grown very short; from now on, let those who have wives live as though they had none, and those who mourn as though they were not mourning, and those who rejoice as though they were not rejoicing, and those who buy as though they had no goods, and those who deal with the world as though they had no dealings with it. For the form of this world is passing away" (I Cor. 7:29–31).

90. Chap. II, pp. 71–4.

POSTSCRIPT

The Essene Faith and
the Christian Gospel

IN DRAWING ON the Qumrân library in the discussion of Christian origins, we have dealt primarily with parallels, with data which reveal continuities between the Essenes and the early Church. We have noted common language, common doctrines, common institutions. We have made no attempt to draw up systematically the differences between Christianity and Essenism.

Some few comments on the relation of Essenism to Christianity may be in order, however, in light of the current popular discussion of the scrolls. We have discovered the greatest similarities between these in their common apocalyptic point of view. Both were apocalyptic communities which in their common life attempted to bridge the gap between the Old Age and the New Age. There are, however, distinctions to be made between Essene apocalypticism and New Testament eschatology.

The Essene and the Christian live in the Old Age, yet by anticipation in the new. Thus in some sense we can speak of the "overlapping" of the ages in their existence as members of the New Covenant. For the member of the early Church, however, the time is "later." He stands on a new ground. The Messiah has come. He has been raised. The resurrection is not merely an anticipatory event. It shows that the New Age has come. Professor Stendahl has expressed the distinction by saying that "the degree of anticipation" is greater in the New Testament, its eschatology "higher."[91]

This "later moment" of the Christian's existence, this "greater degree of anticipation" of the early Church has radical effects upon Christian doctrine. The legal framework of Judaism, including Essene Judaism is smashed. The New Age is one in which the law is engraved in the heart. The gift of the Holy Spirit—anticipated in Essene doctrine—is poured out on the early Church, so that life is Spirit-dominated, and a new freedom replaces or rather fulfills the law.

The peculiarly priestly flavor of Essene apocalypticism is largely missing in early Christianity. "The hour is coming when neither on this mountain nor in Jerusalem will you worship the father . . . the hour is coming and now is when the true worshipers will worship the Father in spirit and truth." (Jn. 4:21–23.) The destruction of the Temple caused no strain upon early Christianity. The work of the old sacrificial system was completed in Jesus' sacrifice.

To be sure, the rejection of the priestly laws of purity, separations from sinners, the hierarchical distinctions in rank, and the dominance of the priesthood rests, however, on factors other than the "lateness of the hour" in which the early Christian existed. Christian eschatology is more directly rooted in Old Testament prophetism, the Essene in Old Testament priestly traditions. The sure signs of the New Age, according to Jesus, were the healing of the sick, the blind seeing, the dead rising, the dumb speaking. God gathered the poor, the maimed, the abandoned, the sinner into his banquet. The Essene excluded from the eschatological banquet all the unclean, those distorted in body and spirit. Such were unworthy of the New Age. Jesus' "poor" were the humble outcasts of

91. "The Scrolls and the New Testament, an Introduction and a Perspective" in *The Scrolls and the New Testament*, pp. 1–17. This is perhaps the best short discussion of this topic; I am indebted at many points in the following remarks to my colleague's paper.

Palestine. The Essene "poor" were in some sense an "artificial" poor, the elite of desert who shared their goods.

But to return to our central theme. The Christian lived in that "later moment" in the history of redemption when the Gentiles were to be brought into the Kingdom of God.[92] Hence Christianity turned out to the world. The Essenes, of course, looked forward to the day when Israel would atone for the sins of the world[93] and the nations would flow to Jerusalem. But they lived in an "earlier" moment, before the full manifestation of God's Kingdom, when salvation was to be preached only to the Jews. Priestly separatism and what is inaccurately called Jewish "particularism" belong to one phase in the history of redemption. Freedom and what is wrongly called Christian "universalism" to a later phase of the history of redemption . . . after the Messiah has come.

All this is to say that the "event" of Jesus as the Christ, his exaltation, his resurrection, the gift of his Spirit, distinguishes the two eschatological communities. It is possible that the Righteous Teacher of the Essenes was *expected* to return as a Messiah. But for the Church, Jesus had been resurrected as Messiah.[94] The event was past. The New Age was fully begun. The Messiah *had* come, had been resurrected and enthroned, though he would come again in glory.

We should emphasize that the New Testament faith was not a new faith, but the fulfillment of an old faith. The Church is precisely Israel in its own self-understanding.[95] Jesus did not propose to present a new system of universal truths. He came to fulfill the past work of God, to confirm the faith of the fathers, to open the meaning of the Law and Prophets. The New Testament does not set aside or supplant the Old Tes-

92. Cf. Stendahl, *op. cit.*; J. Jeremias, *Jesu Mission für die Völker*, Chap. III; Munck, *Paulus und die Heilsgeschichte* (Copenhagen, 1954), pp. 242–76.

93. 1QS 8:10.

94. Compare Stendahl's remarks in this connection, *op. cit.*, pp. 14 f.

95. Cf. the writer, the *New Republic*, April 9, 1956, p. 18.

tament. It affirms it and, from its point of view, completes it. Lines of continuity between Moses and Jesus, Isaiah and Jesus, the Righteous Teacher and Jesus, John the Baptist and Jesus should occasion no surprise. On the contrary, a biblical faith insists on such continuities. The biblical faith is not a system of ideas, but a history of God's acts of redemption.

It is not the idea of redemption through suffering but the "event" of the crucifixion understood as the atoning work of God that distinguishes Christianity. It is not the doctrine of resurrection but faith in the resurrection of Jesus as an eschatological event which forms the basis of the Christian decision of faith. It is not faith that a Messiah will come that gives Christianity its special character, but the assurance that Jesus rules as the Messiah who has come and will come. It is not the hope of a New Creation that lends uniqueness to Christianity, but the faith that Jesus is the New Adam, the first of the New Creation. Finally, it is not a "love ethic" that distinguishes Christianity from Judaism—far from it. The Christian faith is distinguished from the ancient faith which brought it to birth in its knowledge of a new act of God's love, the revelation of His love in Jesus' particular life and death and resurrection.